La Reine Blanche

La Reine Blanche

Mary Tudor: A Life in Letters

SARAH BRYSON

AMBERLEY

For the strong women in my life.
Thank you for your never-ending love and support.

First published 2018

Amberley Publishing
The Hill, Stroud
Gloucestershire, GL5 4EP

www.amberley-books.com

British Library Cataloguing in Publication Data.
A catalogue record for this book is available from the British Library.

ISBN 978 1 4456 7388 2 (hardback)
ISBN 978 1 4456 7389 9 (ebook)

Typesetting and Origination by Amberley Publishing.
Printed in the UK.

Contents

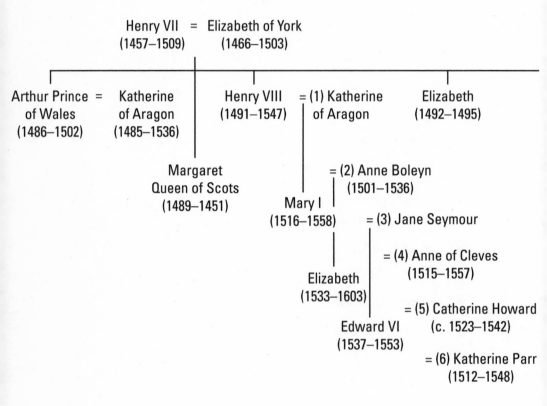

Henry VII = Elizabeth of York
(1457–1509)   (1466–1503)

Arthur Prince = Katherine   Henry VIII   = (1) Katherine   Elizabeth
of Wales   of Aragon   (1491–1547)   of Aragon   (1492–1495)
(1486–1502)   (1485–1536)

                    Margaret   = (2) Anne Boleyn
                    Queen of Scots   (1501–1536)
                    (1489–1451)   Mary I
                                         (1516–1558)   = (3) Jane Seymour

                                                            = (4) Anne of Cleves
                                                               (1515–1557)
                                          Elizabeth
                                         (1533–1603)
                                                            = (5) Catherine Howard
                                          Edward VI   (c. 1523–1542)
                                         (1537–1553)
                                                            = (6) Katherine Parr
                                                               (1512–1548)

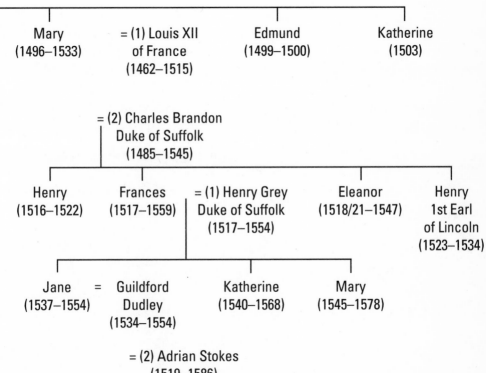

Mary
(1496–1533)

= (1) Louis XII
of France
(1462–1515)

Edmund
(1499–1500)

Katherine
(1503)

= (2) Charles Brandon
Duke of Suffolk
(1485–1545)

Henry
(1516–1522)

Frances
(1517–1559)

= (1) Henry Grey
Duke of Suffolk
(1517–1554)

Eleanor
(1518/21–1547)

Henry
1st Earl
of Lincoln
(1523–1534)

Jane
(1537–1554)

= Guildford
Dudley
(1534–1554)

Katherine
(1540–1568)

Mary
(1545–1578)

= (2) Adrian Stokes
(1519–1586)

Introduction

✣

Late in the evening of 1 January 1515 Mary Tudor became a widow when her husband, King Louis XII of France, died. At just eighteen years of age Mary retired to the Hôtel Cluny and as tradition dictated she donned white for mourning. While there she was given the title 'La Reine Blanche' or 'The White Queen' and it is this time in Mary's life, perhaps more than any other, that defined who she was as a woman.

In an age where women were considered to be inferior to men, their duty to serve their husband, to bear many children and be a good Catholic, the stories of women such as Mary Tudor, Dowager Queen of France are often overshadowed by those of men. The Tudor age was a period dominated by men and yet there were so many women of the age who were strong, independent, intellectually gifted, and extremely successful in many different ways. Women like Lady Margaret Beaufort, Elizabeth I, Katherine of Aragon, Anne Boleyn, Katherine Parr – and Mary Tudor.

As the youngest surviving daughter of King Henry VII and his wife Queen Elizabeth of York, Mary Tudor would have been aware from an early age that her future was not in her own hands. Mary was considered to be one of the most beautiful women in all of Christendom. Her first husband, King Louis XII of France described his wife as a 'nymph from heaven', her beauty and affability warranting the expression.[1] Young, beautiful, talented in all the accomplishments that a woman of the time should have – dancing, singing, playing a musical instrument and most of all faithfully serving her husband, Mary was a great marriage prize.

Her father would make a diplomatic alliance with a foreign country which would involve Mary marrying a man she had most likely never met. She would leave her home and family, travel to another country to marry and live out her life, risking all the perils of childbirth hopefully to provide her husband with many healthy sons. Her path was set out before her by her father and was not her own to follow.

Mary's younger years are overshadowed by the men in her life: her father, the new Tudor king Henry VII who claimed the throne from King Richard III at the Battle of Bosworth Field; her eldest brother, Prince Arthur, heir to the Tudor throne, and her beloved brother who became King Henry VIII. She was groomed to be a dutiful wife and mother and that is just what Mary was. At the age of eighteen Mary married a French King thirty-four years her senior. While she may seem young by modern standards, during the Tudor period the legal age for marriage was twelve years for a girl and fourteen for a boy.[2]

Yet when her husband died only three months later, Mary did what so many other women of the time could not – she took her life into her own hands and shaped her destiny. It was then, as a young widow, that Mary blossomed; or perhaps for the first time in her life she had the opportunity to show the strong, self-willed, determined woman she always had been.

It was during her time in France that Mary became a prolific letter writer. She wrote many letters to various people, including her brother and thankfully these letters still survive today. A letter may seem outdated today but during the Tudor age could convey a thousand meanings. Letter writing was a skill. A letter was a way to impose oneself on another person, to express one's wishes and desires, to seek assistance or support or to simply keep oneself in the mind of another. Mary was an extremely skilled writer and examining her letters opens up a deeper and more meaningful understanding of who this fascinating woman was. Through studying Mary's letters I have come to know a woman who was not simply the daughter, sister or wife of a king, but a strong, determined woman who knew her own mind and what she wanted from her life. A young woman who was passionate and most of all, who knew how to manoeuvre the men around her to get exactly what she wanted. In an age where women were seen as inferior versions of men, not as quick of wit or as intellectual, Mary used her letters to further her own desires and wishes and to seek assistance and support for those in her service.

Mary would not have been able to challenge men verbally, or publicly speak her mind. To do so would have been to step out of the mould that had been so carefully created for her by the men in her life and the culture of the time. Many men held the belief that to publicly challenge a man meant that a woman was not in fact a true woman, or that the woman was somehow mentally unbalanced. There were even physical and humiliating punishments for women who dared to challenge or speak ill of their husbands. Therefore Mary influenced the men in her life by using what skills and means she had at hand – in her case it was letter writing.

Mary Tudor's letters are a fascinating and captivating look at how a woman could wield power without publicly challenging the patriarchy. They show how Mary was able to manoeuvre those around her to follow her heart – marrying her second husband for love, rather than being dragged back to the international chess game as a marriage pawn. They are also, on occasion, a way of looking into Mary's life whereby the layers of princess and queen are stripped back and only the woman remains.

I have tried to include as many of Mary's letters as possible, as well as other letters that various people of the period wrote about her. By using Mary's own words my aim is that the reader will gain a deeper understanding of this Tudor princess. I hope that by considering Mary's letters in their original form, you are able to gain a deeper and more intimate understanding of who this fascinating woman was; to explore the woman beneath the majesty and to see that despite being viewed as inferior, Mary was strong, determined and intelligent.

To move forward with Mary Tudor's life I have had to take a step back. I have chosen to start this book not at Mary's birth but over fifty years earlier, before her father's great battle against King Richard III and his victory at Bosworth Field. I believe that to gain a greater understanding of what Mary's childhood would have been like, the ideas, ideals and events that would have influenced and affected her life, it is vital that I set the scene of what England was like leading up to Mary's birth. This I believe helps to gain a deeper understanding of how the national and international political climate would have influenced Mary in her formative years.

I would like to take a moment to thank those that have helped me. To Melanie V. Taylor for her never-ending support, advice, encouragement, laughs, guidance and for always keeping me on track; you are like a mother to me and I treasure you deeply. To Heather R. Darcie for always being there to listen to my thoughts and for always encouraging me. Melanie and Heather, our travels around England and our conversations have inspired me greatly. To all my dear Tudor friends, thank you for your friendship and inspiration. Also I must say a very big thank you to Nathen Amin and Geoffrey Munn for allowing me to use your photos. To my wonderful husband I must thank you a thousand times over for helping around the house and supporting me while I lost myself in fifteenth- and sixteenth-century documents, I promise I'll come back to the real world one day! To my daughter, who is already a strong little girl, I hope you grow to become a strong woman. And to my amazing best friend Amanda Reinman, thank you for listening to my constant Tudor babble with love and grace. I love you deeply; you will forever and always be my sister.

1

The Rise of the Tudor Dynasty

⚜

'Judge me, O Lord and favour my cause'
Psalm 42

Born in early 1496[1] Mary Tudor was the fifth child and third daughter born to the new Tudor king, Henry VII and his beautiful wife, Elizabeth of York.[2] While Henry VII had been king for almost eleven years at the time of Mary's birth, his journey to the throne of England had not been easy, nor was his current position as King of England free from threat. To understand fully the time that Mary Tudor was born into it is vital to go back almost fifty years earlier to explore the turbulent period into which her parents were born.

England was far from stable, with unrest simmering throughout the country. The uncertainty had caused major turmoil throughout England not only for the common people but for those who attempted to claim the throne and rule. Uprisings, rebellions, challenges to the throne, executions, sickness and the constant threat of danger lurked close by.

When Henry Tudor was born on 28 January 1457 the Wars of the Roses were extant, upheaval resonating throughout England. The great factions of York and Lancaster battled for the throne, each side believing it was their Divine right to rule England. The Lancastrian side was headed by King Henry VI, his wife Queen Margaret of Anjou and his son Prince Edward. The king was suffering from some form of mental illness that made him completely incapable of ruling for long periods, requiring his wife and other members of the council to step in and govern while he was incapacitated.[3] The Yorkists were headed by Richard of York, 3rd Duke of York and his son Edward. Richard was the great-grandson of King Edward III and governed England as Lord Protector while King Henry VI hallucinated or fell into a torpor. Soon the duke and the queen fell out with one another and the duke sought to take the throne for himself and his heirs, declaring his own royal ancestry.[4]

The two factions battled fiercely, with many losses. After Henry VI's death on 22/23 May 1471[5] the Lancastrian faction was crushed. Edward IV claimed the throne and became king, bringing a semblance of stability once more to England. There was a new Yorkist king on the throne, but there was someone else who felt he had a stronger claim. Henry Tudor was the son of Edmund Tudor, 1st Earl of Richmond and his wife Lady Margaret Beaufort. Edmund Tudor was captured in one of the battles of the Wars of the Roses and died of what some historians suggest was the plague, on 3 November 1456, just two months before his son's birth.[6] Edmund was the eldest son of Owen Tudor, whose wife was the Dowager Queen Catherine Valois. Catherine's first marriage was to King Henry V and her son, the late Henry VI, was the half-brother of Edmund Tudor. As one of the last male heirs in the Lancastrian line Henry Tudor and his mother both strongly believed that Henry had a claim to the English throne.

Henry, together with his Uncle Jasper, 1st Duke of Pembroke, had escaped to Brittany in 1471 when Edward IV had come to the throne.[7] It was here that Henry and his uncle would spend most of the next fourteen years. Despite being warmly welcomed by Duke Francis of Brittany it was soon clear that young Henry Tudor and his uncle were pawns in a strategic game amongst Brittany, France and England. Edward IV, the new Yorkist King of England, wanted Henry and his uncle to be returned to England to neutralise any threat Henry's Lancastrian blood may cause to the throne. In attempting to see both Tudor men returned King Edward pledged money and troops to Duke Francis to aid him in the fight against French troops.[8] Duke Francis restricted Henry and Jasper Tudor's movements so they could not flee to King Louis XI of France, an ally who had previously sheltered Jasper Tudor.[9]

While Henry and Jasper were in Brittany, Edward IV died on 9 April 1483. Edward's successors were his two young sons, Edward and Richard. Understanding the turmoil that a young boy might have in his early reign, Edward left his own younger brother, Richard, Duke of Gloucester, as protector to guide his son the future Edward V. To keep the young king and his brother safe after the death of their father Richard took the boys to the Tower of London. Just before Edward V's coronation Richard had the boys declared illegitimate. He claimed that his brother was pre-contracted to marry Lady Eleanor Butler and thus the children Edward IV had with his wife, Queen Elizabeth Woodville, were illegitimate.[10] As his brother's only legitimate heir, Richard claimed the throne for himself and on 26 June 1483 was crowned king.[11] Both Edward and Richard, the young princes of the Tower, were never seen nor heard from again. Their fate is explored in more than a few books!

Many of those who had previously supported Edward IV turned on King Richard III for what they believed was a betrayal of the previous king. They fled England heading for Brittany and Henry Tudor. With a small group of loyal supporters Henry Tudor attempted to claim the English throne. Funded by Francis, the Duke of Brittany, Henry and a small army headed for England. At the same time a rebellion was formed in England, headed by the Duke of Buckingham, who had previously been loyal to King Richard III.[12] Buckingham raised the rebellion in the name of Henry Tudor. However, due to horrific storms many of Henry Tudor's small fleet ships were cast back to France and forced to make their way slowly back to Brittany. Without support, Buckingham's rebellion was crushed and after a summary trial the Duke was executed. Henry Tudor and a few of his men beat the storms and arrived at Plymouth where they were greeted by soldiers pretending to be part of the Duke of Buckingham's rebellion. Hearing of Buckingham's execution and the fall of the rebellion Henry and his men quickly turned around and headed back to Brittany.[13]

At Christmas in 1483 in the Cathedral of Rennes Henry Tudor made a vow to marry Elizabeth of York, daughter of the late King Edward IV and niece of Richard III. By marrying her, he would unite the houses of Lancaster and York and bring unity to

England.[14] It has been suggested that the prime mover behind this union was Henry's mother, Margaret of Beaufort.[15] Margaret was a woman who was willing to play the long game. Extremely smart and cunning, she had already endured many trials throughout her life. It was her desire to see her only son take his rightful place on the English throne and a union with the oldest daughter of the late King Edward IV would help not only to secure the Yorkist supporters, but also to unite the two warring houses of Lancaster and York. Margaret's doctor, Lewis Carleon, was able to pass messages to Queen Elizabeth while she was in sanctuary at Westminster proposing the idea of the marriage between Elizabeth and Henry.[16] Queen Elizabeth appears to have agreed to this union. If Henry Tudor returned to England and claimed the throne, then Elizabeth's daughter would be queen.

Immediately on becoming king, Richard III entered into negotiations with Duke Francis of Brittany to seek the return of Henry and Jasper Tudor.[17] Sensing danger, Jasper and Henry Tudor fled from Brittany, just managing to escape the Duke of Francis' soldiers who had been following close behind. They made it across the border into France where they were warmly welcomed by the young French king, Charles VIII.[18] English exiles that had flocked to Henry Tudor's side followed the young man into France and a mere eight months later, Henry Tudor set sail once more to lay claim to the English throne.

After fourteen years of exile, on 1 August 1485, Henry and approximately 2,000 soldiers sailed from Harfleur and on 7 August they landed at Mill Bay, 6 miles west of Milford Haven. When Henry made it to the shoreline he knelt down, kissed the sand and uttered Psalm 43, 'Judge me, O Lord and favour my cause' before making the sign of the cross.[19] Henry was welcomed by his half-uncle, David Owen, the illegitimate son of Henry's grandfather, Owen Tudor. When the army was unloaded and formed up, Henry and his soldiers headed towards the village of Dale.

The castle surrendered easily and it was here that the army stayed for the night. The next day the army marched to Haverfordwest, Cardigan, and then to Llwyn Dafdd. Henry and his men defeated the garrison at Aberystwyth and then turned inland. By 13 August the troops had reached Machynlleth and the following day they began the 30-mile march over rough terrain to Dolarddun. From there the army headed to Long Mountain where Henry was met by Rhys ap Thomas. Thomas was held in high regard by the Welsh people and he openly pledged his loyalty to Henry Tudor, who claimed Welsh ancestry through his father. Thomas committed around 2,000 men to Henry's cause.[20]

Henry Tudor's growing army marched towards Shrewsbury. When they arrived, they found that the portcullises were closed. The following day Henry sent a man to negotiate passage through Shrewsbury and shortly after this, a mysterious message was sent to the mayor of the town. All of a sudden Henry and his troops were allowed to pass through the town and many men from Shrewsbury joined Tudor's army.[21]

From Shrewsbury Henry and his army travelled through Shropshire to Staffordshire, where Henry was met by Sir Gilbert Talbot and around 500 men. With his army growing in size, Henry travelled to Stafford. There he was met by Sir William Stanley, the younger brother of Henry's stepfather, Thomas Stanley. The Staffords had not openly declared if they would support Richard III or Henry Tudor. However, Thomas Stanley had been following Henry's army under the guise of watching their movements; and it had been William Stanley who had sent the mysterious message to the mayor of Shrewsbury, which convinced the mayor to allow Henry and his troops through the town.[22]

After the meeting, Henry's troops marched through Lichfield and on 20 August they arrived at Tamworth. The following day they marched over the Anker River to Atherstone. It is rumoured that Henry held a secret meeting there with his stepfather, at which Stanley apparently pledged his support for Henry's cause.[23]

On 22 August Henry knighted several of his most loyal supporters including Sir John Jastoy, Sir John Trenzy, Sir Richard Guildford, Sir John Sisley, Sir Thomas Milborn, Sir William Typer and, Sir William Brandon, father of Mary Tudor's second husband.[24] In addition, he sent a message to Thomas Stanley asking for his men to join forces with his own troops. Stanley sent a message back saying that he needed to prepare his men and would not join Henry's troops.[25]

The Battle of Bosworth is one of the most well-known battles in English history and cannot be described in detail here. However, an outline of the battle is important to understand Henry Tudor's victory and how he became king. Richard III's army, consisting of 12,000 to 20,000 men faced the army of Henry Tudor, around 5,000 to 8,000. The combined forces of Thomas and William Stanley consisted of around 6,000 men; but neither man had yet to move into position to support Richard III or Henry Tudor.[26]

There has been a great deal of debate over the centuries as to where exactly the battle took place. It is commonly believed that Richard III held the higher ground on Ambion Hill and Henry Tudor occupied the flat ground close to the marshes. Historian Michael Jones proposes that the battle took place 80 miles away towards the west and closer to the town of Atherstone.[27]

Henry lacked experience in battle and so he wisely appointed the Earl of Oxford to lead the vanguard and command his men. Henry and a group of men followed the vanguard flanked by Sir Gilbert Talbot and Sir John Savage.[28] Next to Henry rode Sir William Brandon, Henry's standard bearer. To hold the standard was a great responsibility and the standard Henry had chosen was the Tudor white and green, with the red cross of St George, patron saint of England and soldiers, and the Welsh dragon.

For his part Richard III had the Duke of Norfolk and Sir Robert Brackenbury leading his vanguard. Following the vanguard came the king, his personal bodyguard and other soldiers, and behind them were the Earl of Northumberland and his troops.[29]

When the battle started the vanguards commanded by the Earl of Oxford and the Duke of Norfolk clashed violently. The pair were old rivals and the stakes were as high as they could get – whoever won claimed the English throne. After a fierce battle both sides paused for a moment, regained their breath so far as possible and reformed. Oxford ordered his men to form a wedge and he drove them forward crashing into Norfolk's men. At the attack Norfolk's vanguard faltered and in the fighting Norfolk was killed.[30]

Richard III and his troops began to advance and it is believed that Henry Tudor dismounted in order not to make himself a visible and easy target. With the men around him now under attack, the French pikemen whom Henry had hired in France were quickly called on to surround Henry. Richard III's mounted army charged straight into these pikemen and many of his men were killed in the sudden and violent clash.[31]

It is most likely that, seeing Richard III's mounted troops fall to the French pikemen, William Stanley chose to throw in his lot with Henry Tudor. Stanley and his army rode toward Richard III and Richard's most loyal supporters begged the king to flee the battle. Richard III would not be seen as a coward and seeing Henry Tudor before him, he continued to push forward. The king managed to kill William Brandon, Henry's standard bearer. However, he never made it to his enemy. Richard III was cut down and killed.[32] Henry Tudor and his army were victorious and after the battle the new English king ordered that the dead were taken to be buried at the nearby church of St James, Dadlington.[33]

Despite winning at Bosworth, Henry Tudor still had a great deal to achieve if he wished to create a strong, stable dynasty. Henry and his victorious army headed towards London. On the way he worked quickly to ensure that everyone knew he was the new King of England; he wished to set aside the past and bring a new, glorious future to the country. Henry ordered that none who had left the battle (on either side) should be attacked or harmed. Crowland states:

> Since it was not heard nor read nor committed to memory that any others who had withdrawn from the battle had been afterwards cut down by such punishments, but rather than he had shown clemency to all, the new prince began to receive praise from everyone as though he was an angel sent from the kingdom through whom god deigned to visit his people and to free them from the evils which had hitherto afflicted them beyond measure.[34]

On 3 September 1485 Henry Tudor was welcomed by the people of London. He was led through the streets in a magnificent procession to St Paul's Cathedral where Mass was heard and the *Te Deum* sung. After this he returned to Baynard's Castle before moving to Guildford where Henry met his mother, Margaret Beaufort, for the first time in fifteen years.[35] Henry had fled England when he was just fourteen years of age, now he was twenty-eight. One can only wonder what the reunion between mother and son was like. Margaret had worked hard over the years to see her son's lands and properties restored to him and to provide support for his claim to the throne. It was soon clear to many just how influential Margaret had been and would continue to be in her son's life. It was also during this time that Henry Tudor assembled his new council, declaring before them his desire to honour his pledge to marry Elizabeth of York.

Henry Tudor's coronation was held in Westminster Abbey on 30 October 1485. Henry wished for as many people as possible to witness his elevation as the newly anointed King of England. The event was to be spectacular and stands were set up for people. For the people of the late fifteenth century it was important that a king looked the part. Displays of great wealth and prosperity were a sign of a king's power and right to rule. Henry would not disappoint. A lavish procession headed out from the Tower of London filled with trumpeters, heralds, high-ranking members of the city of London, members of the king's new court and of course the future king himself. Henry Tudor rode his horse caparisoned with a cloth of gold and purple, a sign of royalty. Along the way there were banners and signs of the new Tudor dynasty. Henry Tudor was crowned king by Thomas Bourchier, the Archbishop of Canterbury,[36] at Westminster Abbey. After years of exile and struggle, Henry had achieved his ambition. After the ceremony King Henry VII travelled to the Tower of London to enjoy his coronation feast. On 13 November the traditional jousts were held to celebrate England's new king.[37]

Henry Tudor wasted little time in using his first Parliament to his own benefit and to the benefit of those that served him. He used Parliament to reverse all Acts of Attainder that had been placed on his loyal servants by the late kings Edward IV and Richard III. In addition, Henry VII issued a general pardon to all those that had offended him as king.[38]

Henry VII also went about rewarding those who had served him during the tumultuous years in exile and at the Battle of Bosworth. Lord Thomas Stanley (Henry VII's stepfather), was created Earl of Derby and granted a number of manors as well as being created the Master Forester and Steward of the King's Game North of the Trent and Chief Steward of the Duchy of Lancaster. Sir Rhys ap Thomas was created Chamberlain of South Wales, while Henry's Uncle Jasper Tudor was granted the titles of Duke of Bedford and Earl of Pembroke as well as being appointed to the post of Chief Justice in the South of Wales. A number of other Welshmen who had supported Henry were greatly rewarded.[39]

Even those lesser people, who were not directly involved with Henry during his exile, or in battle, were rewarded. Andrew Oterborne, a former tutor when Henry was a boy, was granted twenty marks and Lewis Carleon (Margaret Beaufort's doctor) was granted £40 a year for the great risks he had taken in passing notes between Margaret and Elizabeth Woodville while Elizabeth claimed sanctuary at Westminster.[40]

The Earl of Oxford, who had been so influential before and during the Battle of Bosworth, was highly rewarded, being appointed to the office of Great Chamberlain, in addition to being created the Admiral of England and the Constable of the Tower of London. Henry also went about appointing other men who had served him faithfully and whom he trusted to occupy important roles throughout England.[41]

In addition to such appointments to secure vital positions throughout his new kingdom, King Henry sent out a proclamation that excluded some of Richard III's supporters from the pardon that he had previously released after the Battle of Bosworth. Henry wanted to quickly stamp out any lingering loyalty to the late king. By an Act of Parliament King Henry VII backdated his rule to 21 August 1485 – the day before his victory at the Battle of Bosworth. Through this Act, Henry was declaring that he was the lawful King of England at the Battle of Bosworth and that Richard III, now known as Richard, Duke of Gloucester, was the usurper. By backdating the commencement of his rule Henry would be able to attaint all those who had supported Richard III and, take their property and titles. Despite such an all-encompassing Act, he only had twenty-eight men attainted, eight of whom were already dead.[42]

Less than three months later, on 18 January 1486, Henry Tudor finally fulfilled the oath he had sworn to marry Elizabeth of York. Why did Henry wait so long after being crowned to marry Elizabeth? There were several stumbling blocks that had to be dealt with before the couple could marry. During his rule King Richard III had declared Elizabeth of York and her siblings illegitimate.[43] One of Henry VII's first acts was to repeal this and restore legitimacy to his future wife and her siblings.[44] In addition, two dispensations to marry were sought from the Pope because Elizabeth and Henry were related within the fourth degree of consanguinity. The grant was received on 16 January and two days later Elizabeth and Henry were married at Westminster Abbey.

This marriage was more than the simple joining of a man and a woman; it was the unification of the houses of Lancaster and York. By marrying in Westminster Abbey Henry Tudor would have ensured the event was magnificent and as richly decorated as possible, so that all who witnessed the wedding could report the union between the two houses.

Henry Tudor was twenty-nine, Elizabeth of York a month shy of her twentieth birthday. Both had faced great adversity in their lives; Henry fleeing into exile for fourteen long years before he returned to England to lay claim to the throne. Elizabeth had witnessed her uncle claim the throne from her brother and the mysterious disappearance of her two brothers before she, her mother and sisters fled into sanctuary. With uncertainty looming all around her, it may have seemed to her that she would never find her rightful place in life. Yet on 18 January Elizabeth became not just a wife, but Queen Consort of England. Unfortunately, no records survive describing the marriage ceremony.

Elizabeth was reported to be 'intelligent above all others, and equally beautiful. She was a woman of such character that it would be hard to judge whether she displayed more of majesty and dignity in her life than wisdom and moderation.'[45] Henry hoped the marriage would bring an end to the dramatic and devastating Wars of the Roses that had raged for decades. Henry's marriage to Elizabeth would help to align himself with the Yorkist faction, cementing the validity of his rule.

It is unknown exactly how much contact Henry and Elizabeth had before their marriage; what is known is that Henry desired to see his future bride before their wedding as 'for the lady Elizabeth, she received also a direction to repair with all convenient speed to London, and there to remain with the Queen Dowager her mother;

which accordingly she soon after did, accompanied with many noblemen and ladies of honour.'[46]

It is completely understandable that Henry would wish to see the woman he was to marry. It is interesting to note that their first child, a son they named Arthur, was born eight months after their marriage on 20 September. It may have been that that Arthur was premature.[47] Or it may be possible that Henry and Elizabeth undertook a simple handfasting ceremony before their more public wedding in Westminster. The ceremony would have been conducted in front of a few witnesses and would not have needed a priest. Instead the couple would have held hands and agreed to marry one another, exchanging simple vows in which they promised to be each other's respective husband and wife. Legally, according to the law and the Church, the couple would have been married.[48]

Whatever the exact circumstance of Elizabeth's pregnancy, Henry Tudor had claimed the English throne due to his Lancastrian blood and his right as victor at the Battle of Bosworth Field. He was the last king to win the throne on the field of battle. He had entered London with great pomp and ceremony and been crowned king in Westminster Abbey. He had married Elizabeth of York, daughter of the late King Edward IV, and in doing so had united the houses of Lancaster and York. Henry Tudor was God's anointed king and his rule would usher in a new era for England. However even as king and with his wife pregnant with the future heir, Henry Tudor had a long way to go before he could ensure the stability and peace of England. During his reign he would face several rebellions and usurpers; and as these dramatic events were unfolding, a little girl would be born who would one day become Queen of France. On 18 March 1496 Queen Elizabeth of York had done her duty once more and given birth to a fifth child, a healthy baby girl, at Sheen Palace.[1]

2

A Rose Blooms

❧

'*Hodie nata Maria tertia filia Henricis VII 1495.*'

At approximately nine o'clock on the night of 29 December 1497 at Sheen Palace 'began a great fire within the king's lodging and so continued until twelve of the night and more ... a great part of the old building was burned and much harm done in hangings, as in rich beds, curtains and other appertaining to such a noble court.' It is thought that the fire may have been started by a wooden beam in the queen's lodgings catching alight, perhaps from a candle. Mary and her parents, siblings and grandmother Margaret Beaufort, were all present but escaped unscathed.[2]

With much of Sheen Palace destroyed, Henry VII took the opportunity to rebuild it in greater splendour. Using what was left of the existing ground plan, he built a lavish three-storey palace in a rectangular shape. Each floor had twelve rooms; the top two floors were for private apartments and state rooms while the ground floor was for servants. There was a bridge over the moat, which linked these privy lodgings to a large courtyard, Great Hall and Chapel. The Great Hall contained two fireplaces with chimney flues, and a hammer beam roof. The Chapel was built of stone, beautifully decorated with Tudor roses and the Beaufort portcullis, and had buildings on either side containing privy closets for the king and queen. There were other buildings surrounding the court that held apartments for courtiers and kitchens. The new palace was surrounded by orchards and magnificent gardens. Henry VII named his new abode Richmond Palace in honour of his previous title of Earl of Richmond.[3]

Before Mary's birth it may have been possible that Queen Elizabeth sought a physician to inform her if she was carrying a boy or girl. A son was naturally preferred, an heir to carry on the father's name and bloodline. It was believed that a child was formed from the seed of a man and some 'matter' from the woman and that life within the womb did not begin until the soul entered the foetus, which happened at forty-six days for a male and ninety days for a female.[4]

The Franciscan, Friar Bartholomew, wrote that if a baby grew on the woman's right side it would become a male and if it grew on the woman's left side, a female. It was also believed that if a woman's right breast was larger the baby would be a male, if her left breast, a female would be born.[5] Girls took longer to develop as they were made from cold humours, and boys from hot humours, which were the same as the womb in which the baby grew. Such predictions seem crazy and irrational; but the desire to know if the unborn baby was a boy or girl was overpowering and led to such nonsense, and it is why Elizabeth may have sought to find out if she was carrying another son.

Margaret Beaufort outlined a strict set of protocols and necessities required for Elizabeth's labour and birth. These protocols covered everything from the number and rank of the women allowed within the chambers, to the number and even the colour of the cushions used by the queen![6] Approximately one month before the child was due to be born, it was customary for the queen to withdraw from the world. After a church service in which people prayed for the safe delivery of the child, Elizabeth retired to a series of rooms known as the 'lying-in chamber'. The purpose of these rooms was to recreate a womblike effect, warm, safe and shut off. To do this, thick tapestries depicting happy images so as not to upset or distress the mother and in turn harm the unborn child, were hung on the walls and over the windows. Only a single window was left open to allow in fresh air as it was believed that bright light could bring in evil spirits. Carpets would have been placed over the floor and a fire would have burned constantly.

Elizabeth may have also have had two beds, one in which she could rest and sleep in before the birth and a second in which to give birth. This second bed would have been full of pillows and covered in crimson satin, the colour helping to hide any blood stains. A birthing stool may have also been provided as another means to give birth.[7]

The queen would have been accompanied by her female servants; men – including male physicians – were strictly barred from the lying-in chamber. Elizabeth's mother, Elizabeth Woodville, had supported the queen during her first three pregnancies, but she had died on 8 June 1492, before Mary was born.[8]

During her labour Elizabeth would have trusted in her Catholic faith. It is known that she asked for the Girdle of Our Lady to be brought to her from Westminster Abbey. The girdle would have been laid over Elizabeth's stomach while she and her ladies prayed for the Virgin Mary to help the queen's labour pains and to bring about the safe delivery of her child.[9] Elizabeth may have also called on St Margaret, the patron saint of pregnant women and childbirth, to aid her in her labour and the birth.[10]

Legend states that St Margaret of Antioch was the daughter of a pagan priest who converted to Christianity. Upon fleeing her home, Margaret became a shepherdess who was captured and tortured for being a Christian. While she was in prison, she had an encounter with the devil who came to her in the form of a dragon. The dragon swallowed Margaret, but was irritated by the cross she wore and spat her out. Due to her delivery from the dragon because of her faith in Christ she became a popular figure for pregnant women to address in their prayers.[11]

It is quite probable that Elizabeth of York's midwife for Mary's birth would have been Alice Massey, who was also the midwife for her previous pregnancy as well as her last pregnancy (which would take place in 1503).[12] Friar Bartholomew wrote that a midwife

...takes the child out of the womb, and ties the navel-string four inches long. She washes away the blood on the child with water, anoints him with salt and honey (or salt and roses, pounded together) to dry him and comfort his limbs and members, and wraps him in clothes. His mouth and gums should be rubbed with a finger dipped in honey to cleanse them, and to stimulate the child to suck.[13]

A midwife had to be 'pleasant and merry, of good discourse, strong'[14] and have a good reputation. The profession of midwifery was not taught at schools, but rather by time and experience. Women would have learnt the trade from other women, and by assisting a midwife attending a woman in labour. Since childbirth was such a dangerous time for both mother and baby, the midwife was also granted by the Church the ability to baptise a baby should it appear that it would not live. Therefore the midwife had to be a good Catholic woman, dedicated to Christ and the Church.[15]

The little girl Elizabeth of York gave birth to was named Mary, possibly after the Virgin Mary as she was born so close to the Tudor New Year, 25 March, known as Lady Day or the Feast of the Annunciation of the Blessed Virgin (the date that Mary was told she was pregnant with Jesus). The date of her birth was recorded by Elizabeth in her psalter.[16] Margaret Beaufort recorded Mary's birth in her book of hours. Next to 18 March Margaret wrote: '*Hodie nata Maria tertia filia Henricis VII 1495*', 'Today was born Mary, the third daughter of Henry VII 1495.'[17] Margaret recorded the date as 1495 because during the early Tudor age, the new calendar year did not start until Lady Day, 25 March,[18] so we would say that she was born in 1496, referring to the modern Gregorian calendar.[19] Henry VII states that Mary was born in 1495 when he wrote to the Duke of Milan on 2 March 1499 rejecting a marriage proposal between Mary and the duke's son. Mary was only three at the time; having not quite reached her fourth birthday.[20]

Shortly after her birth, Mary would have been christened. It was vitally important that a new-born baby be christened since it was believed that an unchristened soul would forever be stuck in limbo. A baby could be christened a few minutes after birth, or even during the birthing process should the midwife believe that there was a chance it may die and the midwife was able to touch any part of the child, such as the top of its head or a limb.

There are no records of Mary's christening, but it is most likely that it followed the strict rules set out by Margaret Beaufort and was similar to that of her older siblings. A stage would have been set up at the front of the chapel on which stood a silver gilt front covered by a beautifully decorated circular canopy. Margaret Beaufort's rules dictated that a duchess carry Mary to the font while a second duchess held the chrisom cloth. Following behind would be a countess who carried the ermine-lined train which would have hung from Mary's tiny shoulders.

Naturally the christening of a member of the royal family would be attended by the highest members of the nobility and it was vitally important that all could see the little princess being christened. After the ceremony Mary was taken back by royal procession to her mother who awaited her daughter in her chambers. Elizabeth of York would not have been able to participate in Mary's christening as it was forbidden for a mother to appear in public until she was churched, which happened thirty days after she had given birth.[21]

Queens did not breastfeed their own children and therefore Mary would have been given to a wet nurse.[22] It was thought breastfeeding slowed the time in which a mother could conceive again and since it was a queen's primary duty to have children, the quicker she could start to lie with her husband the better. A lady by the name of Anne Crown was chosen to breastfeed young Mary, a woman of impeccable reputation.[23] It was believed that a child's personality and character was passed to the child through the breast milk,[24] therefore a woman without a stain on her character had to be sought – especially if she were to feed a royal child. The midwife also had to be in extremely good health and her daily food intake and activities were closely monitored.[25]

Not everyone agreed with the idea that a woman's baby should be given to another to be breastfed. In fact some thought it an unnatural act. Thomas More, writing in his book *Utopia*, believed that a baby boy would take the woman who breastfed him as his mother.[26] Spanish humanist scholar, Juan Luis Vives in his book *Instruction of a Christian Woman*, advised women to breastfeed their own children if they could since the act passed on not only nourishment and love to the child, but also the mother's disposition.[27] Desiderius Erasmus, humanist, Catholic priest and theologian, was rather more insistent on the subject:

If you would like to be a complete mother, take care of your baby's little body, so that after it has freed itself from vapors, the spark of reason may have the support of good and serviceable bodily organs. Every time you hear your boy squalling, believe that he's asking this of you. When you see on your breasts those two little swollen fountains, so to speak, flowing with milk of their own accord, believe that Nature is reminding you of your duty. Otherwise, when your baby is ready to speak and with his sweet baby-talk calls you 'mamma,' what will be your reaction, hearing this from him to whom you refused the breast and whom you banished to a hired nurse, just as if you had put him under a sheep or a goat? What if he calls you 'half-mother' instead of 'mother' when he can talk? You'll fetch the rod, I dare say. But the woman who refuses to nurse what she bore is scarcely a half-mother. The better part of childbearing is the nursing of the tender baby, for he's nourished not only with milk but by the fragrance of the mother's body as well.[28]

How Elizabeth of York felt about such condemnation remains unknown. It may have stung her deeply to be shamed for not breastfeeding her own children or she may have shrugged and accepted her role as queen and sought a suitable wet nurse. Whatever her personal thoughts Elizabeth was queen; it was her duty to provide her husband with many strong, healthy children.

Mary was not the first daughter to be born to Henry VII and his queen. In fact Mary was the fifth child born to the couple. The couple's first child, Arthur, had been born on 20 September 1486 at Winchester. Arthur's birth was recorded by his grandmother Margaret Beaufort as being after midnight and just before one o'clock. Giving birth to a son less than a year after Henry VII and Elizabeth's marriage was seen by some as a sign from God that the new Tudor dynasty was blessed. Arthur was christened on 24 September in Winchester Cathedral.[29]

Almost three years later, on 28 November 1489 at around nine o'clock in the evening, Elizabeth had given birth to her second child, a healthy baby girl named Margaret.[30] The little girl was christened in Westminster Abbey on 30 November using the traditional silver font from Canterbury Cathedral.[31]

Elizabeth of York continued to accomplish her wifely and queenly duties and gave birth to her third child, a son, at Greenwich on 28 June 1491. The new baby boy was named Henry; he was strong and healthy. King Henry VII now had an heir and a spare to secure his newly founded dynasty. Of all her siblings it would be her brother Henry that Mary would grow closest to over the years, being spoiled by her brother with lavish, expensive clothing as well as being able to manipulate him into agreeing of her marrying a man of her own choosing.

Just over a year later, on 2 July 1492, Elizabeth gave birth to her fourth child, a daughter named Elizabeth. Sadly Elizabeth would not survive infancy. During the Tudor age there was a high infant mortality rate and Elizabeth died at just three years of age of what was believed to be a wasting disease. She is buried at Westminster Abbey.[32]

Mary did not meet her older sister, Elizabeth, since the new princess was born after Elizabeth had died. It is often believed that the birth of a daughter was a great disappointment to a king and queen as the continuation of the family line and a dynasty relied on strong, healthy and competent sons. In the case of Mary's birth, there is nothing to suggest that her being female was a disappointment to her parents. Her father already had two sons and Elizabeth of York had proven herself to be fertile so more than capable of conceiving and giving birth to more. In fact, the birth of a daughter would have been seen as beneficial. As a new king seeking to bring stability to England, the birth of a daughter provided the means for future marriage alliances and a chance to strengthen political alliances with other countries.

Elizabeth of York would not give birth again for another three years. In February 1499 at Greenwich Elizabeth gave birth to a son named Edmund. Despite the great joy of another son, the little boy died at just fifteen months of age. He, like his sister Elizabeth, is buried at Westminster Abbey.[33]

Elizabeth of York would give birth one last time on Candlemas Day, 2 February 1503, in an attempt to give her husband another son after the tragic death of their oldest child, Arthur, in 1502. Her labour came on suddenly and she gave birth to a daughter, named

Catherine, at the Tower of London. Catherine died on 10 February and the queen died the next day.

In 1496 Elizabeth's death was still eight years away and little Mary had her whole life ahead of her. As a beautiful, healthy baby, Mary would have been moved to the royal nursery at Eltham Palace where she would be cared for and closely watched over. It was here at Eltham that Mary was brought up with her older siblings; Margaret aged six-and-a-half and Henry, four-and-a-half. Her eldest brother Arthur, aged nine years and heir to the Tudor throne, would not have been present because he had been taken to Farnham in Hampshire to be raised in his own establishment.[34]

Eltham Palace is a lavish building with a long and rich history. In 1295 Anthony Bek, Bishop of Durham, acquired Eltham and rebuilt the manor house. In 1305 Bek presented the manor to the future Edward II and Eltham stayed in royal hands, being extended. In the 1470s Mary's grandfather, King Edward IV, ordered the building of the exquisite Great Hall with a hammerbeam roof.[35] As a child, Mary would have become familiar with the Great Hall as well as the lavish gardens surrounding the palace.

Baby Mary would have been swaddled tightly and laid in a cradle containing a wool mattress and down pillows. Swaddling was a common tradition, a process believed to be vital to the newborn child's development. Mary would have been wrapped in a linen shirt and then a breech cloth (nappy) would have been put on. The swaddling bands were narrow pieces of linen approximately 3 yards long. These were wrapped tightly around the baby's body. The idea was that swaddling would keep a child warm as well as ensuring that their arms and legs grew straight. Swaddling bands could be quite simple, or in the case of a royal baby, elaborately decorated.[36]

The Tudors believed that infancy lasted until a child was seven.[37] During these first seven years of her life Mary would have spent a great deal of time at Eltham with her older siblings. She would have been under the care of Mistress Elizabeth Denton, who supervised all the royal children; her duties included ensuring each child was fed according to their age, was well dressed and that their establishments were properly furnished. A few years later, when Mistress Denton became a gentlewoman to Queen Elizabeth of York, her place was taken by Mistress Anne Crowmer.[38]

As a princess, Mary's clothing would have matched her status. On 16 November 1497 at less than two years of age Mary received three pairs of hosen, eight pairs of single-soled shoes and four pairs of double.[39] In 1499, lavish clothing was ordered for the five-year-old princess including 'a gown of green velvet, edged with purple tinsel and lined with black buckram; a gown of black velvet, edged with crimson; kirtles of tawny damask and black satin edged with black velvet; and two pairs of knitted hosen';[40] as well as two pairs of knitted hosen and linen socks,[41] which would have helped to keep Mary warm during the winter months. In 1500 'a dress of crimson velvet, requiring 4 1/2 ells of material, one of blue velvet, and another of black, furred with ermine'[42] were ordered for the princess. To dress a young child in miniature adult clothing was not at all unusual up until the nineteenth century. Despite these multiple layers of expensive material, the opportunity to play would have been a natural part of Mary's life.

Mary would have been able to play with a wide range of toys including dolls with dresses matching the fashions of the day. She may have had doll furniture and other accessories to go with her favourite dolls. If so, examples of these have not survived. Other items such as a simple ball in cup, and rattles, would have been available for young the Mary to explore and play with.[43] Despite the common misconception that young children were subject to strict rules, playing was common, especially for the upper class who could afford to let their children have free time.

At around the age of four or five Mary would have been provided with her own establishment, which included ladies-in-waiting to serve and play with the young princess, a teacher and a wardrobe keeper who were each paid 66*s* and 8*p* per quarter. Mary's physician was paid 1*s* 5*d* per day to tend to any ailments.

Mary seems to have suffered with fragile health from quite a young age. Richard Babbam, the royal apothecary, received payments throughout the period from 1504 to 1509 for medicines for the princess. Unfortunately, what these medicines were for and how frequently they were administered is unknown. In December 1513 a

Doctor Robert Yaxley was paid the sum of £13 6s 8d for ten weeks' service to Mary. With a doctor attending on Mary for such an extensive period of time it appears Mary's health was a concern.[44] Most frustratingly we do not know what the doctors were treating. It may have been simple and quite common illnesses of the time or something more complex that required greater attention and care. Mary's health in the last years of her life was also of great concern and she was troubled with toothache in adulthood and a constant, agonising pain in her side, which flared up frequently.

Mary's establishment at Eltham was lavishly decorated with carpets, wall hangings, and other expensive items.[45] Despite being only five years of age Mary had a reputation as a daughter of the king to uphold and it would appear that King Henry VII was not about to skimp when it came to the raising and education of his children. Henry VII personally signed off items such as furniture, clothing, blankets, cushions, bedding, napkins and even ribbons of silk and gold[46] for all his children.[47]

As a future player on the international marriage stage, Mary would have received the highest quality education. She learned French and Latin. A young Frenchwoman named Jane Popincourt was placed within Mary's establishment not only for companionship, but primarily to teach the young princess French through conversation. There are few details relating to Jane's age and date of birth; it is commonly believed that the Frenchwoman was in her early teens when she was placed with Mary. Jane would later become a maid of honour to Queen Elizabeth of York and during the early reign of Henry VIII it was rumoured that the Frenchwoman became the new king's mistress for a time.[48]

In 1512 a tutor by the name of John Palsgrave was assigned to Mary to support her efforts to learn French in a more formal fashion. Palsgrave was paid £6 13s 4d a year for Mary's education.[49] Little is known of Palsgrave's early years. He was most likely educated at Cambridge before travelling to Paris where he obtained his Master of Arts degree. On returning to England he entered Mary's establishment. Palsgrave would end up travelling to France with Mary in 1514 on her marriage to the French king, Louis XII. Later Palsgrave would become the tutor of Henry VIII's illegitimate son, Henry Fitzroy.[50]

Mary would have also been taught other skills necessary for a woman of the time including dancing, singing, playing cards, playing a musical instrument and embroidery.[51] Mary was able to play the lute and clavichord with great skill. In 1506, when Prince Phillip and Juana of Castile visited England, Mary was able to impress the guests with her skills on each instrument. She was a skilled dancer and at the same banquet Mary danced and again received great praise for her talents.[52] Mary was taught social etiquette appropriate to her status as a princess and a woman; manners, rules at table, polite conversation and most importantly, how to dress and present herself.[53]

It was commonly believed at the time that women did not need to be as well educated as men. Women were not considered able to handle the deep theological questions posed by education, nor to comprehend fully what they were being taught. Instead it was believed that the role of a woman was to be a good and loving wife. A woman was to be obedient, loving, chaste, and God-fearing. Education and learning were therefore not seen as high priorities.

In his work *The First Blast of the Trumpet Against the Monstrous Regiment of Women*, published anonymously in 1558 against the accession of Mary I, John Knox stated that women are

> ...weak, frail, impatient, feeble, and foolish; and experience has declared them to be inconstant, variable, cruel, lacking the spirit of counsel and regiment. And these notable faults have men in all ages espied in that kind, for the which not only they have removed women from rule and authority, but also some have thought that men subject to the counsel or empire of their wives were unworthy of public office.[54]

And later:

> Woman in her greatest perfection was made to serve and obey man, not to rule and command him. As St. Paul does reason in these words: 'Man is not of the woman, but the woman of the man. And man was not created for the cause of the woman, but the woman for the cause of man; and therefore ought the woman to have a

power upon her head' (1 Cor. 11:8-10) [that is, a cover in sign of subjection]. Of which words it is plain that the apostle means, that woman in her greatest perfection should have known that man was lord above her; and therefore that she should never have pretended any kind of superiority above him, no more than do the angels above God the Creator, or above Christ their head. So I say, that in her greatest perfection, woman was created to be subject to man.[55]

Against God can nothing be more manifest than that a woman shall be exalted to reign above man; for the contrary sentence he has pronounced in these words: 'Thy will shall be subject to thy husband, and he shall bear dominion over thee' (Gen. 3:16). As [though] God should say, 'Forasmuch as you have abused your former condition, and because your free will has brought yourself and mankind into the bondage of Satan, I therefore will bring you in bondage to man. For where before your obedience should have been voluntary, now it shall be by constraint and by necessity; and that because you have deceived your man, you shall therefore be no longer mistress over your own appetites, over your own will or desires. For in you there is neither reason nor discretion which are able to moderate your affections, and therefore they shall be subject to the desire of your man. He shall be lord and governor, not only over your body, but even over your appetites and will.' This sentence, I say, did God pronounce against Eve and her daughters, as the rest of the scriptures do evidently witness. So that no woman can ever presume to reign above man, but the same she must needs do in despite of God, and in contempt of his punishment and malediction.[56]

Despite such declarations, there were several European women of this period who stood against such standards set upon them. Louise of Savoy (1476–1531), mother of the future King Francis I (who would inherit the throne from Mary's husband in 1515), ensured that both her daughter and her son received a high quality education. Louise was politically astute and an extremely adept diplomat. When her son, now King of France, was captured at the Battle of Pavia in 1525 by the Holy Roman Emperor, Charles V, Louise acted as Regent and successfully negotiated her son's release.[57]

Another politically astute woman was Margaret of Navarre (1492–1549), the daughter of Louise of Savoy. Margaret was as skilled in diplomatic relations as her mother. She was a writer, author, patron of the arts, humanist and reformer. Her court was known to be a place that attracted the highly educated and sophisticated as well as a refuge for humanists and reformers. Patricia and Rouben Cholakian write of Margaret that,

> ...she was a leading figure in the intellectual and religious movements of the time, a stalwart and unremittingly generous patron of the major writers and thinkers of the French Renaissance. She was a key figure in the reformist movement, often risking her own position in her fearless battle against corruption and abuse, a cause to which she committed herself throughout her entire life.[58]

Margaret of Austria, Duchess of Savoy (1480–1530) was another strong and influential woman. It would be Margaret and her father, the Holy Roman Emperor Maximilian I, who would, in the early part of the sixteenth century, negotiate a marriage between Mary and Charles, Prince of Castile, Margaret's nephew. Thrice widowed, Margaret dedicated her life to ruling the Netherlands. She was active in the daily workings of government: negotiating trade agreements, undertaking war and creating peace treaties, as well as devoting herself to the upbringing of her nieces and nephews. When her nephew Charles became Holy Roman Emperor in 1519, Margaret supported him in the running of the Low Countries as regent from 1507 until Charles reached his majority in 1515. Charles re-appointed her as regent in 1519 and she ruled the Hapsburg Netherlands until her death in 1530. Margaret's court was well known for its sophistication and many fathers sought to place their young daughters at her court.[59]

Mary's own grandmother, Lady Margaret Beaufort, was a deeply devout and influential woman. It has been suggested Lady Margaret, an imposing figure who outlived her son, played a role in supervising her grandchildren's education and upbringing. She founded the Lady Margaret Professorships of Divinity at the universities of Oxford and Cambridge. In addition to this she founded Christ's College, Cambridge, and on her death left a great sum of money for the building and endowment of St John's College. Lady Margaret was a prominent member of her son's court and took great pride and effort in laying out the guideline and rules relating to childbirth and christening of her royal grandchildren.[60]

Despite not having a classical education, Mary did not lack intellect, as her future letters will show. It may well have been Margaret Beaufort's early influence that guided Mary to use her wit and feminine skills to follow her desires and ultimately to get what she wanted out of life.

Unfortunately, we do not know what role Mary's mother played in Mary's formative years. There is hardly any mention of Mary in her mother's accounts, except for a note in her book of wardrobe for 20*d* to be paid to a tailor to make Mary a black satin gown and a payment of 12*d* for a letter of pardon in 1501 for an upcoming jubilee – that is a letter of participation.[61] This is not to say that Elizabeth did not care deeply for her daughter or any of her children, but as a queen her duty was to her husband the king. It was vital that she was by his side, not only to continue providing her husband with healthy children but to present herself as a unified force within the house of Tudor.

In addition to such a formal education, religion and faith were at the very core of a Tudor person's being. During the formative years of her life Mary would have been taught all the important aspects of the Catholic faith. She would have been taught about participating in the Mass and also the Eucharist and the miracle of transubstantiation, where the bread and wine of communion are believed to be turned into the actual flesh and blood of Christ. She would have learnt about confession and the need to admit sins to a priest and repent for her sins. She would have been taught about the idea of doing good deeds for others and the concept of taking pilgrimages. Mary took the belief in doing good deeds deeply to heart and during her teenage and later years she worked hard to support and provide for those in her service. Mary would have also believed that the Pope was the head of the Catholic Church and had been appointed to the papal throne by God.

A woman's virginity and chastity were highly treasured. It was vital that a woman go to her future husband a virgin (unless of course she was to remarry after the death of her first husband). It was extremely important that a woman's virginity be protected and a young girl be kept from anything that may have a negative influence on her lusts or desires. The concept of a woman being intellectual and chaste did not go hand in hand. In fact, many believed that if a woman were learned then she would abandon both her femininity and chastity.[62]

We know nothing of Mary's sexual knowledge or experiences (if any) growing up. The ideal of the Virgin Mary, chaste and devoted to God, would have been emphasised to Mary from a young age. However, it is highly unlikely that she would have known nothing about what awaited her in the marriage bed and as a wife. Mary would have had to have been deaf and blind not to have known that women gave birth or to be completely oblivious to any courtly gossip. It may have been a close friend, such as Jane Popincourt or even her governess Mistress Anne Crowmer, who educated Mary on menstruation, sexual intercourse and childbirth.

We gain the first glimpse of Mary's early years in 1499, when Mary was just four years of age. Desiderius Erasmus – he who criticised mothers who did not breastfeed their own children – was invited by William Blount, 4th Baron Mountjoy, to accompany him to England. Erasmus visited Eltham Palace, and wrote of his experience:

> I was staying at Lord Mountjoy's country house, when Thomas More came to see me, and took me out with him for a walk as far as the next village, where all the King's children, except Prince Arthur, who was then the eldest son, were being educated. When we came into the hall, the attendants not only of the palace but also of Mountjoy's household were all assembled. In the midst stood Prince Henry, then nine years old, and having already something of royalty in his demeanour, in which there was a certain dignity combined with singular courtesy. On his right was Margaret, about eleven years of age, afterwards married to James, King of Scots, and on his left played Mary, a child of four. Edmund was an infant in arms. More, with his companion Arnold, after paying his respects to the boy Henry, presented him with some writing. For my part, not having expected anything

of the sort, I had nothing to offer, but promised that on another occasion I would in some way declare my duty towards him. Meantime I was angry with More for not having warned me, especially as the boy sent me a little note, while we were at dinner, to challenge something from my pen. I went home, and in the Muses' spite, from whom I had been so long divorced, finished the poem within three days.[63]

Frustratingly, Erasmus writes nothing more of Mary than a mere side note in relation to her older brother Henry, another example that women were far less important than men. It is interesting to note that Erasmus writes that Mary 'played' by Henry's side. At only four years of age, Mary may have been too distracted by a favourite doll or toy to focus on an important visitor.

As mentioned earlier, shortly before Mary's fourth birthday she had received her first marriage proposal. Duke Ludovico Sforza, Il Moro from Milan wrote to King Henry VII seeking Mary's hand in marriage for his son Massimiliano who was the Count of Pavia. The duke was the head of one of the richest states in Italy and sought an alliance with England in the hopes that he would have England's support against France.[64] The duke wrote to his ambassador, Don Raimundo de Raymundi of Soncino, asking him to return to England and seek Henry VII's youngest daughter in marriage for his son.

As we desire to tighten our friendly relations with his Majesty, we shall gladly receive the Order of the Garter, and you will take steps so that it be sent. Nor does this bond, though a strong one, satisfy our desire, but as his Majesty has two daughters, and we understand that the younger is of an age corresponding to that of the Count of Pavia, our firstborn, you will tell his Highness that if it pleases him to give his younger daughter as wife to the Count, we shall gladly receive her as our daughter-in-law.[65]

Henry VII was not inclined to have his youngest daughter married to the Count of Pavia, especially since at the time England and France were at peace. In addition to this, Henry VII was not willing to marry his daughter off to a wealthy Italian state; the English king was looking for a grander marriage alliance for his daughter, one that would hopefully unify England with a far greater European power.

The prospect of marriage was still some time away for Mary. In the meantime the young princess would face two deaths in her family and her father would face a rebellion that threatened to topple him from the English throne.

3

Of Deaths, Marriages and Rebellions

✠

'The same year was fatal, as well for deaths as marriages, and that with equal temper.'

Outside the walls of Mary's establishment, her early years were far from peaceful. Her father, Henry VII, was still a relatively new king and by the time of Mary's birth in 1496 had been on the throne for eleven years. Although he had a son and heir, there were people who sought to bring him to ruin. Some of the old Yorkist faction sought revenge for the death of Richard III. Additionally, England's old enemy, Scotland, was always looking for an opportunity to invade.

In February 1487, less than two years after Henry VII claimed the throne at the Battle of Bosworth Field, a young boy had appeared claiming he was Edward Plantagenet, Earl of Warwick and that he was the rightful heir to the English throne. Edward, Earl of Warwick was the son of George, Duke of Clarence, the late brother of King Edward IV. The problem with the pretender's claim was that the real Edward, Earl of Warwick (aged eleven), was a prisoner in the Tower of London. Henry VII had taken the young Earl and imprisoned him immediately on taking the throne, fearing that Edward, as a Yorkist born and bred, would be a candidate for others to rally behind.[1] It would seem that King Henry VII's suspicions were correct and in retaliation for the young pretender's claim, he had the real Edward, Earl of Warwick, brought out of the Tower of London and marched through the streets of London. Not all believed what they were seeing and soon Yorkist supporters appeared out of the woodwork to provide aid for the pretender.

One of these supporters was John de la Pole, Earl of Lincoln and nephew of Edward IV. It is unknown if the Earl of Lincoln believed the boy was the heir of George, Duke of Clarence and true claimant to the English throne, or if Lincoln simply saw an opportunity to rise in rebellion against Henry VII. Either way, the Earl worked with his aunt, Margaret, Duchess of Burgundy, another sister of Edward IV, to raise an army consisting of Swiss and German mercenaries to travel to England in rebellion.[2] Landing in Ireland, Lincoln and his men were warmly greeted by Gerald Fitgerald, Earl of Kildare, who was no friend of Henry VII. In Dublin on 24 May 1487 the boy claiming to be Edward Plantagenet was crowned King Edward VI.[3]

In reality the pretender was one Lambert Simnel, a baker's son. He was the pupil of Richard Simon, a priest who saw potential in the young boy. Simnel was handsome, reasonably well educated and held himself well; Simon clearly believed that he could pass off the boy as Edward Plantagenet. It is believed that at first the priest wished for Simnel to play the part of Richard, youngest son of Edward IV and one of the mysterious princes in the Tower. Simon soon changed his mind and quickly went about educating and training young Simnel to play the role of Edward, Earl of Warwick.[4]

With an army behind him, the newly crowned pretender landed at Furness, Lancashire, before moving eastwards gathering supporters along the way. Soon there were approximately 4,000 Irishmen, 1,500 German and Swiss mercenaries, and a large number of Yorkist supporters, all marching south.[5]

In an attempt to disperse the army, Henry VII issued a pardon for any of those that had risen in rebellion against him. The people were to admit their offences to the king and then disband.[6] It is unclear if any of the Yorkist supporters took up this offer. Perhaps they felt it was too late and that it was better to move forward with their claim, or perish in the attempt. Henry VII was not about to let his hard-won crown slip away, raising his own army and gaining the support of Thomas Stanley, Earl of Derby, his stepfather and his men.[7] The king was also supported by the Earl of Shrewsbury and his own uncle, Jasper Tudor, and their men. In all Henry VII had approximately 6,000 men behind him, a far superior number than the supposed 'Edward VI'.[8] Both armies met near the village of East Stroke in Nottinghamshire. Of the Battle of Polydore Vergil wrote:

> Both sides fought very stoutly and fiercely, nor did the Germans in the forefront, rough men and exercised in arms, yield to the English, just as not many men excelled their captain Martin Schwartz in power of mind and body. On the other hand the Irish, although they conducted themselves with great courage, yet since in accordance with their national custom they fought with bodies unprotected by any armor, they fell more than anybody else, and their slaughter was a great source of fear to the others. The battle was fought on equal terms for more than three hours, when at length the king's first battle-line, by far the strongest and best manned, which alone had joined and continued the fight, made such a vigorous attack on the enemy that first it killed the opposing captains, then turned all the rest to rout, and in the flight these men were killed or captured. But when the battle was finished, then it was more evident how much courage had existed in the enemy army. For their leaders John Earl of Lincoln, Francis Lovell, Thomas Broughton, Martin Schwartz and Thomas Fitzgerald, the commander of the Irish, all died at the posts they had occupied while fighting when alive. About 4,000 men were killed, and among these the five leaders I have named. The king lost less than half as many of his men, who had launched the first attack.[9]

Henry VII was victorious and had suppressed his first major rebellion. John de la Pole, Earl of Lincoln, had put his support behind a young man that he probably knew to be a pretender. In doing so he had lost his life in the Battle of Stoke Field on 16 June 1487. As for Lambert Simnel, Henry VII took pity on the boy, perhaps realising that he was nothing more than a pawn in a larger game, and put the boy to work in the Tudor kitchens turning the spit. It was hot, exhausting work but at least Simnel was alive. He would end up working his way up to becoming the King's Falconer, a strange twist of fate for a young boy who once sought to claim the English throne.[10]

There was little time to rest because soon Henry VII would again be fighting to keep his crown and throne. This time the threat went by the name of Perkin Warbeck. Warbeck asserted that he was the long lost Richard, Duke of York, the youngest son of the late Edward IV and one of the princes in the Tower. He stated that his older brother Edward had been killed while in the Tower, but he had managed to escape and flee to Europe where he had been raised by York sympathisers. He had previously been sworn to secrecy about his identity, but, now he was older, believed it was his right to claim the throne.[11]

The truth was that Warbeck was the son of Jehan de Werbecque, a burgher of Tournai. Born in 1474, Warbeck worked in several households before starting work for a Breton silk merchant by the name of Pierre Jean Meno. In autumn Warbeck travelled on one of Meno's ships to Cork, Ireland. Upon seeing young Warbeck many claimed that he was the true Edward Plantaganet, Earl of Warwick. Warbeck denied this, but instead stated that he was the long-lost Richard, Duke of York the younger of the two princes in the Tower.[12]

Despite the falseness of his claim there were a number of European rulers who either believed Warbeck or simply wished to take the opportunity to rally against Henry VII. They included Charles VIII of France and Maximilian I, Holy Roman Emperor. Both men publicly declared that Warbeck was Richard, Duke of York, and the true heir to the English throne. In addition Margaret, Duchess of Burgundy and sister of the late Edward IV, also declared that Warbeck was her nephew and sought to support and educate him. Polydore Vergil writes that Margaret, Duchess of Burgundy,

> ...could not help hating Henry worse day by day, and she brooded day and night about inflicting some plague upon him so that someday this man might be ruined and destroyed, she might satiate her hatred with her enemy's blood, and the rule

would come to some man of her faction. Then, after seeing all the strivings of Earl John of Lincoln and herself come to naught a little earlier, she returned to her ancient practice and began to weave an inextricable net for Henry.[13]

With another opportunity presenting itself Margaret wasted little time taking Warbeck into her care. At her court she began to teach him the history of the House of York and the manners and history of England.[14]

On Saturday 1 November 1494, in an attempt to counter Perkin's threat of invasion, Henry VII bestowed the title of Duke of York on his youngest son, the three-year-old Henry Tudor, in a lavish ceremony.[15] This did not stop Warbeck and soon he was preparing to invade England.

With the financial aid of his 'Aunt' Margaret, Duchess of Burgundy, Warbeck sailed with fourteen ships and approximately 6,000 men to England. Warbeck's ships attempted to land at Sandwich, Kent, on 3 July 1495, but the soldiers were routed before they could even make it to the shore. Warbeck and his men fled to Ireland and then to Scotland, where they were greeted by King James IV. With an English alliance with Castile and Aragon in the form of a marriage between Henry VII's son Prince Arthur and Princess Katherine of Aragon, James VI needed to strengthen Scotland's ties with France. The Scottish king supported Warbeck's claims that he was Richard, Duke of York, and even organised a marriage between Warbeck and Lady Catherine Gordon, a distant cousin of the king. In addition, James IV granted Warbeck an annuity of £1,200. It is doubtful that James IV believed Warbeck was the real Richard, Duke of York, but used this as an opportunity to again go to war with England.[16]

In September 1496, Warbeck, supported by James IV and a Scottish army, crossed the border and invaded England. James IV claimed the attack was to place Richard, Duke of York, as the rightful King of England, on the throne. It was hoped that those in the north of England would support the venture. However, this support did not materialise and soon the Scottish army was defeated. Warbeck fled to Ireland.

In September 1497 he returned to England to make another attempt to claim the throne. Warbeck and a small group of supporters landed in Cornwall. The place was chosen because Henry VII had recently levied huge taxes in the area to pay for dealing with the two rebellions. It was hoped that the Cornish would rise up against Henry VII and join with Warbeck. The plan worked and soon Warbeck was being proclaimed 'King Richard IV' and had gathered an army of around 8,000 men. The army travelled from Cornwall to Exeter and then to Taunton. While in Taunton Warbeck heard reports that Henry VII's army was closing in; terrified, Warbeck panicked and fled, but was captured at Beaulieu in Hampshire.

In June 1498 at Westminster and Cheapside, Warbeck was forced to announce to the public that he was not Richard, Duke of York, and that he was nothing more than an imposter. He was asked as to why he was impersonating the duke and in response Warbeck blamed Margaret, Duchess of Burgundy.[17] After the public confession Henry VII treated Warbeck with some kindness, keeping him at court and even making Warbeck's wife, Lady Gordon, a lady-in-waiting to Queen Elizabeth of York. However Warbeck tried to escape and when he was captured he was imprisoned in the Tower of London. It was within the Tower that Warbeck met Edward Plantagenet, 17th Earl of Warwick, the son of George, Duke of Clarence, and together they planned their escape. The plan was discovered and with Henry VII not wishing to take any more chances, Warbeck was charged with trying to escape from the Tower. On 23 November 1499 he was taken to Tyburn Hill where he was hanged. Although the official charge was trying to escape from the Tower, the truth was that while he was alive Warbeck posed a threat to Henry VII. The first Tudor king simply could not let any such threat to his throne and his dynasty live.[18]

While trying to suppress Perkin Warbeck's rebellion Henry VII was also trying to negotiate a marriage for Prince Arthur, Prince of Wales, Duke of Cornwall, Earl of Chester. Mary would have known little of her eldest brother, as Arthur had his own establishment at Farnham, Surrey. In November 1489 at just three years of age Arthur had been formally created Prince of Wales.[19] As Prince of Wales and heir to the English throne, Arthur would learn how to govern.

Is seeking a suitable wife for his son Henry naturally sought an alliance with a strong foreign power. Marriage negotiations had begun only a few years after Arthur's birth and Henry VII had turned to King Ferdinand of Aragon and his wife Queen Isabella of Castile. Rulers of Aragon and Castile respectively the couple provided a great powerbase, an alliance with which would greatly strengthen Henry VII's standing as the new Tudor king. He sought the hand of Ferdinand and Isabella's youngest daughter, the beautiful Katherine of Aragon, in marriage for Arthur.

On 26 March 1489, when Arthur was just two-and-a-half years of age and Katherine only a year older, the children were contracted in marriage. Part of the negotiated marriage treaty was that each party promised friendship and that they would support the other if they were attacked. Neither party would support rebels of the other – this last clause was vital for Henry VII as he desperately desired the return of John de la Pole, Earl of Lincoln and Yorkist nephew of the late King Edward IV, who at the time also held a strong claim to the throne and was free in Europe. With regards to the marriage between Arthur and Katherine the treaty stated:

In order to strengthen this alliance the Princess Katharine is to marry Prince Arthur. The marriage is to be contracted per verba de futuro as soon as Katharine and Arthur attain the necessary age. The marriage shall be contracted per verba de prœsenti and consummated as soon as the Prince and the Princess attain the necessary age for it. Henry and Ferdinand and Isabella shall swear to employ all their influence with their children that the marriage be contracted as stipulated.[20]

All was set to ally England with Castile and Aragon; yet the actual marriage would not take place for another twelve years. In the meantime King Ferdinand and Queen Isabella had been watching events in England through the eyes and contacts of their ambassadors. With several rebellions taking place during Henry VII's early reign they worried about the stability of the Tudor dynasty. With the death of Perkin Warbeck, and Simnel Lambert kept secure in the king's kitchens, there was only one more threat in England that the Spanish couple worried about – Edward Plantagenet, Earl of Warwick.

Despite being held in the Tower of London since he was just a boy, his mere existence still appeared to be too much for Ferdinand and Isabella. As Simnel Lambert proved, anyone could rise claiming to be the Earl or perhaps the real Earl of Warwick could escape the Tower and seek to gather Yorkist supporters to his cause. The Spanish rulers strongly hinted to Henry VII that the marriage treaty would not go ahead until all threats to the throne had been removed, and that included Edward, Earl of Warick.[21]

It is said that Henry VII debated his decision for some time before finally relenting. Edward, Earl of Warwick, was beheaded in August 1499. Polydore Vergil writes that 'Earl Edward, who had been imprisoned since childhood, [was] so far removed from the sight of man and beast that he could not easily tell a chicken from a goose.'[22] Whether Henry VII believed that Edward, Earl of Warwick, posed a genuine threat is unknown. Either way, the young man was dead and the union between the Tudors and the great rulers of Castile and Aragon could go ahead.

Before Mary could see her distant elder brother married, she was to be confronted with the first death in her family. In February 1499 Elizabeth of York went into confinement at Greenwich to give birth to her sixth child. The baby was a boy and named Edmund, perhaps in honour of Henry VII's father Edmund Tudor who had died before Henry was born. Despite appearing strong and healthy at birth the little boy would only live for fifteen months before he died in 1500,[23] cause unknown. His passing meant that, once more, Mary was the youngest of the Tudor siblings.

Sadness would eventually turn to joy when Katherine of Aragon arrived at the English harbour of Plymouth at three o'clock on Saturday 2 October 1501.[24] Katherine made her formal entry into London on the 12th. It was in an upper-storey room, out of sight of the crowd, where Mary and the other women in her family, including her older sister Margaret, caught their first glimpse of their new sister-in-law. Mary was now five years of age and had been granted two new gowns for the lavish occasion, 'one of russet velvet trimmed with ermine backs and furred within with miniver, and another of crimson velvet with tabard sleeves trimmed with the same; a kirtle of tawny satin with a pair of green satin sleeves'.[25] There are no records of Mary's first impressions of her sister-in-law,

Katherine. She may have been in awe of the beautiful young Spanish princess but certainly in the following years Mary and Katherine would form a close friendship which would last Mary's lifetime.

Arthur and Katherine were married in a spectacular ceremony at St Paul's Cathedral on 14 November 1501. As the bells of all the churches in London tolled in celebration, a great wedding feast was held and it is assumed that Mary attended with the other members of her family. The celebrations and feasting lasted for several days. A great tournament was held at Westminster. Katherine, the new Princess of Wales, sat with Queen Elizabeth, Lady Margaret Beaufort, the king's mother, and the princesses Margaret and Mary. On the other side of the stands were the king, Prince Arthur and Prince Henry. The newly married couple and members of the court watched the king's champion, the Duke of Buckingham, joust against the Sir Guillaume de la Riviere who led the challengers. The whole event was organised by Sir Thomas Brandon, uncle of Charles Brandon, who would become Mary's second husband.[26]

After the wedding it was decided that Arthur and Katherine would return to Ludlow Castle, the prince's main residence in Wales. There was some discussion over this since Arthur was only fifteen and Katherine seventeen. However, the decision had been made and on 21 December Katherine and Arthur departed for Ludlow. On their journey they stayed at Bewdley and then at Woodstock in Oxfordshire where they celebrated Christmas. After this they made their way to Ludlow where Arthur and Katherine began to settle into their new life and the prince, together with his council, returned to the duty of governing Wales.[27]

Less than a month later, on 24 January 1502, Mary's elder sister Margaret was betrothed to King James IV of Scotland. Despite previous strained relationships, negotiations had been taking place for some time for a marriage between the eleven-year-old Margaret Tudor and the twenty-nine-year-old James IV, King of Scotland. The marriage was beneficial for both parties, James IV would receive 30,000 golden nobles (£10,000)[28] which was an extraordinary sum in those days and equates to £6,224,000 today.[29] Henry VII secured peace with Scotland, which ensured that James IV would not support any rebels or wage war against England.[30] The following day a proxy marriage took place at

Richmond Palace. High Mass was celebrated before the wedding and King Henry, Queen Elizabeth, Prince Henry and Princess Mary attended. Following this Margaret was married to James IV with the Earl of Bothwell standing in for the king.[31]

With little warning, on 2 April 1502, Prince Arthur died. Toward the end of March, Arthur and Katherine had become ill. As their health deteriorated they were both instructed to go to their beds, attended by doctors. Prayers were said for the prince and princess, but no amount of medicine or prayers could save the prince and Arthur died.[32]

There are many theories put forward surrounding the cause of the prince's death. Suggestions such as cancer or tuberculosis have been put forward as possible causes. However, when examining the recorded symptoms of both Arthur and Katherine, the most likely reason is the sweating sickness.

Appearing in 1485 and then on and off throughout the century until 1551, the sweating sickness was one of the worst diseases to strike England since the Black Death. In 1557 it was described as 'so sharp and deadly that the lyke was never hearde of to any manne's remembrance before that tyme'.[33]

The symptoms are closely associated with modern-day influenza or viral pneumonia. First, people would start to ache all over their body, they would get headaches, become thirsty, vomit, and most notably, and where the name came from, start to sweat profusely. They would also experience a rapid pulse, chest pain and the struggle to breathe. So sudden was the illness that many of those who caught it were dead within twenty-four hours.

When Henry VII heard the news that his son was dead, he was overwhelmed with grief. Elizabeth of York was called to comfort her husband and she tried to reassure him that they were both young enough to have more children. Elizabeth was also devastated at the loss of her son and after she left her husband she broke down in tears, with Henry now coming to console his wife.[34] Edward Hall, in his *Chronicle of the History of England*, wrote of Arthur's death:

For that noble prince Arthur, the kynges fyrst begotten sonne, after that he had bene juaryed to the lady Katheryn his vvyfe.

v. monethes, departed out of this transitory lyfe, i-u his castel of Ludlowe, and with a great funerall obsequy was buryed in the cathedral churche of Worcettre.[35]

Following his death, Arthur's body was disembowelled and filled with spices before being embalmed. On 25 April the coffin was taken to Worcester Cathedral, a journey of 40 miles. The weather on the day was so bad and the rain so strong, that the cart carrying the coffin repeatedly got stuck in the mud and oxen were brought to pull out the cart.

Arthur Tudor had been the heir to the throne and his funeral was a lavish and respectful affair. More than 1,000 candles burned in Worcester Cathedral and the funeral was attended by approximately 550 people, with 2,400 yards of black cloth having been purchased for the mourners. William Smith, Bishop of Lincoln, conducted the funeral service while the coffin was buried in the south end of the high altar. Smith sprinkled holy water and earth into the coffin and then the Comptrollers of Arthur's household ceremoniously broke their white staves in half and placed them into the grave to show their service to the late prince had ended. Henry VII ordered a tomb to be erected.[36]

There are no records of Mary attending her brother's funeral and it is highly unlikely that she would have done so. It was not usual for royal members of the deceased's family to attend. For the rest of the year, Elizabeth of York wore black. Her account books show that Margaret and Mary also wore black; several items in black material being ordered for the girls, including in June, 'a black satin gown' for Mary.[37]

Elizabeth became pregnant with her seventh child shortly after Arthur's death. She gave birth one last time on Candlemas Day, 2 February 1503. Her labour came on suddenly and after a difficult labour Elizabeth gave birth in the Tower of London to a daughter who was named Catherine. Neither mother nor daughter would live long. Elizabeth of York died in 1503, on 11 February, which was also her birthday. Baby Catherine had died the day before.[38] The exact cause of Elizabeth's death remains unknown. After giving birth to her first child Arthur, the queen suffered from an ague, a type of fever and sweats. It may be that with her last pregnancy

Elizabeth contracted puerperal fever, an infection of the womb or vaginal passage, or perhaps with the difficulty of labour there was some internal injury or heavy bleeding.[39] Mary Tudor, at eight years of age, had lost her beloved mother.

Such was Henry VII's grief over the loss of his wife he ordered 636 Masses to be said for her soul. Elizabeth of York was buried in the Lady Chapel at Westminster Abbey, also known as the Henry VII Chapel. Each year on the anniversary of Elizabeth's death Henry ordered that a requiem Mass be sung, bells tolled and 100 candles to be burned in his late wife's honour. Not long after Elizabeth's death the king fell ill and it was reported that his sickness was owing to a broken heart caused by the loss of the woman he loved.[40]

We have no knowledge of how Mary reacted first to the death of her brother, then to the loss of her mother. Arthur was ten years older than Mary and although the siblings would have known one another it is highly doubtful that they would have been close. Mary was raised at Eltham Palace with her other siblings and spent most of her time either there or travelling from court to court. The loss of her older brother probably did not touch Mary as deeply as the loss of her mother.

Despite her mother's death, Margaret's wedding to King James IV of Scotland went ahead. Without her mother, Margaret's grandmother, Lady Margaret Beaufort, stepped in to ensure that all was prepared and made ready for her granddaughter's departure. Margaret was married in person to her husband King James IV of Scotland on 8 August 1503.[41] It would be many long years before Mary saw her sister again.

At just eight years of age Mary had known a great deal of death: her oldest brother Arthur, and her two younger siblings, Edmund and Catherine as babies, as well as the death of her mother. Mary had also, in essence, lost her older sister Margaret as Margaret was now queen of Scotland and living far away. Her father had managed to stop two major rebellions against his throne, yet despite these victories such rebellions showed that there were those who resented the Tudor king and the house of Tudor. Although brought up in splendour, Mary's early years were far from stable.

4

Princess of Castile

❧

'Nature has never formed anything more beautiful; and she excels no less in goodness and wisdom.'

Before Mary suffered the devastating loss of both her older brother and her mother, at the age of five she was a married woman, by proxy. This of course was not uncommon, especially for a royal princess. Marriages between children were regularly arranged to create alliances and unite families, the children, while technically married, were not expected to live together as man and wife until they came of age. For a girl this was twelve years and for a boy, fourteen.[1] For Mary's marriage it is important to step back and examine the marriage haggling that would take place between Henry VII of England and Philip, Duke of Burgundy for several years until finally, after Philip's death, only weeks after he was crowned king, *juris uxore*, of Castile, a treaty would be signed which would see young Mary married to her even younger husband, Philip's son, the future King Charles V of Spain and Holy Roman Emperor.

In early June 1500 Henry VII and Philip, Duke of Burgundy negotiated a treaty of friendship. The first part of this treaty established that Henry VII's second son, Henry Tudor, Duke of York, would be promised in marriage to Philip's eldest daughter Eleanor;[2] the second that the English king's younger surviving daughter Mary, would be pledged to marry Philip's son Charles. Charles was just four months old.[3] The details of the treaty were sketchy; Henry VII did not appear to ponder greatly on the smaller details. For now, a tentative treaty was in place and he was strengthening England's ties with Europe's greatest leaders.

The treaty would not last long. Events throughout Europe would see constant changes in alliances and soon Philip was seeking a French bride for his son Charles, namely Princess Claude, the daughter of Louis XII of France. The political winds changed again and soon Louis XII withdrew from the treaty with Philip and married his daughter Claude to Francis of Angoulême, son of Charles, Count of Angoulême and Louise of Savoy.[4] Yet again the Duke of Burgundy was on the lookout for a beautiful and influential bride for his son and it would seem that fate would intervene.

On January 16 1506 Philip, now king of Castile through his wife Joanna, *suo jure* queen regnant of Castile, were sailing for Spain when a fierce storm blew them off course and they had to take refuge in England. Never one to overlook an opportunity, Henry VII jumped at this one and welcomed his royal guests warmly. Philip I and Joanna would be wooed with almost three months of entertainment and lavish celebrations. While this was happening Henry VII and Philip I of Castile negotiated a new treaty of friendship and a renewed discussion of marriage between Mary and Charles took place.[5] On the evening of Sunday 1 February a celebration was held at Windsor Castle. Mary was presented to her future father-in-law in order to impress him with her beauty, grace and skills.

> And when the King heard that the King of Castile was coming he went to the door of the great chamber and there received him, and desired him to take him by the arm, or else the King of Castile would not have taken so much upon him, but by the King's desire; and so both together went through that chamber, the King's dining chamber, and from thence to an inner chamber where was my lady Princess and my lady Mary, the King's daughter, and divers other ladies. And after the King of Castile had kissed them and communed with them, and communed a while with the King and ladies all, they came into the King's dining chamber, where danced my lady Princess and a Spanish

lady with her in Spanish array, and after she had danced two or three dances she left ; and then danced my lady Mary and an English lady with her : and ever and anon the lady Princess desired the King of Castile to dance, which, after he had excused himself once or twice, answered that he was a mariner "but yet" said he, "you would cause me to dance" and so he danced not, but communed still with the King. And after that my lady Mary had danced two or three dances, she went and sat by my lady Princess on the end of the carpet which was under the cloth of estate and near where the King and the King of Castile stood. And then danced one of the strange lords and a lady of England. That done, my Lady Mary played on the lute, and after upon the claregulls [a type of early piano]. who played very well, and she was of all folks there greatly praised that in her youth in everything she behaved herself so very well.[6]

With her beauty and display of talent and skills, Mary had made a very good impression. The Treaty of Windsor was officially signed on 9 February 1506. England and Castile were bound to support one another should one party be attacked or go to war and aid would be given to the country under attack. The treaty also stated that each country should not do anything that would be detrimental to the other and that any rebels of one country should not be supported or housed by the other, but returned to their home country immediately.[7]

The clause regarding political refugees was an oblique reference to Edmund de la Pole, the nephew of Henry VII's late queen. Pole was a staunch Yorkist and had a powerful claim to the throne.[8] As previously mentioned, to have Pole returned to English soil – and undoubtedly quickly despatched – would have been a huge boost for the new Tudor dynasty's tentative hold on the throne.

While a marriage alliance between Mary and Charles was discussed during Philip and Joanna's time in England, an agreement was never officially put to paper. A marriage between the widowed Henry VII and Margaret of Austria, Regent of the Netherlands, was also discussed, yet it does not appear that either party was deeply invested in such an arrangement.[9] Philip and Joanna left England on 23 April 1506.

On 25 September 1506, Philip died aged just thirty, having been confirmed as King of Castile earlier in the month. His wife Joanna had inherited Castile through her late mother, Queen Isabella, and was considered mad and not fit to inherit, let alone rule.[10] Henry VII, eager to maintain the peace treaty, continued to keep friendly relations with the Holy Roman Emperor Maximilian, (the late Philip's father), and Margaret of Austria, regent of the Netherlands, Philip's sister, who was proposed as the new bride for the English king. Margaret was not at all interested in remarrying; from 1507 she was appointed guardian of the young Charles V. Having no new bride, Henry pushed even harder for a marriage between his daughter Mary and the young Charles, now heir to both the kingdom of Castile and the Hapsburg Netherlands. The Holy Roman Emperor Maximilian I sought to maintain an alliance with England to ensure that Henry VII would not join forces with France.[11]

In May and June 1507 several grand jousting celebrations were held in memory of Philip and Joanna's stay in England the previous year and perhaps in hope of keeping the prospect of a marriage between the young Charles V and princess Mary alive. These jousts were organised by the sixteen-year-old Prince Henry, now the sole heir to the English throne.

The jousts took place at young Henry's manor in Kennington and it was not the prince, but his younger sister Mary, who was the star of the events.[12] Mary (now aged eleven) played the role of Lady May, the servant of Dame Summer. 'Lady May' had been told about recent jousts that celebrated her enemy Lady Winter and her servant Dame February. She wished therefore that these jousts held in the months of May and June would represent her own honour. Dressed in a gown of green embroidered with spring flowers and surrounded by her ladies (also dressed in green), Mary as Lady May addressed the contestants that wished to joust for her honour:

Most highe and excellent Princesse under your patient supportac'on I which am called the Ladye Maie in all monethes of the yeare to lustye hearts most pleasant certifie your Highness howe that under signe and scale fully authorized by the hand of my Ladye and SovVaigne Dame Somer, I have free licence during

the tyme of my short Raine to passe my tyme and a ffortnight in
the moncth of my sister June as shalbe to my Comfort and most
solace. Wherefore I have sailed in the scouring seas in this shippe
I have cast out myne anchors under the supportac on of your
gratious licence to rest me and my said servants which have long
been travailed in the stormy seasons of March and Aprill for I see
in mynde that noble couragious hearts are determined to have my
Ladye Somer in exercise of Chivalric.[13]

With only a short speech and at the age of eleven, Mary played her
role in the courtly ideals of chivalry perfectly. Young and beautiful,
she presented herself as the servant of Summer who had battled
great seas to find anchor and safety among the brave jousters who
fought for her honour. She had come to see who would fight for
her Lady Summer and in turn for her. Mary was placing herself
under the protection of brave, strong men who would do their
chivalric duty and fight to protect her. This game of courtly love and
chivalry is one that Mary would play well throughout her life, using
her weak position as a woman to gain what she wanted from the
men around her. After acting the role of Lady May in this specific
joust, further jousts during May and June provided Mary with the
opportunity to practise skills that would aid her later in life.

Every Sunday and Thursday in May and June of that year,
superb jousts were held between two o'clock on the afternoon and
six o'clock in the evening when the church bells rang. Courtiers of
great stature and skill would charge along the tilt at one another,
trying to break their lances and see their opponent fall. Mary,
as Lady May and the centre of the celebrations, sat in a pavilion
strewn with flowers. Next to this was a hawthorn tree in blossom,
an emblem of the Tudors, the flowers symbolising Henry VII's
children, on which was a shield quartered with the Tudor colours
of green and white. Mary sat with her brother Henry overseeing the
celebrations and fierce jousting.[14]

On 21 December 1507 at Calais, commissioners, with the
assent of the Holy Roman Emperor Maximilian, and Henry VII of
England, finally signed a treaty.[15] The treaty was set out in two
parts, the first detailing the military alliance and support that
Henry VII and Archduke Charles would provide one another.

Fourteen points were negotiated and agreed on, stating that neither party should show harm to the other, that both parties would come to the aid of the other should they be harmed or attacked, that neither party should assist or support rebels of the other party, that neither party should conclude a peace treaty with the enemy without consent of the other party and that Henry VII should act as a good father to Charles and Charles as a good son to Henry VII.[16]

The second part of the treaty focused on the marriage of Mary Tudor and Archduke Charles. This part of the treaty consisted of twenty points that seemed to have been haggled over at some length, detailing what would happen to each person in the proposed marriage should the other renage and who was to pay what money to whom and when.

The Archduke Charles is to conclude the marriage with the Princess Mary, either in person or by proxy, before the feast of Easter next coming.

The King of England consents to the marriage of his daughter.

Within forty days after the Archduke Charles shall have completed the fourteenth year of his age, he is to contract the marriage by ambassadors sent for that purpose to England.

The King of England promises to permit the marriage to be contracted *per verba de præsenti* on that occasion.

The Archduke Charles is to contract the marriage *per verba de præsenti* with the proxies of the Princess Mary as soon as he shall have completed the fourteenth year of his age.

The King of England is to send the Princess Mary to the Archduke Charles within three months after the marriage shall have been contracted *per verba de præsenti*.

The dowry is to consist of 250,000 crowns, which are to be entrusted to the keeping of merchants in Bruges.

Conditions on which the payment of the dowry is to take place, and on which it is to be restored:

The King of England gives the usual securities for the payment of the dowry. Moreover, the Mayor of Calais, for himself and the Merchants of the Staple, is to give security for the payment.

The King of the Romans, the Archduchess Margaret, Charles de Croy, Henry, Count of Nassau, &c., and the towns and counties of Flanders, bind themselves to pay 250,000 crowns to King Henry if the Archduke Charles refuses to contract the marriage. The King of England, his noblemen, counties and towns of England, bind themselves to pay an equal sum of money to the King of the Romans if the Princess Mary refuses to contract the marriage.

All the documents respecting this marriage are to be exchanged in London before the feast of Easter next coming, and before the ambassadors of the King of the Romans go to London, in order to contract the marriage.

The King of the Romans and the Archduke Charles are to assign to the Princess Mary all the towns, castles, lands, &c., as her jointure, which the Duchess Margaret has held.

The noblemen and vassals of the Archduke are to be security for the jointure.

The Princess Mary is to have a jointure, not only in the dominions which the Archduke at present possesses, but also in those which he shall hereafter inherit according to the custom of the country.

The right of inheritance in England is reserved to the Princess, as though she were living in that country.

The dowry is, after the death of the Princess, to remain with the Archduke Charles, whether they should have children or not.

All the jewels, ornaments, &c. of the Princess are in such a case to become property of the Archduke.

The King of the Romans and the Archduchess Margaret are to procure within [blank] days the consent of King Ferdinand to this marriage.

Both parties renounce all exceptions against this treaty, of whatever nature they may be.

The contracting parties are to ratify this treaty before the feast of Easter next coming.[17]

With Easter only a few short months away it would seem that both parties were eager to see the young couple married, at least by proxy. For Henry VII the future of the Tudor dynasty was looking strong. His eldest daughter was married to King James IV of Scotland, securing peace, at least for a time, along the Scottish borders. His son and heir, Henry, was still in the marriage market and negotiations were on and off again for the young prince to marry his brother's widow Katherine of Aragon to strengthen ties with King Ferdinand of Aragon. Now his daughter Mary was tied in marriage with Archduke Charles, heir to the throne of Castile and possible claimant to the great and powerful Holy Roman Empire. The borders of England appeared to be strong and trade agreements cemented. All that the new Tudor king had worked so hard to obtain had finally come to fruition.

Henry VII was not about to let such a momentous occasion pass without ensuring it was celebrated throughout England. As soon as news reached England that the marriage treaty had been signed, Henry VII issued letters to the Mayor and Aldermen of the City of London, as well as other notable and important men from various towns throughout England, that 'by his great labour, study and policy, this great and honourable marriage was concluded.'[18] In celebration of the great union a ballad was composed,

> Arouse yourselves, ye sleepy spirits
> Whoever are friends of the English,
> Let us sing AVE MARIA!
>
> Dame Mary shall join the fleece of gold,
> And the enclosure of the castles, eagles and lilies,
> Arouse yourselves,
>
> Mary, daughter of the true lily,
> Henry the seventh, that King of worth,
> Prince over all Princes,
> Arouse yourselves,
>
> Shall deliver all Flanders
> From the great annoyance of its enemies,
> Reinstating the churches,
> Arouse yourselves,
>
> Rejoice again I say
> Sing Burgundians, all unitedly,

At this lofty marriage,
Arouse yourselves,

For during ten thousand years from this
There will not be, nor has been in the country,
Such a peace, such an alliance,
Arouse yourselves,

We all pray, great and small.
That the kings may all be good friends,
And peace through all the world,
Arouse yourselves,

And that at last in Paradise
All may sing
With voice and heart purified,
Arouse yourselves.[19]

The people of England obviously held high hopes for the union of their princess and the grandson of the Holy Roman Emperor. Peace and friendship between nations were what the common people hoped for from this marriage. For Henry VII he wanted all of England to know that he was a strong, reliable king who was successfully negotiating strong alliances with the great factions of Europe. Whichever way the people of England looked, be it north to Scotland or across the Channel to Europe, England was supported by powerful allies, which Henry VII had worked hard to secure using his daughters as pawns in marriage. His people could see he was not an upstart king who had claimed the throne, but there by divine right, appointed by God, and was serving his people and protecting them.

At twelve years of age Mary was officially betrothed to the one who would inherit the rule of most of the countries of Europe on the death of his grandfather in 1519. Unfortunately, there are no records of what Mary thought about her forthcoming marriage or about her future husband. As a woman, and even more so as a princess, she knew it was her duty to follow her father's wishes. She would not have been blind to the fact that sooner or later a marriage would be arranged for her, and most likely one to secure a political alliance with another country. Her sister Margaret had been married at thirteen to King James IV of Scotland, a man some fifteen years her senior. Mary would have accepted her duty; her personal feelings were kept just that, personal. Outwardly, Mary presented the picture of a beautiful young princess ready and eager to become a wife.

It is also unknown what Mary's second husband, Charles Brandon, thought about this dynastic marriage. At twenty-three years of age it is doubtful that Brandon had any romantic feelings towards the young princess. He was after all was caught up with his own marital problems at this time. Brandon first attracted the attention of Anne Browne, daughter of Sir Anthony Browne, around 1505 or 1506 a few years before. Brandon proposed marriage to Anne and the couple slept together, conceiving a daughter who would be named Anne after her mother. However, Brandon saw better prospects for himself with Anne's aunt and he broke off the marriage proposal and made a proposal to Margaret Neville, Dame Mortimer, a widow of some wealth. On 7 February 1507 Brandon had licence of Dame Margaret's lands and began to sell them off in quick succession, profiting more than £1,000. (£483,770)[20] However, with the land sold and a healthy profit made Brandon was looking to annul his marriage to Dame Margaret on the grounds of consanguinity, due to his previously relationship with the dame's niece and also being related to the grandmother of Dame Margaret's first husband.[21] In 1508 Brandon returned to Anne Browne and the couple married in secret at Stepney Church. They later repeated the marriage ceremony publicly at St Michael Cornhill. In 1510 Anne gave birth to the couple's second daughter, named Mary. Anne died shortly after and Brandon was left a widower with two young daughters at the age of twenty-seven.[22]

It is quite possible that by then Brandon would have been aware of the beautiful Mary. Brandon had participated in the celebratory jousts for the wedding of Arthur Tudor and Katherine of Aragon and participated in other sporting events at court. The chances that Brandon and Mary had seen and knew of each other therefore would have been quite high. Although there would be little doubt that Brandon, not yet knighted even though he was an Esquire of the Body, would not have had cause to speak with or spend time with a princess.

Down through the centuries it has been reported that even as a teenager, in her most formative years, Mary desired to take Brandon as her husband. There are romantic stories of the teenager admiring the dashing, much older, Brandon, dressed in his armour and ready to joust. If, even at thirteen years of age, Mary had any lustful or romantic feelings towards Brandon, these have not been recorded. Perhaps this was for the best since Brandon was far beneath Mary's social position and she was officially betrothed to a boy who was an archduke, prince, future king and most likely to become the most important person in Europe, the Holy Roman Emperor. Mary's future would take her down a different path and it would be another five years before she would find herself in Charles Brandon's arms.

On Saturday 17 December 1508 at Richmond Palace, just before midday, Mary was finally and officially married by proxy to Archduke Charles. No expense was spared. The Great Hall of Richmond was draped with silk and decorated with expensive plate and ornaments to show Henry VII's, and therefore England's, wealth. In the chapel where the Mass was to be held, the altar was decorated with gold and silver gilt statues of saints, all studded with gems. To prepare for the proxy wedding, Mary was allocated a chamber in which cloth of gold was hung and expensive furniture was set out. The entire event was recorded by Pietro Carmeliano, the king's Latin Secretary:

> And thus, the kinges highnes beyng under his clothe of estate, the Ambassadoure of Aragon and the lordes spirituell syttynge on his right hande downewarde, and my lorde the Prynce with other Lordes temporall syttynge in like wyse on the lefte hande, and the sayd Ambassadours syttynge also directely before his grace, the president of Flaundres purposed a proposicion containgnynge the cause of their commynge ; which was for the parfect accomplissement of all thynges passed and concluded for the sayde amitie and Mariage at the towne of Calays.[23]

With her father the king and her brother watching, Mary arrived escorted by her former sister-in-law Katherine of Aragon and followed by other noble ladies. She was led up to an elevated dais where she stood under a canopy of cloth of gold. Katherine stood close by on a lower platform.[24] An attendant recorded his personal thoughts on Mary's bearing:

> Now to declare and announce in words the splendid beauty of this princess, the modesty and gravity with which she bore herself , the laudable and princely gestures, befitting so great a princess, which, at that time, were found in her, would be out of my power to make comprehensible by any word or page. I will pass it by therefore, only saying that never could there be any, or only the most splendid, comparison with any other virgin princess, in so tender an age; for she was about eleven years old; her regal courtesy, and noble and truly paternal gravity were shown before all. Such was the composure of her dress, habit, and manners, that I may truly affirm that no princess, exercised in these great mysteries, would show so many splendid and royal virtues. Whatever in short of reverence, or humble subjection, of gravity, and respect was due to her most serene father, whatever of courtesy and affability to the orators, that she showed forth, like a most wise princess.[25]

Standing in for the young Charles was Sieur de Berghes. After an address by the Archbishop of Canterbury in Latin, both Mary and de Berghes exchanged vows under the canopy of cloth of gold. De Berghes recited the vows on behalf of Charles and then placed a ring on the middle finger of Mary's right hand. Mary did likewise, taking de Berghes by the hand and gracefully reciting her wedding vows:

> I, Mary, by you, John, Lord of Berghes, commissary and procurator of the most high and puissant Prince Charles, by the grace of God Prince of Spain, Archduke of Austria, and Duke of Burgundy, herby through his commission and special procuration presently read, explained and announced, sufficiently constituted and ordained, through your mediation and signifying this to me, do accept the said Lord Charles to be my husband and spouse, and consent to receive him as my husband and spouse. And to him and to you for him, I promise that henceforth, during my natural life, I will have, hold, and repute him as my husband and spouse; and herby I plight by troth to him and to you for him.[26]

Berghes stepped forward and pressed a kiss to Mary's lips. With the wedding now performed all that was left to do was to ratify the marriage. This ratification was signed by both Berghes and Mary was well as a number of foreign dignitaries who had attended the wedding, the Archbishop of Canterbury, four bishops, one duke (either the Duke of Norfolk or Buckingham), nine earls and eleven barons. The reason for the horde of witnesses is obvious: there now would be no questioning as to whether the wedding had gone ahead.

Afterwards the members of the party went to the Chapel Royal where they attended High Mass performed by the Bishop of London. A lavish and expensive feast was enjoyed and again Henry VII spared no expense. Meals were served on plates of gold and silver gilt. Other table utensils were made of precious metals and encrusted with pearls and fine stones. Wine flowed and it was reported that 'delicate and sumptuous' meats were served.[27]

Following the wedding and wedding feast there were a further three days of celebrations and jousting.[28] Mary (now styled the Princess of Castile) and her former sister-in-law, Katherine of Aragon, watched the jousts from a gallery. Opposite where they sat in another gallery were the heralds, who recorded all that happened and ensured that everything went according to plan, and musicians.[29]

On the evening of the third and final day another banquet was held, which is reported to have been even more spectacular than the one following the wedding. During the banquet Mary was presented with three magnificent pices of jewellery The first was a gift of a balas ruby, which was pale rose in colour, garnished with pearls and given to Mary by her new aunt-in-law, Margaret of Austria. The second, a brooch consisting of a large diamond and ruby surrounded by pearls, was from her grandfather-in-law, Maximilian I. The last present, a gift from Mary's new husband Charles, was a ring with the monogram K that stood for 'Karolus', the Latin form of Charles, surrounded by diamonds and pearls.[30]

As well as the royal celebrations, the people of London joined in with their own rejoicing and entertainment. Bonfires were lit and men, women and children danced and celebrated around the flames, singing the young princess's praises, drinking wine and eating sweets provided by the king. Some played musical instruments until night fell.[31]

Henry VII made Charles a Knight of the Garter before the foreign ambassadors returned home. The day after the proxy wedding Charles wrote to Mary:

My dear companion ['mate']

With good grace and as cordially as I can, I recommend myself to you. I have charged the Lord of Bergues, and my other ambassadors ordered to your country, to inform you of the good condition of my person and my affairs, begging you to believe the same and to let me know by them of your health and good tidings, which is the thing I most desire, as knows the blessed Son of God, whom I pray, my good mate, to give you by his grace your heart's desires. At Malines, the 18th day of December.[32]

Ma bonne compaigne,

Le plus cordialement que je puis a v[ostre] bonne grace me recommande. Jay charge le Sieur de Bergh\"ez] et autres mes ambassadeurs ordonnez par de la vous deviser [de la] disposition de ma personne et de mes affaires, vous priant l[es] vouloir croire et par eulx me faire savoir de vostre sante [et autres] bonnes nouvelles, qui est la chose que plus je desire, c[omme] scet le benoit Filz de Dieu, auquel je prie, ma bonne com[paigne], vous dormer par sa grace ce que desirez. A Malines, [ce] xviij 6 jour de decembre.

Vostre bon mary

CHARLES.[33]

Written the day following Mary's proxy wedding, Charles's letter is written in French, the common language of court and in which Mary and Charles were both fluent. The letter, although containing sweet words, is nothing more than cordial, recommending himself to Mary, confirming his health and then inquiring as to Mary's.

Pietro Carmeliano, the king's Latin secretary who recorded in great detail Mary's proxy marriage to Charles, officially wrote his notes into the piece 'The spousells of the Princess Mary, daughter of Henry VII, to Charles Prince of Castile, A.D. 1508'. This was translated into Castilian and Catalan and a copy was presented to King Ferdinand of Aragon by Henry VII's ambassador to that court, John Stiles.[34]

Ferdinand was not happy about the new marriage arrangement. Ferdinand had been included in the Treaty of Perpetual Peace, but his inclusion was more a formality than an actual consultation with the king. Charles was his nephew; the young boy's mother, Joanna of Castile, was the third child of Ferdinand's marriage to his late wife, Isabella of Castile. Ferdinand desired the lands which once belonged to his wife and wished to rule them in place of his grandson, at least until he reached an appropriate age. Ferdinand was furious that no mention of his other daughter, Katherine of Aragon, who was still living in England after the death of her husband Prince Arthur Tudor, had been included in the treaty.[35]

At the end of April 1509 Ferdinand wrote a hasty letter to his ambassador at the English court. In this letter Ferdinand accused Henry VII of doing whatever he wanted because Katherine of Aragon had remained in England and was thus under Henry's control. Ferdinand claimed that Henry VII demanded that the plate and jewels from Katherine's dowry should not be included. He then demanded all her dowry be returned to Spain. Henry VII had then demanded that the marriage between Charles and his daughter Mary be ratified. Ferdinand claimed that with every demand that was granted, Henry VII asked for more. He went on to suggest that he was being blackmailed by the English king. Ferdinand held no love for England and their alliance.

Ferdinand instructed his ambassador to say that he would not enter into any agreement for the marriage between Charles and Mary until Katherine of Aragon was married to the Prince of Wales, (Prince Henry having been created Prince of Wales in 1503). Ferdinand covered his back by stating that he had never declared himself against the marriage between Mary and Charles, just that he wished for his daughter to marry first. Should Henry VII not agree to this, then Katherine was to prepare herself to return to Spain.[36]

From Ferdinand's letter it is clear that his thoughts were on his youngest daughter's future marriage and the belief that perhaps she was being held by Henry VII in England against her will. Henry VII denied these accusations and told the Spanish ambassador that Katherine was being treated well and that he only wished for the marriage between his daughter Mary and Charles for the great love he held for Charles's grandfather, Ferdinand. He wished for this marriage to tie their countries together in union and so that no other country would see them as enemies, but close friends.

While Ferdinand was not openly against the marriage of the young couple, he clearly would not consent to it happening without an agreement of marriage between his daughter Katherine of Aragon and Henry VII's son and heir Henry, now Prince of Wales. The king of Aragon's agreement to any marriage treaty was dependent on what happened to his daughter. Unfortunately what Ferdinand thought, felt or demanded counted for little – the proxy marriage between Mary Tudor and Charles had already taken place.

He may have noticed that while the wedding ceremony was conducted *per verba de praesenti*, that is, the words were spoken in the present tense and thus were legally binding, it was yet to be consummated. Although proxy marriages were legal, the Catholic Church often did not consider them binding until the couple had consummated their marriage, which in Mary and Charles' case could not take place until Charles was of the legal age of fourteen. This too may have caused concern for Ferdinand because his grandson had entered into the marriage as a minor and thus had no legal say in his own wedding. Whatever Ferdinand's reservations, Mary would be Princess of Castile for six years – never once meeting her husband.

5

Thy Brother the King

✤

'Henry was greatly attached to his sister, and found her so joyous a sharer in all his frolics and festivities, that he seldom permitted her absence from a court of which she was the loveliest ornament.'

The marriage of Henry VII's youngest daughter to Prince Charles of Castile was a huge diplomatic success for Henry VII. Despite the loss of his eldest son and heir, the first Tudor king still had Prince Henry and was grooming the new Prince of Wales to succeed him as King of England. His elder daughter Margaret was now queen of Scotland, thus creating an alliance with England's bothersome northern neighbours. Mary's marriage to Prince Charles created a hugely successful alliance since it not only aligned England with Castile and Aragon, it also saw his daughter set to one day become queen of Spain; a country that was due to be one of the greatest political players in all of Europe. King Henry VII would not live to see the fruit of his ambitions.

On 19 March 1509 King Henry VII paid forty shillings to a clerk to draw up his will.[1] By this time the first Tudor king was gravely ill and perhaps realised that he would not live to see his youngest daughter leave England for Spain. In his will Henry outlined his desires for Mary's marriage to Prince Charles and her future.

ALSO whereas for the more affured confervacion and encreace of the ftate, and honour of us, our Herres and Succeffours, and of our

Reame, and th'advacement of the profperitie, vtilitie and comoditie of our Subgiects, it is by our conducte and moyne couvenanted, accorded and concluded, betwixt us on the oon partie, and the mooft facrede Prince Maximilian, elect Emperour, afwel for hymself and in his owen name, and as then King of Romains, as alfo as graundfader, tutor and governour, of the perfone, lands and countreis, of the right high and mighty Prince Charles Prince of Spayne, Archiduc of Aufrich, Duc of Bourgoyne, Brabant etc. and Counte of Flandres etc. his nepheu, and the fame Charles Prince of Spayne, by th'affent of his faid tutour, and the right noble Princeffe the Lady Margarete Ducheffe of Savoie, Awnte to the faid Prince on th'oder partie, for marriage by Godds grace to be had, and folempnely in the face of the Churche to be contracted, betwixt the faid Prince of Spaine, and our mooft dere doughter the Lady Mary, at fuche tyme as the faid Prince of Spaine fhall be of fuch perfite and full age, as the lawes of the Churche require for that porpofe, vnder fuch maner and fourme, and in fuche tyme and place, and with fuche condicions, as in the treatie thereupon paffed and concluded betwixt the Commiffioners of bothe fides, and afterward afwel by us as by the faid Emperour, Prince of Spayne and Ducheffe, by our and their feveral Letters Patents, under our and their grete feals, fubfcribed with our and their hands, ratified and confermed, it appereth more ample and at length; according whereunto fpowfells by words of the prefent requifite due and convenient in that behalve, by oure moynes, and at our right grete coft and charges, have been folempnely and openly contracted betwixt the faid Prince of Caftell, by his Proctour in that parte fufficiently conftituted, ordeigned and deputed on the oon partie, and our faid doughter in her perfone on th'oder partie, in our Manour of Richemount, the [blank] daie of the moneth of Decembre, in the xxiiii yere of our Reigne, our felf in our perfone, and th'Ambaffadours of the faid Prince of Caftell, with many other of the mooft honorable Lords Spirituall and Temporall, Laidies, and other Nobles of our Royme in a grete nombre then being prefent, with diverfe and many mooft folempne and honourable Jufts, Tourneys, Fefts, and other triumphes and ceremonies, to fuch an acte convenient and requifite, enfuyng the faid contractie of efpoufellis, and by a long fpace of tyme contynuyng and enduring.

AND whereas we for the Dote and mariage of our faid doughter, over and above the coft of her traduccion into the parties of Flandres, and furnifshing of Plate and other her Arraiments for her perfone, Juelxs, and garnifshing of her Chambre, which wol extende to no litle fome nor charge, muft paie and content to the faid Prince of Spaine, the fome of fifty thoufand pounds in redy money, at certaine termes expreffed in the faid Treatie; for the whiche paiement, by th'advife of our Counfell, we have by our Letters vnder our great Seale fubfcribed with our hande, bounden our felf, our heires and Succeffours, Reames, Lands, Countreis, and all other goods moevable and immovable, and in like wife the perfones and goods of all and every our Subgects, movables and imovables where foever thei fhall be founden; and that in like wife the Maire and Fellifhip of our ftaple of Calais, have at our defire bounden theim and their fucceffours , for the paiement of the faid Some; we vndoubtedly trufte and have our full confidence, that the thre Eftats of our Reame, according to the laws and auncient cuftumes provided, and inviolably tyme oute of mynde obferved and ufed, for the mariage of the Kings children of the Reame, fhall and wol by auctoritie of Parliament, fufficiently ordeyne and provide for the full paiement and contentacion of the faid L.M, to the faid Prince of Spayne, according to the porpointe of the faid treatie; and fee us our faid Staple difcharged of the faid bands and obligacions. Confidering fpecially, that the perfection of the faid mariage, fhall redounde to the gretteft honour, fuertie, tranquillitie, refte, peace, prouffite and commoditie, vniverfally and particularly of our faid Reame and fubjetts, and that thei and their goods, by our said bande as before is faied ftande bounden for the fame.

AND in cafe it foo fortune, as God defende, that the faid mariage, by the dethe of the faid Prince of Caftile, or by any other chaunce or fortune whatfoever it be, take not effect, but vttrely diffolve and breke, or that our faid doughter be nat married by us in our life, nor after the fame have fufficient provifion for her Dote and mariage by the faid thre Eftates; we then wol, that our faid doughter Mary have for her mariage, fift thoufand poundes paiable of our goods, yf fo moch remaigne after the perfourmance of fuch thinges and charges as in our Wille is above and before exprefed and fpecified, which thinges and chargies, we wol furft and before all other matiers be doon and perfourmed, of and with our faid goods as farre as thei wol extende; and that doon and fully perfourmed, yf any thing then remayne of our faid goods, we wol then that they for the payment of the faid L.M take of the faid goods as farre as thei wol goo. And if the faid goods wol not perfourme the faid L.M, we then wol that that lakketh and cannot be levied of our faid goods for the paiement of the faid L.M, bee levied of the faid rentes, revenues, prouffits and emoluments, by the hands of our Executours , foo and in noon other wife, that in her faid mariage fhe be ruled and ordred by th'advife and confent of our faid Sone and Prince, and our faid Executours; and foo that fhe be maried to fome noble Prince out of this our Reame.[2]

Henry VII's will states that when Charles Prince of Spain reaches maturity, as dictated by the Church, he wishes for the marriage between his daughter Mary and Charles to go ahead and be consummated – as outlined in the treaty signed on 21 December 1507 and consented to by himself and Emperor Maximilian I. For Mary's dowry Henry VII sets aside £50,000, roughly the equivalent of £24,188,000,[3] on top of the expenses and items that he is already providing for his daughter such as her jewels, plate, clothing, and items for her chamber. Henry VII then binds his heirs and realm to pay this sum. Clearly Henry sees his daughter, Mary, as a valuable asset and one worth investing in. He is willing to set aside a large sum for her dowry, making her even more desirable in the marriage market. Should he die before the sum is paid then he orders that once all his other debts have been paid, his goods should be sold to the sum of £50,000. If there isn't enough to get to the figure then he asks that the common people be taxed for the remainder. He then goes on to remind his subjects that Mary's marriage is for the good of the realm, so they should not mind being taxed!

Henry VII does make a note that if the marriage, for whatever reason, including Prince Charles's death, does not go ahead then Mary should still have the £50,000 for her dowry for her next marriage. Lastly, Henry VII orders that if he dies before Mary is married that she should be ruled by her brother, Prince Henry, and his council. He specifically desires his daughter to marry a noble prince outside of England.

Henry VII died on 21 April 1509 at his palace of Richmond. He was fifty-two years of age. The late king's death was kept quiet from the public for two days before being announced after supper on the 23rd, St George's Day.[4]

No record survives of how Mary was informed of her father's passing or of her own personal thoughts concerning this event. There does not appear to have been a close bond between father and daughter. The two did see each other regularly, especially as Mary grew and became a more prominent member of the court. This is not to say that Mary did not grieve. It was, as described, common for babies and children to be raised at a nursery away from the court.

Henry VII was buried in the Lady Chapel at Westminster Abbey next to his late wife Elizabeth of York. An effigy of the king, crowned and holding the royal sceptre, was placed on the coffin and placed on a chariot drawn by five horses draped with black velvet. Above the chariot was a cloth of gold. Henry VII's body was taken to the abbey where services were held to honour the late king. As part of the funeral procession Mary rode a horse, her saddle, pillion and the horse's coverings were all covered by or made from black velvet costing 17*s*. Henry's funeral cost a staggering £8,500 (£4,112,000) and Mary was granted new clothing for the solemn occasion. She received 'four new mantelets from Paris, two at 20*s* a piece, and two at 26*s* 8*d*, with six handkerchiefs to match at 9*s* each'.[5]

On 14 May King Ferdinand wrote to Gutier Gomez De Fuensalida, Knight Commander of Membrilla. His concerns were for his daughter, Katherine, and he was willing to use the marriage between Mary and Prince Charles as a bargaining tool to ensure that Katherine would be married to the next Tudor king:

…John Stile has sent unfavourable reports to England. Has spoken with him and has told him to write henceforth only good news. Has, likewise, said to him that he is willing to ratify the marriage between Prince Charles and the Princess Mary, and to grant all the demands which he had denied the late King of England.

Told him that the best thing that can be done is to conclude an alliance between himself, the Emperor, and the King of England. John Stile answered that he believed the marriage of the Princess Katharine would soon be concluded, and he promised to send a favourable account to his master. The letters of John Stile which are enclosed must be delivered to the King immediately.

Is really disposed to ratify the marriage between Prince Charles and the Princess Mary, on condition, however, that the wedding of the Princess Katharine takes place without delay. He must reconcile himself with the Princess Katharine, and arrange with her the line of conduct to be observed. She can give him valuable advice. She wrote formerly that there was no doubt her wedding would soon be celebrated, if the old King of England were to die.

He cannot render him a greater service than to bring about the consummation of the marriage of the Princess Katharine.[6]

Ferdinand then wrote to his daughter personally, assuring her that if her marriage to Henry went ahead, he would gladly consent to the marriage of Mary and Prince Charles and withdraw any stipulations that were holding the marriage back.

Had refused, as long as the late King of England lived, to ratify the marriage of Prince Charles with the Princess Mary, to renounce his eventual claims on her dower, or to pay the whole remaining 100,000 scudos of her dower in money. Had done so, because he knew that the late King Henry was neither his nor her friend. But now that he is dead, the marriage of Prince Charles with the Princess Mary will be ratified, all his claims on her dower renounced, and the whole 100,000 scudos paid in coin. Thus, all impediments to her marriage are removed.

Her marriage, and that of Prince Charles, are of great political importance, since they will secure an alliance and friendship between himself, the Emperor, Prince Charles, and the King of England. The present state of Europe renders this alliance highly desirable and even necessary.[7]

King Ferdinand need not have worried about his daughter, nor was there any need for him to use his objections against Mary's marriage to Prince Charles as a bargaining tool. The almost eighteen-year-old Henry, now King of England, wasted little time in marrying Katherine of Aragon, still young and beautiful at twenty-three years of age. On 8 June 1509 Archbishop Warham issued a licence allowing the marriage of Henry and Katherine to be sanctified in any church in England.[8] A mere three days after this decree on 11 June, Henry and Katherine were married in a quiet ceremony in the oratory of the Friar Observants' Church.[9]

There has been great debate over the centuries whether, on his deathbed, Henry VII instructed his son to marry the widowed Katherine. It is possible that Henry VII played no role in the decision, but that Henry VIII took it upon himself to marry Katherine since he had once been betrothed to her and now desired her for his wife. Whatever the reason for the young couple's marriage, Katherine was now finally Queen of England.

In marrying Katherine, Henry's ministers sought a papal dispensation from Rome because of Katherine's marriage to Henry's late brother, Arthur. Polydore Vergil argues that this marriage was valid since Arthur and Katherine had not had children together.[10] Katherine would later claim that she and Arthur never had sexual intercourse and that she was a true maid when she married Henry. In June 1509 this matter almost seemed trivial, such details were more or less ignored amidst the great joy and excitement of the young couple's wedding.

Mary did not attend her brother's small and intimate wedding. However, she did witness her brother's magnificent coronation. On 23 June 1509, Henry, dressed in white damask and cloth of gold, progressed from the Tower through the streets of London to Westminster. He was followed by his new bride, riding in a litter and dressed in a gown of white damask and cloth of gold, trimmed with miniver.[11] Mary and her grandmother Lady Margaret Beaufort watched the procession from behind a latticed window in a house in Cheapside that Lady Margaret had rented for the day for the price of 2*s* 10*d*.[12] One can only wonder if Mary, now fourteen years of age, thought about her own wedding, still a few years away. Or maybe she recalled the time she had seen Katherine enter London seven years earlier.

The following day, 24 June, Katherine and Henry were crowned King and Queen of England at Westminster Abbey. There are no records of Mary attending her brother's coronation. It is reasonable to assume that as a member of the royal family she did, and sat with her grandmother Margaret Beaufort in the choir.[13] After the coronation the newly crowned king and queen and other noble members of court returned to Westminster Hall for a spectacular banquet. The Duke of Buckingham was the Lord Steward for the celebrations and rode up and down the length of Westminster Hall on horseback, leading the procession of extravagant dishes. The feasting and celebrations lasted until midnight. Several days of jousts and celebrations followed. There were traditional jousts as well as a tourney where knights battled each other with swords.[14]

The celebrations were cut short five days later when on 29 June Margaret Beaufort died. She was sixty-eight years of age and had watched both her son and grandson become kings of England. She was reportedly active and in full possession of her faculties until her death. Margaret Beaufort had been greatly loved and respected by the people and London went into deep mourning. Churches and chapels were draped with black fabric and church bells tolled for six days.[15] Margaret was buried at Westminster Abbey on 9 July, her dear friend and chaplain Bishop John Fisher giving the funeral sermon.[16]

Lady Margaret's estate was valued at around £18,000 (£8,708,000).[17] She left only £18 8s 4d[18] (equivalent to £39,870.71)[19] to her granddaughter Mary. It is unclear why Margaret left her granddaughter so little. Perhaps she believed that she would be taken care of by her brother, the new king, or that Mary would soon travel overseas to reside permanently with her husband Prince Charles.

Lady Margaret had been a constant figure in Mary's life, often overseeing the organisation of the royal nursery and events at court. Mary and her mother, along with Lady Margaret, had watched Katherine of Aragon's procession into London together in 1502. Mary and her grandmother had surveyed Henry and Katherine's coronation procession just a few weeks earlier. It is reasonable to assume that the pair would have sat together at banquets or suppers throughout the years. Now Mary's final connection with her childhood was gone. Both of her parents had died and now her influential and powerful grandmother had too. Her sister Margaret had been in Scotland for several years and her brother Henry was now a married man and King of England. Mary may have felt overwhelmed at the sudden changes; or alternatively, perhaps she was excited about the future.

Just three days after his marriage Henry VIII wrote to Margaret of Austria regarding his new marriage and that of his younger sister's marriage to Prince Charles:

> Is writing to the Emperor, whom, in consideration of his love towards the late King his father, he makes the participator of his news. Was charged by Henry VII., on his death bed, among other good counsels, to fulfil the old treaty with Ferdinand and Isabella of Spain by taking their daughter Katharine in marriage; now that he is of full age, would not disobey, especially considering the great alliance between Aragon, the Emperor, and the house of Burgundy by reason of the marriage concluded between the Prince of Spain and the King's sister Mary, and considering also the dispensation obtained from the Pope by Henry VII., the King of Aragon, and the late Queen of Spain. Accordingly the espousals were made between him and Katharine on the 11th inst. On St. John the Baptist's day they were both crowned in Westminster Abbey in presence of all the nobility. The realm is in as good peace as in the late King's time. Begs she will forward his letter to the Emperor, and certify him frequently of news. Westm., 27 June.[20]

At this early stage of his rule it appeared that Henry was willing to continue with the marriage treaty his father had worked so hard to obtain. However, the new king had greater and more pressing matters on his mind.

At the time of his death Henry VII had amassed vast wealth and the royal coffers were overflowing. A great deal of this money had been gathered through the years using a series of bonds from people who had to pay the king money in order to show their loyalty and keep themselves out of jail. While the justification behind the early bonds started off as genuine breaches of the law, soon any excuse was being used to hold a wealthy person to ransom. False accusations were being made and people were not given the chance to defend themselves. People were intimidated and threatened until they paid the sums demanded.[21] The bonds had made the late king very unpopular, but the intimidating brutality employed in the collection of the monies was blamed on two of his leading councillors, Edmund Dudley and Richard Empsom.[22]

Henry VIII wasted little time in getting rid of Dudley and Empsom, which made him popular. He then began to spend the vast sum of money his father had amassed. Henry spent a great deal of his time following pursuits such as jousting, archery, hawking, and one of his favourite pastimes, hunting.[23] There was no lack of entertainment and festivities at court and often there were banquets, dances and masquerades. One of the new king's great pranks was to dress up with his men as various characters and 'surprise' his wife and her ladies.[24] Katherine had to feign surprise every time Henry pulled off his mask. The sophisticated new queen must surely have found this constant charade tiresome. The king wished his favourite sister to be present during all the entertainments.

During Henry VIII's early reign, when Mary was away from court he would send her small presents and requests for her return.[25] Henry spent a great deal of time with Mary, enjoying her company in the regular court entertainments.[26] One such occasion was on Shrove Tuesday of 1510. Henry VIII organised a lavish banquet to honour his foreign ambassadors. He led Katherine to his own royal seat situated under a canopy of cloth of gold at the high table. Once seated, Henry talked to his guests for a time before he suddenly disappeared. He returned a short time later with Henry Bourchier, Earl of Essex. Both men were dressed in the Turkish fashion wearing robes of baudekin powdered with gold, wearing crimson velvet hats and carrying scimitar swords. Henry's companions followed dressed in Russian and Prussian clothing. They were all escorted by torchbearers who wore crimson satin and had their faces blackened with soot as though they were Moors. Henry and his companions then performed for the gathered company.[27] Henry disappeared again. A short time later the Chronicler Hall records:

There came in a drumme and a fife appareiled in white Damaske and grene bonettes, & hosen of the same sute, than ceratyn gentlemen followed with torches, apparayled in blew Damaske purseled with Ames grey, facioned lyke an Awbe, and on their heddes hodes with robes and longe tippettes to the same of blew Damaske visarde. Then after them came a certayne number of gentlemen, wherof the kyng was one, apparayled all in one sewte of shorte garments, litle beneth the poyntes, of blew Veluet and Crymosyne with log sleues, all cut and lyned with clothe of Vrolde And the vtterparte of the garmentes were powdered with castels, & shefes of arrowes of fyne doket gold. The vpper partes of their hosen of lyke sewte and facion, the nether paries were of Scarlet, poudred with tymbrelles of fyne golde, on their heades. bonets of Damaske, syluer flatte oueninthe stole, and thereupon wrought with gold, and ryche fethers in them, all with visers. After them entred. vi. ladyes, wherof twoo were appareyled in Crymosyn satyne and purpull, embroidered with golde and by vynyettes, ran fioure delices of. gofde, with marueylous ryche strange tiers on their heades. Other two ladvcs in Crymosyne & purpull, made like long slops enbroudered and fret with gold after antike fashion: and ouer that garment was a short garment of clothe of golde scant to the knee facioned like a tabard, all ouer, with small double rolles, all of flatte golde of Damaske, fret with fiysed golde, and ontheyr heades skayns and wrappers of Damaske golde with flatte pypes, y straunge it was to beholde. The other two ladies were in kyrtels of. Crymosyne and purpul satyr), enbroudered with a vynet of Pomegraneltes of golde, all the garmetes cut compasse wyse, Lauyng but demy sleues, and naked doune from the elbowes, and ouer their garmentes" were vochcttes of pleasantes, rouled with Cryrnsyne veluet, and set \V letters of golde lyke Carectes, their heades roulded in pleasauntes and typpers lyke the Egipcians, enbroudered with gold. Their faces, neckes, armes & handes, couered with fyne pleasaunce blackc: Some call it Lumbcrdynes, which is merueylous thine, so that the same ladies seined to be nygfost or blacke Mores. Of these foresayed. vi. ladyes, the lady Mary, syster vnto the kyng was one, the other I name not. After that the kynges grace and the ladies had daunsed a certayne tyme they departed euery one to his lodgyng.[28]

One of these six ladies was Mary, although which one she was and what costume she was wearing Hall does not state. Her face, neck, arms, and hands were covered in black and her outfit was made out of expensive material. Mary danced with the other ladies and men before leaving with everyone to go to Henry's lodgings.

Records show that Henry frequently spent great sums upon his sister, an outward sign of his love and favour. On 13 October 1509 Henry signed a warrant for the Great Wardrobe to deliver gowns to the Princess of Castile.[29] On 5 November Henry once again wrote to the Great Wardrobe ordering 'unto our welbeloved sister the Lady Mary: gown of tawney cloth'[30] be delivered. Just nine days later on the 14th Henry ordered material of russet to be delivered to Mary.[31]

The following year on 26 May[32] and again on 29 November Henry again wrote to the Great Wardrobe and ordered that it deliver cloth and gowns to Mary.[33] Unfortunately there are no accounts of how much Henry spent on such clothing and material; however, as princess of both England and Castile and a frequent member of the royal court, it can be safely assumed that Mary's gowns were made out of the finest cloth to reflect her status and position at court.

Henry VIII continued to spend money on his sister in 1512. On 5 March Henry ordered that broadcloth gowns be delivered to Mary[34] and on 23 March he signed a warrant to deliver to Anne Jernyngham, one of Mary's gentlewomen, black satin for a gown.[35] A week later on 1 April Henry purchased her a crimson satin gown.[36] At the end of the month Henry ordered from the Great Wardrobe russet for 'watching clothing'[37] for Mary. It is unclear what watching clothing consisted of, but again it was in russet, which appears to have been a colour favoured by Mary or Henry. The following year on 28 November 1513 Henry wrote to the Great Wardrobe ordering vestments of crimson velvet, robes used in ceremonial or religious services. On 3 December Henry ordered a gown of cloth of gold, an extremely expensive and difficult material to make, to be prepared for Mary.[38]

On 13 April 1513, with Mary's marriage to Prince Charles still going ahead, Mary wrote to her future aunt, Margaret of Austria, Regent of the Netherlands and Dowager Duchess of Savoy: 'Madame la Duchesse de Savoye ma bonne tante – Thanks her for some patterns of costume of the ladies of her court. Hopes to introduce the same fashion for herself.'[39]

It may be that the cloth Henry was purchasing for his sister was for her maids to create gowns in the fashion that were worn at the Spanish court. Previously, in 1511, Margaret of Austria had sent a Flemish man by the name of John Cerf to serve Mary. This was in order to educate Mary on the ways of the European court and to prepare her in both style and dress.[40]

On 15 October 1513 a new treaty was signed between Henry VIII and Margaret of Austria, on behalf of Maximilian I, the Holy Roman Emperor. Part of the treaty was in relation to military tactics against France and the second was to set a marriage date and location for Mary and Prince Charles.

Declaration by Henry VIII. that he and Margaret of Savoy, acting for the Emperor, have concluded certain articles (recited) of agreement for defence against France by the Emperor's supporting the garrison of Tournay with 4,000 horse and 6,000 foot in Artois, Hainault, &c., paid by the King (200,000 cr.), during the winter, and invasion of France before 1 June next, and also for the marriage of Prince Charles with the Princess *Mary* at Calais before 15 May next.[41]

Maximilian wrote to Margaret of Savoy stating that he was 'satisfied with her arrangements for the household of the Princess Mary in the appointment of the wife of Charles Ourssin, Margaret's controller, as her femme de chambre, and John Glennet, nephew of De Sallans, treasurer of Burgundy, who is now with Margaret's secretary Marnix, as controller'.[42]

The French were not so happy with the alliance and Spinelli, the Venetian ambassador, wrote to Henry on 15 November 1513:

The French say that Margaret of Savoy was the sole cause of the aid given by the Emperor to England, but as soon as the Prince comes to the age of fifteen, and is out of his minority, 'if here been not taken other way and better council in the matter, they shall compel him by force to do it'; that the alliance of marriage between the Prince and my Lady Mary is *contre le bien publique;* that he shall have no other than the second daughter of the French King, or they will give her to Don Fernando his brother, and trouble the succession.[43]

Whatever the French thoughts on the marriage were, Charles was still writing to his bride and on 18 December 1513 he dictated a letter to Mary inquiring as to her health and informing her of his current state.[44] After much discussion back and forth it was finally decided that Mary and Prince Charles would be married and have consummated their marriage by the middle of May 1514.[45] Henry had spared no expense on his little sister and had provided her with everything that she could desire for her life as Princess of Castile. Her clothing had been carefully prepared in the Flemish fashion, right down to the type of cloth and colour that was used. She had

> ...dresses and robes, bonnets, jewels and jewel cases, a mirror, gold necklaces and chains, ornate girdles of 'as goodly fashion as may be devised,' and for the wedding day a gold coronet set with precious stones. Her apartment furnishings and stable equipment were of the same regal quality; besides gold plate, china, and silver she had tapestries, wall hangings, cushions, coverings for chests and cupboards, and various sized carpets, some for window seats and others for floors. Cloth of gold walled her bedchamber, which contained an upholstered chair and 'a large trussing bed' with celure, tester, and counterpane also of cloth of gold, and damask curtains. Two gentlewomen who were to sleep in her room had pallet beds and fustian sheets, but hers was a 'feather bed of fine down,' with linen sheets, a bolster, and two pillows. For traveling she was given a 'rich litter of cloth of gold lined with satin or damask,' chariots, three wardrobe cars for her clothing, and beautifully caparisoned palfreys and horses. Candle sticks, a silver crucifix, purple and crimson vestments, a private pew, and a missal 'of fair print' for furnishing her chapel.[46]

In addition Mary had about a hundred people to serve her including two ladies-in-waiting, five gentlewomen, three women of the chamber, twelve gentlemen of the chamber, three chaplains, fifteen yeomen, twenty grooms, an almoner, and thirty-six people set to serve the attendants.[47] Mary appeared to have everything she could have ever wanted, yet she was still in England. After six years of being married by proxy and styling herself as Princess of Castile, Mary's marriage to Prince Charles was not to be.

Maximilian I began a series of excuses as to why his grandson could not get married. First he was ill without any specification of the ailment; and then the excuse was that Charles had caught a fever from the moon![48] Knight, Henry VIII's ambassador in Spain, wrote to his king stating 'those about the Prince of Castile would gladly hinder his marriage with the Lady Mary, saying, he is a child, and she a woman full grown.'[49] While there was an age gap of approximately five years, this had not hindered the proposed marriage until now.

While these excuses were being made during 1514, The Holy League against France was created between the Holy Roman Empire, Spain, the Papal States, and England, culminating in war with France.[50] Maximilian I continued to request money from England, stating that his empire was poor and that it cost a great deal of money to go to war.[51] King Ferdinand did not hold up his side of the previous agreement in providing England support in the war against France and this left Henry VIII feeling betrayed. Then, to Henry's fury, Ferdinand signed a one-year truce with the French king.[52] At the same time Pope Julius II died and when Pope Leo X succeeded he showed no wish to continue the Holy League's feud with France.[53] In the midst of all this, Thomas Wolsey, Henry VIII's right-hand man, was attempting to create peace throughout Europe for England.

Henry was also growing angry with the emperor for the delay in the marriage between his sister and Prince Charles. Soon Henry VIII was looking for an alliance elsewhere and Mary would play a vital role in this. Henry VIII turned his attention away from a treaty with the Roman Empire and sought one with France. King Louis XII of France was eager for an alliance with England. Part of this new alliance was to be a marriage between Henry's sister Mary and the fifty-two-year old King Louis XII.[54]

Born on 27 June 1462 Louis XII had been king for seventeen years when the marriage was mooted. He was the son of Charles, Duc d'Orléans and Mary of Cleves. Louis succeeded to his father's dukedom at just three years of age. When he was fourteen he was obliged to marry the French King Louis XI's daughter, Joan the Lame. It was believed that due to her disability she would not have been able to bear children. After Louis XI's death his son Charles VIII came to the throne. Charles VIII had previously aided the late Henry VII when he had fled from Brittany and then made his claim on the English throne. Charles' reign lasted only five years and during that time Duke Louis rebelled against his king. He was defeated and taken prisoner at St Aubin du Cormier in 1488. King Charles VIII set him free three years later in 1491. Louis regained Charles VIII's favour and soon was leading the French royal army against Italy.[55]

In 1498 Charles VIII died without any heirs and as closest relative, Louis succeeded to the French throne. In 1499 papal dispensation was granted annulling his fruitless marriage to Joan the Lame and he immediately married Anne of Brittany, Charles VIII's widow. This marriage annexed Brittany to France and guaranteed peace between the two.

When Anne of Brittany died in 1515 Louis only had two daughters, Claude and Renée. Under Salic law a woman could not succeed to the French throne. Therefore Louis married his daughter Claude to Francis, son of Charles, Count of Angoulême, and Louise, eldest daughter of the Duke of Savoy. This meant that if Louis had no surviving sons he would be succeeded by Francis because the Count of Angoulême was a cadet branch of the French royal house of Valois and marrying his daughter Claude to Francis secured a Valois heir – if they were to produce a son. His lack of a male heir was one reason why Louis XII was so eager to marry Mary and pushed the treaty ahead.

King Louis XII had a good reputation. He was liked by his people and was determined to maintain order in his kingdom and improve the administration of justice. In 1506 the États Généraux de Tours conferred on him the surname of '*Père du Peuple*' ('Father of the People'). Louis XII was never robust. When he succeeded the throne aged thirty-eight he was said to be sickly, fragile and narrow-shouldered. When he married Mary, Louis XII was suffering with gout.[56] On 7 April 1514 Ambassador Dandolo wrote from Paris:

> The King has told him he will make no agreement that is not to the advantage of the Signory and that he has two practices on hand, one to marry the King of England's sister, the other to give his second daughter to the second born of Burgundy, Ferdinand, and govern Milan until the latter is 13 years of age.[57]

In June the Duke de Longueville, who had been captured in the English 1513 campaign against France and was now unofficial ambassador for Louis XII at the English court, wrote to Henry:

> The King their master also thanks the King of England for consenting to the marriage of his sister. Thinks the alliance of the two Kings will be most profitable to Christendom. Longueville is empowered to conclude it. Trusts it will be a more firm alliance than ever was established. Will give 500,000 crowns, besides the sums mentioned in the treaties of Estaples and London, and also [in the bond] of the late Mons. d'Orleans, all which will amount to 1,000,000 crowns, [to be discharged at the rate of] 40,000 crowns a year, the peace to endure for a year after the death of the first deceased of the two Princes. In the event of Louis having a son by Mary, or Henry by Katharine, who is now enceinte, the alliance will be of equal advantage to both. As to Tournay, though not a very important matter, it must be delivered up, [as the French King] has assured the King of England, by letters under his hand and seal ... Cannot otherwise get the consent of the Estates to the marriage. ... Tournay must be placed in such security that, on the marriage being accomplished, it shall be given up to the King their master without dissimulation. He is surprised that the King of England should wish to marry her without a dowry, she being his sister, which might turn hereafter to her reproach.[58]

The original agreement has a minute regarding certain conditions as to the restoration of jewellery and furniture forming Princess Mary's dowry, which is initialled by Bishop Fox. This demonstrates the agreement of the English King to the King of France receiving these items (that were valued at 200,000 crowns), and if the marriage should prove childless then these items would be returned to England together with the princess.[59]

Mary's dowry for this marriage was 50,000 crowns less than her original dowry to Prince Charles, originally set at 250,000 crowns.[60] Henry must have felt himself fortunate, having to pay less for Mary's dowry while also securing a strong alliance with France.

A trawl of the French archives did not, unfortunately, produce a copy of the English version of the treaty of 1514 where Mary's marriage was included as part of the concordat. However, it did reveal a brief from Pope Leo X to Louis XII, dated 18 May 1514, recording both the treaty cementing the Anglo-French alliance, and that one of the clauses stated the English king's younger sister Marie would marry Louis XII.[61] On 30 July 1514 Mary Tudor formally renounced her marriage with Prince Charles of Spain.

> In the royal manor of Wanstead, and in the presence of Thomas duke of Norfolk, Charles duke of Suffolk, Thomas bp. of Lincoln postulate of York, Richard bp. of Winchester, Thomas bp. of Durham, Charles earl of Worcester, and Sir Ralph Vernay, the Princess Mary solemnly renounced her compact of marriage with Charles prince of Spain.[62]

A week later Louis XII's ambassadors, Louis of Orléans, Duke of Longueville, Marquis of Rothelin, Johannes de Selve, Doctor of Law and President of the Supreme Court of Normandy, and Thomas Bohier, Knight, and Henry VIII's ambassadors, Thomas, Duke of Norfolk, Thomas Wolsey, Bishop of Lincoln, and Richard Foxe, Bishop of Winchester, signed the treaty of 'Peace and Friendship' for their respective kings. From that day forward England and France would be at peace, both nations providing support to the other should they go to war or be attacked.[63] On 12 August at Greenwich Henry VIII wrote to Pope Leo X confirming the forthcoming marriage of his sister to Louis XII and his belief in the benefits of such a union:

> The Princess Mary is to be given in marriage to France. She had been betrothed at thirteen years of age to the Prince of Castile, then nine years old, on the stipulation that when he was fourteen he should send his proxies to England, and solemnly espouse her *per verba de præsenti*. His governors neglected it, and last year when the King was at Lisle, [and again] on the 15th May last he impressed this matter frequently on their attention without effect. Taking the advice of his Council, his sister solemnly annulled the engagement, and was betrothed to the King of France. Thinks their alliance will be of great importance to the

weal of Christendom, and they can now turn their arms against its common enemies.

The following day, on 13 August, Mary was married to King Louis XII. The Duke of Longueville, acted as proxy for the French king [64] accompanied by Johannes de Selve, the President of the Supreme Court of Normandy, and the French general Thomas Boyer. The wedding was held in the Great Hall at Greenwich, the hall was decorated with an arras of gold and laced with a frieze embroidered with the royal arms of England and France. King Henry VIII and Queen Katherine entered first, followed by Mary and her ladies-in-waiting. [65] Mary wore a 'petticoat of ash-coloured satin, and a gown of purple satin and cloth of gold in chequers; she wore a cap of cloth of gold, and chains and jewels like the Queen'. [66] Numerous ambassadors and members of the court attended the wedding. The Spanish ambassadors were conspicuous by their absence. [67]

The wedding was presided over by William Warham, Archbishop of Canterbury, first addressing the French representative in Latin. Johannes de Selve replied that Louis XII was 'desirous' to take Mary as his wife. After this the Bishop of Durham read the French authorization for the proxy wedding. [68]

> The Duke of Longueville, taking with his right the right hand of the Princess Mary, read the French King's words of espousal (recited) in French. Then the Princess, taking the right hand of the Duke of Longueville, read her part of the contract (recited) in the same tongue. Then the Duke of Longueville signed the schedule and delivered it for signature to the Princess Mary, who signed Marye; after which the Duke delivered the Princess a gold ring, which the Princess placed on the fourth finger of her right hand. [69]

With the wedding ceremony over, Mary retired to her chambers to change into a beautifully decorated nightgown. The Duke of Longueville wore a doublet and red hose, leaving one leg undressed to the thigh. Both the duke and Mary lay down in the bed and Longueville touched Mary with his naked leg, symbolising the consummation of the marriage. Archbishop Warham then declared that the marriage was legal and consummated.[70] One can only wonder how Mary must have felt having others watching her as she ceremoniously 'consummated' her marriage, yet as a woman she was subservient to men in all areas and the symbolic bedding was a necessary part of the marriage ceremony.

After this Mary changed into a checked gown of purple satin and cloth of gold with an ash coloured petticoat and a cap of cloth of gold that covered her ears. Once dressed, Mary attended High Mass with her brother, Queen Katherine, the Duke of Longueville, and other members of the court. After Mass there was of course another sumptuous banquet, Henry VIII once more outdoing himself in order to impress the French. Henry and the Duke of Buckingham apparently danced for two hours.[71]

King Louis XII had his own proxy wedding one month later, on 14 September. At the Church of the Celestines in Paris, Louis XII held a similar ceremony where he committed himself in marriage to Mary with the Earl of Worcester standing in for the princess. In attendance were Louis XII's son-in-law Francis, The Duke of Longueville, John Stuart, Duke of Albany and Louis' treasurer, and Florimond Robertet.[72]

Mary received a great number of gifts from her French husband, including two coffers of plate, seals, devices and magnificent jewellery. One of these jewels was the famous 'Mirror of Naples', a diamond as large as a man's finger with a pear-shaped pearl hanging from it said to be the size of a pigeon's egg. Little did Mary know that soon she would be using the 'Mirror of Naples' as a bargaining tool against her brother. In addition to such lavish presents Louis XII sent his artist Jean Perreal to paint Mary's portrait.[73] There is a portrait of Mary attributed to Jean Perreal and it is believed that this was painted while Mary was still in England. These portraits are described in greater detail later.

Charles Brandon, Mary's second husband, was present at both Mary's renunciation of her marriage to Prince Charles of Spain and at her proxy marriage to the French king. For supporting the cause in France and the new alliance between England and France, Charles Brandon was granted 875 livres tournois per annum by Louis XII.[74]

At eighteen years of age Mary was young and extremely beautiful. Her future husband was fifty-two – an age difference of thirty-four years. Many writers of the Tudor age argued that no girl should be forced to marry a man considerably older than herself. Historian Elizabeth Norton found the observation: 'it was unseemly for a young woman to marry an old man that carrieth a countenance rather to be her father than her husband.'[75] But women were expected to serve the men of their household. Hugh Latimer preached that women were 'to be subjects unto your husbands: ye are underlings, and must be obedient.'[76] Mary, as an unmarried woman, was subject to her brother, who just happened to be King of England. She had little choice but to marry the elderly Louis. She had watched her older sister Margaret depart for Scotland at thirteen years of age to marry King James IV of Scotland, aged thirty. Her own grandmother, Lady Margaret Beaufort, was married at twelve years of age and gave birth at thirteen. Perhaps Mary thought little of the age difference, knowing members of her own family had married men much older than themselves.

Love was deemed important in a happy marriage as 'the greatest joy and sweetest comfort that a man may have in this world is a loving, kind, and honest wife.'[77] Mary had not even met her future husband so love was not part of the equation. But there was of course one rather obvious incentive for the young English princess. It was reported by Venetian historian Marino Santuo that 'The Queen does not mind that the King is a gouty old man of _ years and she herself a young and beautiful damsel of _ , so great is her satisfaction at being Queen of France.'[78] Her position would be greatly elevated, she would no longer be subject to her brother's will, but that of her husband. She would have authority as a queen and would command the women of her household. She would be showered with gifts and highly respected, the most important woman in all of France.

She was still subject to the will of her brother, the King of England, and knew that she must abide by his wishes. She had little say in the marriage, although she would, just before she left England for France; use her wits to gain a promise from her brother regarding her future.

Prince Charles did not take well to the news that he was no longer to marry Mary. His councillors tried to reassure the prince that he was young and would find another wife, but since the King of France was the first king in Christendom it was his right to take any woman that he desired as his wife. Charles was furious and allegedly he called for a young hawk to be brought to him and began to pluck the poor bird's feathers. When asked why he was doing such a cruel thing he replied that the hawk was young and did not make great noise. He was like the hawk, his councillors had plucked him and he did not know how to complain. However, he would grow and would remember how cruelly he had been treated.

In September Maximilian sent one of his ambassadors to England to protest against the proxy wedding of King Louis XII and Mary. Andrea Badoer recorded the meeting:

> The ambassador demanded audience of the King, and permission to make whatever statement he pleased; which being granted, he said on behalf of the Emperor, that the King of England had done wrong to break the promise given to his grandson, the Archduke of Burgundy, by marrying the Lady Mary to the King of France, the Emperor's enemy, and that his deserts entitled him to other treatment. To this the King replied, that it was not he who had failed in his faith, but the Emperor, to whom he had disbursed so many thousands of ducats for the raising of troops and the prosecution of the war against France, but that the Emperor took no heed for the observance of his promise, and did nothing at all. The King added other words, blaming the Emperor vastly, so that the ambassador took leave and departed.[79]

There was very little Maximilian could do except grumble. After waiting six years for her marriage to Prince Charles, Mary's new union was rushing ahead. Within two months of her proxy wedding Mary would be in France, and a queen.

6

Nymph from Heaven

⚜

'I think never man saw a more beautiful creature, nor one having so much grace and sweetness, in public or private.'

By the time Mary was preparing for her journey to France, she was eighteen years of age and reputedly one of the most beautiful women in all Christendom. On 5 February 1512, when Mary was just fifteen years of age, the great humanist scholar, Erasmus of Rotterdam, had described her: 'But O thrice and four times happy our illustrious Prince Charles who is to have such a spouse! Nature never formed anything more beautiful; and she excels no less in goodness and wisdom.'[1]

The Venetian Ambassador to the English court described Mary as 'a Paradise – tall, slender, grey-eyed, possessing an extreme pallor.'[2] Thomas More, lawyer, humanist and later Lord High Chancellor of England, considered Mary 'bright of hue.'[3] On 5 March, just before Mary's eighteenth birthday, Philippe Sieur de Bergilies, ambassador to the court of Margaret of Austria, Regent of the Netherlands, saw Mary on the first Sunday of Lent, dressed in the Italian fashion. He wrote that 'never man saw a more beautiful creature, nor one having so much grace and sweetness, in public or private.'[4] With regard to the rumours that Mary was overweight, Philippe Sieur de Bergilies assured Margaret the rumours were false and that Mary was small and sweet.[5]

Just over three months later, on 30 June 1514, Derard de Pleine wrote to Margaret of Austria regarding Mary's appearance and personality:

Madame the Princess [Mary], until I had seen her several times. I can assure you that she is one of the most beautiful girls that one would wish to see; it does not seem to me that I have ever seen one so beautiful. She has a good manner, and her deportment is perfect in conversation, dancing or anything else. She has no melancholy, but is very lively. I am sure that if you could see her you would never rest until you had her with you. She has been well brought up, and it is certain that Monseigneur has been spoken of favourably to her, for by her words and her manner, as well as by what I have heard from those about her, it seems to me that she loves Monseigneur marvellously. She has a picture, which is a very bad likeness, of him, and there is not a day passes in which she does not wish to see him tén times over, so I have been told; and it appears that if one wishes to please her, one has only to talk of Monseigneur.

I might add that she has a good figure, is well grown, and of medium height, and is a better match in age and person for Monseigneur than I had heard before seeing her, and better than any other Princess whom I know in Christendom. She seems quite young, and does not show that in two years she will be far enough advanced for Likerke and Fontaine ... The Princess is so well qualified that I have only to say again that alike in goodness, beauty, and age there is not the like in Christendom.[6]

Less than two months later Dandolo, Venetian Ambassador in France, wrote 'The Queen was very beautiful.'[7] Lorenzo Pasqualigo, wrote to his brothers from London on 23 September 1514 describing Mary as 'very beautiful, and has not her match in all England, is a young woman 16 years old, tall, fair, and of a light complexion, with a colour, and most affable and graceful.'[8] Then on 2 November 1514, on Mary's arrival in Abbeville, France, she was described by one observer as

...very handsome, and of sufficiently tall stature (de statura honestamente granda). She appears to me rather pale, though this I believe proceeds from the tossing of the sea and from her fright.

She does not seem a whit more than 16 years old, and looks very well in the French costume. She is extremely courteous and well mannered, and has come in very sumptuous array.[9]

In a letter written to Antonio Triulzi, the Bishop of Asti regarding Mary's arrival at Abbeville, the writer promises the bishop:

She is generally considered handsome and well favoured, were not her eyes and eyebrows too light; for the rest it appears to me that nature optime suplevit: she is slight, rather than defective from corpulence, and conducts herself with so much grace, and has such good manners, that for her age of 18 years – and she does not look more – she is a paradise.[10]

In another letter written over 8 and 9 November: 'The Queen is said to be from 17 to 18 years old, of handsome presence, not stout, has a beautiful face, and is cheerful.'[11]

Before even meeting his new bride King Louis XII described Mary as a 'nymph from heaven',[12] inspired by the reports of her beauty and affability. Italian chronicler Pietro Martire d'Anghiera described Mary as 'beautiful without artifice … the French couldn't stop gazing at her because she looked more like an angel than a human creature.'[13] Marco Antonio Contarini wrote to Mafio Liom, having seen Mary in March 1515 after the death of Louis, that Mary was 'the most attractive and beautiful woman ever seen'.[14] In 1527, Guillaume Gouffier de Bonnivet, Lord Admiral of France, would describe Mary as 'the rose of Christendom' stating that she 'should have stayed in France. We would have appreciated you.'[15]

It is not surprising to hear that Mary was described as such a beauty. From her portraits and the descriptions of her it would appear that Mary took after both her mother, Elizabeth of York and her maternal grandmother, Elizabeth Woodville. By all accounts Elizabeth of York was a true beauty. Mary also seems to have inherited her mother's slightly taller than average height for women of the time. She had grey eyes and the traditional pale English complexion, a characteristic that was greatly desired. Most striking of all was her golden-red hair, a genetic trait obvious in her brother Henry and dating back to their mother Elizabeth of York and grandfather King Edward IV.

With Mary's marriage to King Louis XII to be undertaken formally on August 1514, Louis XII's 'nymph from heaven'[16] began to write a series of letters to her husband. On 1 August Mary wrote her first letter to Louis XII:

> My lord.
>
> Humbly, with good grace, I recommend me. Because the King, my lord and brother, presently sends his ambassadors to you, I have desired, ordered, and charged my cousin, the Earl of Worcester, to tell you some things from me touching the espousals now spoken of between you and me. So I beseech you, my lord, to honour and believe him as myself; and I assure you, my lord, as I have before written and signified to you by my cousin the Duke of Longueville, that the thing which I now most desire and wish is to hear good news of your, health and good prosperity, as my cousin the Earl of Worcester will tell you more fully. It will please you, moreover, my lord, to use and command me according to your good and agreeable pleasure, that I may obey and please you, by the help of God; who give you, my lord, good and long life.
> By the hand of your very humble companion,
> Mary.[17]

Mary starts off her letter as was common, asking after her new husband's health and wellbeing. The Earl of Worcester, would have been given information from Mary to pass onto Louis XII regarding her own health; all of which would have been very positive. Mary submits herself to Louis promising to obey his commands and to do as he wishes in order to please him. While submitting herself to her husband's wishes Mary is stating her position within the marriage and within the French court. Mary had written a letter to her future husband on the day of her proxy wedding: 'Received the letters written with his own hand and heard with great pleasure what the Duke of Longueville said on his behalf. Will love him as cordially as she can. Longueville will relate how all has been concluded.'[18] She signed her letter '*de la main de votre humble compagne*, MARIE',[19] 'by the hand of your humble companion, Mary'. Having only been married by proxy for a few hours Mary was already playing the role of a loving wife.

On 28 August Thomas Bohier wrote back on behalf of Louis XII that 'the King is in good health – desires news from her every day, but above all things to see her in France.'[20] Clearly Louis XII was smitten with his new bride.

In September Louis XII wrote to Thomas Wolsey, Archbishop of York and Henry VIII's most trusted advisor, inquiring about his beloved wife and the preparations for her journey to France:

My Lord of York, my good Friend,

I very lately received the letter you sent me, and by the contents thereof understand the good and kind intentions that you have, not only to bring about a good peace and mutual amity between the King, my good brother, and cousin, and myself, but also to strengthen and increase it, our honours and estates.

For the which, as affectionately as I can, I give you thanks, and I pray you, my Lord of York, and my good friend, firmly to believe, that there is no alliance in Christendom I hold more dear, than I held, and will ever hold, while I live, that of my said brother and cousin, hoping through your means, to find always in him a corresponding inclination.

And as to what you write about the passage of the Queen, my wife, I give you thanks for the pains that you have taken for providing all things that are requisite and necessary for her voyage, and the extraordinary diligence you have used, and still use, as my Lord of Marigny and Johan de Paris have written, beseeching you to continue your care with as much expedition as you can, because the greatest desire I have at present is to see her on this side the water, and to meet her. In contributing to which without loss of time, as you promised me, you will do me a singular pleasure, and such as I shall always remember, and think myself obliged to you for.

And as to your having detained the said Lord Marigny and Johan de Paris, to assist you in setting out all things a la mode de France, you have done me much pleasure therein, and I have written by these presents to them, that not only in this they should obey you, but also in all other things you shall command, with the same respect as if they were about my person.

And as to the pleasure which you inform me, by your said letters, my wife takes in hearing good news from me, and that the thing which she daily desires is to see me, and be in my company, I desire you, my Lord of York, and good friend, to inform her from me, and make her sensible, that my desires and wishes are the same, and in every respect like hers; and, because it is not possible that I should see her so soon as I could wish, I entreat her that, as often as may be, I may hear from her, and I promise the like on my side.

Moreover, in respect to the very affectionate and cordial assurances that you have given my brother and cousin on my part, and those which you in his name have given me, I return you my thanks with all my heart, and entreat you to say as much to him; and also, that you will be pleased to let me know if there be anything in my realm that would please him, and I will spare no pains to procure it for him.

To conclude, I have seen what you have written to my cousin, the Duke of Longueville, and I have ordered him to send you such an answer as you see I desire you will give credit thereto, and let me hear from you as often as possible, and thereby you will do me the greatest pleasure imaginable. Praying God to have you, my Lord of York, my good friend, in his keeping, I am, Louis.[21]

While Louis XII inquires about the preparations for Mary's journey to France and praises the peace and unity between France and England, he is also subtly asking that preparations are moved forward quickly. It is clear that Louis XII is eager to meet his new bride. He hopes that she will continue to write to him often, since he desires to hear from her if she cannot be with him as soon as he would like. To this letter Mary replied:

My lord.

Very humbly to your good Grace I recommend myself. My lord, I have, by the Bishop of Lincoln, received the very affectionate letters which it has pleased you to write to me lately, which have given me much joy and comfort: assuring you, my lord, that there is nothing I desire so much as to see you. And the King is using all diligence for my journey across the sea, which, may it please God, will be brief. Beseeching you, my lord, to be willing for my very great consolation to make known your news to me, together with your good pleasure, so that I may always obey and please you. May our Creator grant you long life and prosperity.

From the hand of Your very humble Consort, Mary.[22]

As with her other letters this one follows the expected formula. As Louis XII's humble and obedient wife, news of his health is of course the only thing that she desires in this world. Mary then briefly mentions her upcoming journey to France before once more submitting herself to her husband and seeking further news of him before expressing her desire, as always, to please him.

Despite Louis XII's requests for the preparations for Mary's journey to France to be speeded up, Henry VIII was not about to skimp when it came to his beloved sister. No expense was spared for the new French queen's wardrobe and it is reported that Henry VIII spent around £43,300[23] (an almost unthinkable £20,800,000)[24] on clothing. Mary's clothing consisted of a showstopping wedding dress in the French fashion, as well as fifteen other gowns, six of those in the Milanese style and seven gowns in the traditional English style. There were seven kirtles of French design and six kirtles in the English and Milanese styles.[25] Each gown had its own chemise, girdle and accessories. Mary's servants were not forgotten and her six footmen all received new jackets.

In addition to Mary's clothing, liveries for her servants were made, fixtures for her chapel, hangings and tapestries from Brussels, as well as seven hangings detailing the Labours of Hercules. A great seal and private seal that declared Mary's rank were also created. Painted panels spelling out Mary's motto *La volonte de Dieu me suffit* (The will of God is sufficient for me) in gold were designed as well as other similarly necessary trappings were created. Mary could not become Queen of France without looking the part and her jewellery consisted of gold chains and bracelets, carcanets with diamonds and rubies, brooches, rings, medallions, pearled aiguillettes, fontlets studded with gems and fleur de lys ornaments.[26]

Henry VIII ordered beds to be made and delivered for Mary's journey to France[27] as well as a cradle 'covered with scarlet without a frame.'[28] This would prove to be wishful thinking on the part of both Henry VIII and Louis XII! It may have been that other accessories needed for Mary's time as Queen of France were taken from the items ordered when Mary was Princess of Castile.

The entry for 1 October 1514 in Letters and Papers, Foreign and Domestic contains a wonderful reference to all the people that Henry paid for services related to his sister's trousseau.

Henry Delyen, of London, cordwainer, 4l. 16s. (2) 1 Oct., by Th. Foster, of London, broderer, 150l. (3) 1 Oct., by John Godard, tailor to the French Queen, 55s. (4) 1 Oct., by Nic. Maior, the King's saddler, 72l. (5) 1 Oct., by John de Molyne, of Southwark, broderer, 33l. 6s. 8d. (6) 1 Oct., by Wm. Stele, of London, saddler, 4l. (7) 4 Oct., by Ric. Thurston on behalf of his father John Thurston, of London, broderer, 47l. (8) 4 Oct., by Ric. Sylkokes, goldsmith, 75l. for stuff delivered to the broderer. (9) 4 Oct., by George Senesco, gold-wire-drawer, for stuff delivered to the broderer. (10) 4 Oct., by John Warren, bedmaker, 16l. 9s. 11d. for stuff for beds. (11) 4 Oct., by John Worssop, of London, scrivener, 90l. for stuff delivered by Elizabeth his wife, 'concerning silkwoman craft.' (12) 4 Oct., by Margaret Hollyffeld, widow of Thomas H., late merchant-tailor of London, 56s. 10d. for robes. (13) 5 Oct., by Robert Amadas, of London, goldsmith, 134l. for gilt spangles delivered to Wm. Mortymer, broderer. (14) 6 Oct., by Robert Draper, servant 'with' Sir Henry Wyatt, on behalf of Stephen Sawyer, 'cace maker,' 53s. 4d. for 'caces.' (15) 6 Oct., by Thomas Warton, on behalf of Stephen Lynne, chariot maker, 6l., for 'the making of certain charrettes and closse cartes.' (16) 6 Oct., by Th. Tourner, painter, for 5l. (17) 6 Oct., by Wm. Ybgrave, broderer, on behalf of Wm. Mortymer, broderer, 233l. (18) 6 Oct., by Ric. Gybson, of London, merchant-tailor, 3l. 13s. 10d. for robes. (19) 8 Oct., by John Barker, hosier, 10l. 13s. 4d. for hosen delivered to Henry Caleys and John Goodderd for the French Queen's use.[29]

This list shows the extravagant amounts of money that Henry was willing to pay to people such as shoemakers, embroiderers, saddlers, goldsmiths, bed makers, and silk women to ensure that Mary arrived in France with the ultimate trousseau. One can see pride in the amount laid out. Henry refused to have Louis think he could not afford to adorn his sister as befitted her position as Queen of France and the favourite sister of the King of England.

Mary showed her thanks for all the hard work and effort that had gone into preparing her train to France. Shortly before she left England the drapers, mercers and haberdashers in London all gathered to bid their princess farewell. It is reported that Mary appeared in a gown designed in the French fashion and made of cloth of gold. She wore the Mirror of Naples diamond that Louis had given her and personally thanked the workers, and each one kissed her hand. Afterwards she spoke a few words of thanks in French much to the delight of everyone.[30]

Mary also had a number of ladies appointed to attend upon her. These included Mademoiselle Grey, sister of the Marquis of Dorset, Mademoiselle Mary Fenes, daughter of Lord Dacres, Mademoiselle Elizabeth, sister of Lord Grey, Mademoiselles Boleyne (Mary Boleyn, Anne Boleyn would join Mary later in France), Mistress Anne Jerningham, Jean Barnes, Elizabeth Ferrers, Anne Devereux, M. Wotton, and Anne Denys. Lady Jane Guildford was also added to this list of women to attend upon Mary. Lady Guildford had been convinced to come out of retirement to attend upon Mary because she had known Mary since she was a child. Lady Guildford spoke French and would act as Lady of the Bedchamber as well as chaperone and mentor to Mary.[31]

Jane Popincourt had also been suggested to attend on Mary. She had been placed in Mary's household since Mary was a child in order to teach her French and the pair had become quite close. It was logical that a childhood friend, fluent in French, should attend Mary. Yet Louis quickly struck Jane off the list of Mary's attendants. The Earl of Worcester had informed Louis that Jane had conducted an affair with the Duke de Longeuville, who was already married. Louis was disgusted and refused to have a woman of such loose morals about his new wife.[32]

In addition to Mary's ladies it was organised that Dr Denton would attend Mary as her almoner. Her schoolmaster John Palsgrave would serve as her secretary. Henry ordered that Thomas Howard, Duke of Norfolk, Treasurer and Marshal of England, the Marquis of Dorset, the Bishop of Durham, the Earl of Surrey Admiral of England, the Earl of Worcester King's Chamberlain, Thomas

Docwra, Grand Prior of St John of Jerusalem, and Doctor West, Dean of Windsor, should also accompany Mary on her journey to France.[33] Louis signed papers on 8 October stating that as Queen of France Mary would receive 300,000 crowns[34] as well as

> ...the town and castlery of Chinon, the county of Saintonge and town of Rochelle (with great fee, &c., of Saintonge, St. Jean d'Angely and Rochefort), the county of Pezenas (Pedenacii), the lordships of Montigny, Cessenon and Cabrieres, the little seal of Montpellier, the money of St. Andrew and rent of Villeneuve lès Avignon, the rent of the Seneschalcy of Beaucaire, the impositio foranea of Languedoc and the profits of salt of Pezenas, Montpellier, Frontignan and Narbonne to the value of 10,400 livres Tournois; and also, instead of St. Menehould and Moret (which used to be dower of queens of France but are otherwise disposed of by the King's predecessors), Loudun and Roquemaure.[35]

In these papers Louis refers to Mary as his 'beloved consort Marie'. It is clear that without even having met Mary, the French king adored her. He had made her a very wealthy woman as well as queen.

It is interesting to note that at this time Henry also granted Charles Brandon, Duke of Suffolk, £1,000 as his ambassador to the French king.[36] Brandon would not be too far from Mary during her time in France.

Toward the end of September it appeared that all was finally ready for Mary's journey to her new country. On the 22nd, Louis left Paris and travelled to Abbeville where he would meet Mary. On 28 September a grand tournament was held in Mary's honour. Erected in the Rue St Anthoine near the Tournelles was

> ...a Triumphant Arch supported by 5 great Pillars, unto which 5 shields were fastened. Whereof – 1st. One was of Silver, which whosoever touched was admitted to run 4 Courses with a lance, and a 5th pour la Dame if he required it. 2nd. Who touched the Golden Shield, was admitted to one Course with the Lance and coups d'espé sans nombres. 3rd. Who touched the Black

Shield was admitted to fight on foot with a Lance or Pike, and afterwards with a single sword. 4th. He that touched the Tawny Shield was admitted to fight on foot likewise, casting a Lance with one hand and holding a Target in the other, and after this to fight with a Two-handed sword. 5th. They that touched the Grey Shield which the Defendants should keep against all comers with the Arms above mentioned.[37]

Despite being the guest of honour Mary was not present at the tournament in which Francis, Mary's future son-in-law, participated. On 2 September Andrea Badoer had written that Mary 'was to depart on the 15th, that she might cross over and join the King, and would go with a very stately retinue.'[38]

It would not be until 23 September 1514 that Mary travelled from London to Dover where she would depart for France and her new life as queen. Lorenzo Pasqualigo, a Venetian merchant living in London, wrote to his brothers that Mary was accompanied by many great noble men and women including the Lord Chamberlain, the Treasurer, the Chancellor and Lord Stanley (Lord Mounteagle). Mary was also escorted by barons, 400 knights, and around 200 gentlemen, their squires and horses. These men were accompanied by their wives and personal servants. It was estimated that the train comprised 2,000 people.[39]

In his letter Pasqualigo believed that accompanying the princess's entourage were around 1,000 palfreys and 100 carriages. He wrote that the women were wearing beautifully decorated dresses, woven with gold and riding horses draped in expensive cloth. It was not just the women, but also the men wearing expensive clothing; one man's outfit he estimated to be worth around 200,000 crowns![40]

As Mary travelled to Dover she was accompanied by her brother. Katherine of Aragon was pregnant at the time and followed behind in a litter. People from all over the country had come to watch and from time to time the train stopped to accept gifts.[41]

By the time Mary and her entourage arrived at Dover a terrible storm had rolled in. Henry had wanted to sail out around 10 miles in his ship *Henry Grace de Dieu* in order to watch Mary depart, but the weather put a stop to this. In fact the storm was so bad that

Mary was forced to wait until there was a lull before she and her entourage could cross the Channel.

It is believed that during this time Mary sought a concession from her brother. She made Henry promise that should her husband Louis die before her, then she would be free to marry a man of her own choosing. While over the centuries it had been thought that this promise was nothing more than a romantic fairy tale, it is clear from Mary's own letters after Louis' death that Henry VIII did in fact make this promise. After the French king's death Mary wrote to her brother:

Sir, I beseech your grace that you will keep all the promises that you promised me when I took my leave of you by the w[ater s]ide. Sir, your grace knoweth well that I did marry for your pl[easure a]t this time, and now I trust that you will suffer me to [marry as] me l[iketh fo]r to do.[42]

It is interesting to ponder whether Mary's thoughts had already turned to Charles Brandon, Duke of Suffolk. Mary would have been well aware that at eighteen, young and healthy, there was a high probability that her old and sickly husband, riddled with gout, would die before her. Mary and Brandon would have known each other at court and Mary would have been well aware of the handsome, thirty-year-old duke who regularly participated in jousting and other sporting events. Brandon too would not have been able to miss the king's beautiful younger sister who was so often the centre of attention at court.

After Louis XII's death Henry sent Brandon to bring Mary back to England. However, before Brandon left for France, Henry made him promise not to marry Mary.[43] Clearly, the king knew of some level of romantic interest between Brandon and Mary.

However deep Mary's feelings for Brandon may have run, her future, at least for now, was to be in France. On 2 October at two o'clock in the morning the storm finally subsided. Fourteen ships left Dover; however, shortly into the journey the storm picked up again and many of the ships were scattered to Calais and Flanders.[44] Luckily, only *The Elizabeth* was wrecked at sea and even luckier, the ship had only been carrying a small amount of Mary's possessions.[45] On 4 October only four ships managed to arrive in France, leaving the party four days behind their schedule.[46]

The ship Mary was travelling in had to be run into the shore by the ship's master. Mary was then carried onto a rowing boat and rowed to the beach.[47] The storm still raged and by the time Mary reached the shoreline she was soaked to the bone. Sir Christopher Garnish, one of the many knights in Mary's party, picked up the young princess and carried her to shore. For his chivalry Garnish was granted an annuity of £30 and £15 in cash.[48] Upon her arrival Mary was greeted by the Cardinal d'Amboise and the Duke de Vendôme.[49] The following day, on 5 October, Mary reached Montreuil where she stayed at the home of Madam de Moncaverel for two days. Recovered from her ordeal, Mary set out on 7 October for the 20-mile journey to Abbeville.

Mary's arrival in France had not gone unnoticed and messengers were hurrying back and forth between Louis and Mary's entourage. The king was updated on Mary's condition, the people and possessions that she brought with her as well as the distance she was travelling each day.[50] A number of pageants had been set up along Mary's route to Abbeville to welcome and entertain the new queen.[51] Entering the city through the seaport village of Étaples, Mary was welcomed by Francis d'Angoulême, son-in-law of Louis and heir to the French throne should Mary not have any sons by her new husband. She was also greeted by the Duke of Vendôme, Cardinal Amboise, the Duke and Duchess of Longueville, the Governor of Picardy and bishops, abbots and merchants of the city. Mary was welcomed with a song that celebrated the union of the French lily and English rose:

> Princes, try to entertain and keep
> The Rose among the lilies of France,
> So that one may say and maintain –
> Shamed be he who thinks ill thereof.[52]

Several more pageants of welcome had been set up throughout the city. These told the stories of Apollo and Diana, Andromeda and Perseus, Solomon and the Queen of Sheba, Esther and King Ahasuerus, and the Virgin Mary and the Annunciation. Mary was overjoyed by the pageants and the great honour the French people were paying her.[53]

Leaving Montreuil, Mary and her train continued their journey to Abbeville. At two o'clock in the afternoon near the forest of Andres, Mary was surprised by Francis of Angoulême and a small party of his men. Mary and Francis spoke and Francis hinted at the fact that a great surprise would happen soon. The truth was that Louis was keeping a very close eye on his future bride and he had sent Francis to delay Mary. French tradition dictated that a king could not meet his bride immediately before their wedding. However, if he were to meet her by accident that was a different matter!

Louis could not contain his eagerness and while Francis had Mary and her train delayed, the king and his men went hawking. Accompanying the king were the Duc d'Albany, the Lord Steward, the Master of the Horse, the Cardinals of Auch and Bayeaux, and Monseigner de Vendôme as well as 200 members of the French nobility.[54]

Mary and her party were suddenly met by the French King. Louis rode a magnificent Spanish horse, which had been covered in cloth of gold and black satin, while the king wore chequered cloth of gold and crimson, which matched Mary's outfit. Mary had been informed as to what the king would be wearing and changed so that Louis would be able to identify her as soon as he laid eyes on her.

Playing her part, Mary feigned surprise at seeing the king and then blew him a kiss. Louis XII did not understand the meaning of this gesture, though he returned it. He rode over to Mary and leaning from his horse wrapped both arms around her and kissed her.[55] A Venetian report stated that Louis 'kissed her as kindly as if he had been five and twenty. He came in this dress and on horseback, the more to prove his vigour.'[56] The mere sight of his new bride and all the joy and delight that would come with having Mary as a wife had clearly sent a wave of enthusiasm and borrowed vigour through the aged king. After chatting for a short time Louis XII made his excuses and he and his men departed for their supposed hawking trip, allowing Mary to continue to Abbeville. Although the whole meeting had been staged, it appears to have been a great success and Louis was clearly delighted by his future bride.

Before Mary and her party entered Abbeville a sudden storm hit. The party paused for a short time and Mary changed into an English gown made of stiff gold and white brocade. Atop her red hair she wore a tiara containing two large pearls which hung on the left side.[57] At around five o'clock the storm subsided and Mary and her party made their grand entrance into Abbeville. At the front of the party were fifty esquires dressed in multi-coloured uniforms made from silk and wearing gold collars. Next, ordered by rank, came the Duke of Norfolk, noblemen and ambassadors riding in pairs, all wearing clothing of gold or silk and also wearing gold collars. Behind, led by Thomas Wriothesley and John Joyner, came the heralds, trumpeters and macers. Mary then followed, riding a decorated horse and wearing a cap made from crimson silk slightly tilted janutily over her left eye. Francis de'Angoulême rode beside Mary.

Following Mary came her beautiful litter pulled by two horses. The litter was covered in cloth of gold and embroidered with red and white roses signifying the union of the houses of York and Lancaster, together with the white lilies of France. Behind the litter came thirty of Mary's ladies, each wearing beautiful gowns of cloth of gold. Lastly, 200 archers marched at the back of the train as a demonstration and reminder of the military power of England.[58]

In a letter to the Bishop of Asti, French ambassador to Venice, it was written that 'your right reverend Lordship must not be surprised at my representing wellnigh everything in the superlative degree, for the reality exceeds my description, to the great glory of this Queen.'[59] Mary was met by the mayor, the governor, the administrator of justice, thirty chiefs, fifty archers, fifty musketeers and fifty arbalests who were all dressed in red and yellow. Mary was then greeted by the clergy who escorted her to the church of St Vulfan where she heard Mass. She was escorted to the Hôtel de la Grunthuse where the Duke of Norfolk formally introduced Mary to the French king in front of the French and English dignitaries. After their meeting, Claude, Louis's eldest daughter and wife of Francis d'Angoulême, accompanied Mary to Rue St Giles. Here Mary was lodged in the queen's apartments, which were separated from the king's apartments by a picturesque garden.[60]

We have to wonder, if, on their journey to Rue St Giles, Mary and Claude had a chance to converse. Mary was only three years older than her future daughter-in-law. The two were very different in appearance. Mary was considered to be one of the most beautiful women; Claude was plain, short and with a hunchback. Mary may have turned to Claude for advice about the French people and their customs and to seek council about Claude's father. It is unknown if Mary and Claude ever became friends during Mary's short time in France. It may be that the two spent time together, however it is just as likely that Mary was occupied with duties of queenship while her daughter-in-law tended to her own business. In the evening a ball was held in Mary's honour, organised by Francis and Claude. During the ball it was reported that Mary 'delights in hearing singing, instrumental music, and in dancing'.[61] Afterwards Mary retired to her chambers so she could sleep and prepare for the wedding the next day.

Despite the sudden storm delay it was believed by the people that Mary's entrance into Abbeville had been a success. They were delighted with their future queen and Mary was the perfect image of a wife and queen. Young, beautiful and ostensibly completely devoted to her future husband, she was poised, loving and graceful, and conducted herself with great dignity. For his part Louis seemed infatuated and Mary filled him with happiness and appeared to reinvigorate the aging monarchg. Mary had played her role perfectly and she would continue to do so.

The wedding was set for 9 October 1514, the feast day of St Denis, the patron saint of France. Just before dawn Mary and her ladies woke and after a light meal they began to dress and prepare for the ceremony.[62] At seven o'clock Mary left her lodgings. Although her apartments were a short distance from where the wedding ceremony was to be held at the Hôtel de la Gruthuse, the English made sure the short journey was to be a spectacular event. One observer wrote 'if the pomp of the most Christian Queen was great yesterday at her entry, this morning, the 9th, it was yet greater at her wedding, which took place at nine o'clock in the King's house in a large hall.'[63]

At the head of the procession were twenty-six knights marching in pairs, followed by musicians and heralds. Next came Mary wearing a French gown made from gold brocade, trimmed with ermine and dripping in expensive jewels showing off the wealth of England. Mary wore a coronet studded with jewels and her red hair cascaded down over back as a sign of her virginity. Mary's dress was even more magnificent than the gown she had worn the day before.[64]

Walking beside Mary were the Duke of Norfolk, the Marquis of Dorset, the Bishop of Durham, the Earl of Surrey, and Lord Monteagle. Each man was dressed in his most expensive clothing, including cloth of gold, damask and silk and wearing heavy golden chains in order to show their personal wealth. Behind Mary walked noblemen and twenty-four ladies wearing cloth of gold and jewellery. Lastly came thirteen women of Mary's personal staff, each accompanied by a gentleman on either side.[65]

In the hall Louis was already waiting, wearing an outfit of gold and ermine designed to match Mary's gown. Despite his clothing the French king was not as lavishly dressed as other members of his nobility who were each trying to outdo the English. His Master of the Horse spent 116 crowns per yard for cloth of gold for his clothing. It is estimated that his outfit for the day cost the staggering sum of 2,000 crowns.[66]

When Mary finally entered the hall Louis doffed his bonnet and in response Mary curtsied. The king stepped forward and gently kissed Mary before he led her to a seat beside his, under a canopy held by four French noblemen. Florimond Robertet, the King's Treasurer, stepped forward and presented Louis with a necklace made of 'a marvellous great pointed diamond, with a ruby almost two inches long without foil, which was esteemed by some men at 10,000 marks'.[67] The king then turned and gave the necklace to Mary.

Cardinal René de Prie, Bishop of Bayeux, conducted the wedding service. First the nuptial, Mass was sung before the consecrated wafter was broken and shared between Mary and Louis; each kissed the wafer before consuming it. French tradition dictated that the king's son, or nearest male relative, in this case Francis d'Angoulême, Louis's son-in-law, serve the king throughout the marriage ceremony while Mary was attended by her daughter-in-law, Claude.[68]

Once the ceremony was over, Mary stood, curtseyed to her husband and then rose so the two could kiss.[69] Mary was finally a married woman. Mary then left the hall and returned to her apartments where she and her ladies dined together.[70] After dinner a spectacular ball was held, attended by both French and English nobility as well as the newlyweds. Mary wore a dress in the French fashion and Louis was so happy with his new wife that he did not leave her side all evening. All the Enlgish and French nobles were 'banqueting, dancing, and making good cheer'.[71] At eight o'clock Claude led Mary from the banquet to the chambers were she would consummate her marriage.[72]

It was reported at the time that 'the marriage will not be consummated until Tuesday next, and then on Thursday or Friday the King will depart for Paris.'[73] However, there was little truth in such a statement. In fact Louis was eager to bed his beautiful young bride and the next morning 'the King seemed very jovial and gay, and in love, [to judge] by his countenance. Thrice did he cross the river last night, and would have done more, had he chosen.'[74]

Some did not believe the aged king and it is claimed Francis told a friend that 'unless people are lying very hard, I now know that the king and queen cannot possibly have children.'[75] If this statement implied actual impotence or simply that Louis could not father more children is not known. One must bear in mind that until Mary became pregnant and bore her husband a son, Francis was Louis XII's legal heir.

It would be foolish to think that Mary went to her wedding bed having no idea of what awaited her. By eighteen it can be safely assumed that she would have experienced her monthly menstrual cycle and been aware of sexual intercourse and pregnancy. It may have been her own mother who educated her, or perhaps it was her grandmother, Lady Margaret Beaufort, who sternly informed Mary of what awaited her when she wed. Maybe it was her childhood friend Jane Popincourt, sent to teach her French, but who taught Mary more than her language lessons; or perhaps the aged Lady Guildford, deeply beloved by Mary who sat her young charge down and explained what would be expected of her.

If Mary were to believe that all things were settled now that she was Queen of France she was to be mistaken. The morning after the wedding Louis dismissed most of the English women in Mary's household including Lady Guildford, whom Mary held dear to her heart. Mary was quite distressed about having so many of her English women taken from her and on 12 October she wrote desperately to her brother to see if he could convince Louis to reinstate them, or at least Lady Guildford.

> My good Brother, as heartily as I can I recommend me unto your Grace, marvelling much that I never heard from you since departing, so often as I have sent and written to you. And now am I left post alone in effect ; for on the morn next after the marriage my chamberlain with all other men servants were discharged, and in likewise my mother Guldeford with my other women and maidens, except such as never had experience, or knowledge how to advertise or give me counsel in any time of need, which is to be feared more shortly than your Grace thought at the time of my departing, as my mother Guldeford can more plainly show your Grace than I can write ; to whom I beseech you to give credence. And if it may be by any means possible, I humbly require you to cause my said mother Guldeford to repair hither once again. For else, if any chance hap other than weal, I shall not know where nor of whom to ask any good counsel to your pleasure, nor yet to my own profit. I marvel much that my Lord of Norfolk would at all times so lightly grant everything at their requests here. I am well assured that when ye know the truth of everything as my mother Guldeford can show you, ye would full little have thought I should have been thus entreated : that would God my Lord of York had come with me in the room of Norfolk : for then am I sure I should have been left much more at my heart's ease than I am now. And thus I bid your Grace farewell . . . and more heart's ease than I have now. Abbeville the 12th day of October.
>
> Give greetings to my mother Guldeford. By your loving sister, Mary Queen of France.[76]

Mary was distressed at having not only Lady Guildford, whom she refers to as Mother Guildford, removed from her ladies, but also all the other women she felt she could turn to for advice and friendship. Mary had only been married for three days when she wrote this letter. Surely she would need wise women about her that she could trust to turn to for guidance on how to conduct herself with her husband and at other important events and meetings.

It is also interesting that in the letter Mary squarely puts the blame not on her husband, but on the Duke of Norfolk, who clearly discussed the matter with Louis. She is very unhappy with Norfolk and carefully lays all blame on him rather than be seen to be displeased with her husband's actions. This was a very clever tactic. As Louis's wife she could not question his motives or actions, however she could blame a man who was supposed to be looking out for her best interests.

Mary also subtly hopes to evoke a little pity for herself, reminding her brother that she has written to him often because she loves him deeply, but he in return has rarely written. She is trying to pull at her brother's heart strings in an effort to have him take pity on her and see her ladies, or at least Lady Guildford, returned to her service.

On the same day Mary wrote to Cardinal Wolsey. It was Wolsey who had negotiated the treaty between France and England and the marriage of Mary to Louis. Wolsey was the man responsible for much of the administration of the court and Mary believed that writing to him would help her cause.

I recomaund me un to you as hertly as I can, and as schoth .... intreated as the kynge and you thought I schuld have ben, for ... the morn next after the maryage, all my servants, both men and women ... a dyscharged. Insomoch that my mother Guldeford was also dischargyd, whom as ze knowe the kynge and zou willed me in eny wyse to be cowncelled. But for eny thynge I myght do, yn no wyse myght I have any graunt for her abode here, which I assure you my lord is moch to my discomffort ; besyd meny other discomffortis that ze wold full lyttyll have thought. I have not zet seen yn Fraunce eny lady or jentill woman so necessary for me as sche ys nor zet so mete to do the kynge my brother service as sche ys. And for my part my lord, as ze love the kynge my broder and me, fynd the meanes that sche may yn all hast com hither agayn, for I had as lefe lose the wynynge I schall have yn France as to lose her counsell when I schall lacke it, which is not like long to be required, as I am sure the nobill men and jentillmen can schew you more then becometh me to wryte yn this matter. I pray you my Lord gyf credens forther to my moder Guldeford yn every thyng concernynge thys matter. And albehit my Lord of Northfollke h . . b nethyr deled best with me nor zet with her at thys tyme : zet I pray you allwayes to be good lord un to her. And wold to God my had ben so good to have had zou with me hither when I hard c of Northfolke. And thus fare ze weale My Lord. Wryt ile a the xij the daye of Octobr.

My Lord I pray you gyve credens to my ord yn my sorows she have delyve.

Yowr on whyl I lefe

MARY

To my lovynge frend Th'archebischop of Zorke.[77]

Mary addresses her letter to her 'loving friend' immediately creating a warm and personal connection with Wolsey. She reminds Wolsey that it was he and the king who instructed her to consult with Lady Guildford and thus she was only doing as commanded as a dutiful sister. So far she has not found any French women she can trust and take council from and wants Lady Guildford returned to her. Once again, she lays the blame squarely on the Duke of Norfolk.

Chronicler Hall reports that of Mary's women 'some had serued her longe in hope of prefermente, and some that had honest romes lefte them to serue her, & now they were with out scruice, which caused them to take thought in so much some dyed by the way returning, and sone fell mad, but ther was no remedy.'[78] While it is extremely doubtful that the women who were ordered to leave Mary's service and return home either died on the journey home or went mad, their departure was a blow to them. To be placed in the service of a noblewoman, especially a queen or princess, was a highly sought after position. Many mothers asked favours from family members or friends at court in an attempt to have their daughters placed in the service of the queen. To be close to the queen meant status and perhaps even the opportunity to become friends and maybe even ask a favour or two from the queen. To be suddenly told that they were returning home to England would have been a devastating loss of social status for their families.

It may have simply been that Louis, ever aware of potential threat, wished to dismiss any potential spies within his court. It should be unthinkable for the new queen to be harbouring English spies within her household when her future and interests would now lie in France.

When Charles Brandon heard the news he too laid the blame squarely on Norfolk. He believed that Norfolk went along with the French king because most of the women were servants of either Wolsey or Brandon and therefore dismissing them would mean they could not feed information to either man close to Henry VIII. Brandon believed that Norfolk and those who supported him were fiercely jealous of Wolsey's growing influence and the alliance Wolsey had formed with France. Brandon also feared that if Henry found out how unhappy his sister was, Norfolk would not hesitate to lay the blame on either Brandon or Wolsey, or both.[79]

Louis must have sensed his wife's distress at having so many of her beloved and trusted ladies dismissed, or was at least informed. In an attempt to placate his new bride he gave her more fabulous jewellery. He gave her 'a ruby two inches and a-half long, and as big as a man's finger, hanging by two chains of gold at every end, without any foil; the value thereof few men could esteem' as well as 'a great diamond, a tablet, with a great round pearl hanging by it' and 'rings with stones of great estimation'.[80]

Mary was not of course stripped of all her retinue. She still had, among others: 'Le conte de Nonshere, Dr. Denton, almoner, Mr. Richard Blounte, "escuyer descuyerie," the sons of Lord Roos, Lord Cobham, and Mr. Seymour, "enfans d'honneur"; Evrard, brother of the Marquis, Arthur Polle, brother of Lord Montague, Le Poulayn, "pannetiers échansons et valetz trenchans"; Francis Buddis, usher of the chamber, Maistre Guillaume, physician, Henry Calays, "varlet des robes," Rob. Wast. Mesdemoiselles Grey (sister of the Marquis), Mary Finis (daughter of Lord Dacres), Elizabeth (sister of Lord Grey), Madamoyselle Boleyne, Maistres Anne Jenyngham, "femme de chambre," and Jeanne Barnesse, "chamberiere.'[81]

Who is 'Madomoyselle Boleyne'? Both Anne Boleyn and her older sister Mary had been appointed to serve Mary Tudor and it was Mary who travelled from England to France with her queen. Meanwhile Thomas Boleyn, Anne's father, had written to Margaret of Austria to have his daughter released from her service as she had recently been appointed to serve Mary in France. Records tell us that Anne stayed on in France to serve Queen Claude after Louis XII's death and Mary Boleyn return to England, so it is highly likely that it was Anne and not her sister Mary Louis chose to retain in his wife's service.[82] It may have been during this time that Mary came to know Anne Boleyn, a girl five years her junior. Mary and Anne would have a very interesting relationship, both women strongly disliking one another and making public declarations of their disgust.

On 6 November 1514 the Earl of Worcester wrote to Thomas Wolsey regarding the dismissal of Lady Guilford:

My good Lord, as touching the return of my Lady Guildford, I have done to my power and in the best way that I could to the French King; and he hath answered me that his wife and he be in good and perfect love as ever any two creatures can be, and both of age to rule themselves, and not to have servants that should look to rule him or her. If his wife need counsel or to be ruled, he is able to do it ; but he was sure it was never the Queen's mind nor desire to have her again, for as soon as she came on land, and also when he was married, she began to take upon her, not only to rule the Queen, but also that she should not come to -him but she should be with her ; nor that any Lady or Lord should speak with her but she should hear it ; and began to set a murmur and bandying among ladies of the Court. And then he sware that there was never man that better loved his wife than he did, but ere he would have such a woman about her, he had liefer be without her; and he said that he knew well when the King, his good and loving brother, knew this his answer, he would be contented; for in no wise would he have her about his wife. Also he said that he is a sickly body, and not, at all times that he would be merry with his wife, to have any strange woman with her, but one that he is well acquainted withal, afore whom he durst be merry; and that he is sure the Queen, his wife, is content withal, for he hath set about her neither lady nor gentlewoman to be with her for her masters, but her servants, and to obey her commandments. Upon which answer, seeing he in no wise would have her, I answered him again so that he was content, and so I make no doubt but the King's Grace would.be, for the answer was well debated ere

I gave it, as his Grace and you shall know at my coming, which I trust shall be shortly…

My good Lord, the King here hath desired me to write that he heartily desires you, in his name, to desire his good brother and cousin, if God send him a son, that he may be godfather as he was last; for in so doing he shall do him a right great pleasure. And he will send a good and honorable personage to be there against the Queen's deliverance, to represent his person, and to do the act in his name; also the said person shall have authority to speak, commune, and conclude for their meeting, and of other secret matters. And of this he desires you that he may be ascertained of his good brother's mind and pleasure by your writing; for as soon as he hath answer he will dispatch his said ambassador.

My Lord, the French Queen told me that she loved my Lady Guildford well, but she is content that she come not, for she is in that case that she may well be without her, for she may do what she will. I pray God that so it may ever continue to his pleasure, whom I pray to have you, mine especial good Lord, in his blessed keeping. Written at Saint Denis the sixth day of November.

Assuredly yours to my power, C. Worcester.[83]

It is clear from the Earl's letter that Louis XII had put his foot down regarding the possible return of Lady Guildford. He did not trust the woman and believed that not only was she providing ill council to his wife, but also spreading false rumours to the other women of the court. He did not want Mary to be turned against him and, as her husband, it was his duty alone and for no other to provide Mary any council and advice she may need. Despite Mary's letters to her brother and to Wolsey, Louis would not be moved. At the end of Worcester's letter it appeared that Mary had accepted her husband's orders and that Lady Guildford would not be returning. Louis was, in effect, both King of France and king of his wife. As head of the house, obedience by his wife was not just expected, but his right.[84] In his defence, Louis XII's duty was to protect and educate his wife and he was only doing what he believed to be in Mary's best interests. Ultimately, Mary was subject to her husband's wishes and no matter how she felt personally about the loss of Lady Guildford's services, she had to accept her husband's orders. Mary would soon be crowned Queen of France.

7

The French Queen

⚜

'By your loving and most humble sister, Mary, The French Queen.'

With Mary now officially wedded to the King of France, the next step for her was to be crowned queen. The court was due to leave Abbeville shortly after the marriage. Louis was struck with another attack of gout. He had suffered from gout for many years. Mary and the king finally left on 16 October. The court moved slowly and diplomacy and secret matters of war would have to come first before Mary could be crowned Queen of France.

Charles Brandon had been sent to France in mid-October under the pretence of representing the English in the magnificent jousts that would be held after Mary's coronation. Brandon had the illustrious reputation as being one of the greatest jousters in all of Europe, after Henry VIII of course! His public mission was to support Francis in organising the jousting events. However, Cardinal Wolsey and Henry VIII had given him with another, secret, task.

Henry VIII wanted revenge against Ferdinand of Aragon for not holding to his side of the agreement to provide support to England in the war against France earlier in the year. He felt grievously deceived when Ferdinand signed a one-year truce with Louis XII halting any plans for a joint invasion against France. Mary's marriage to Louis was organised in part in retaliation for

Ferdinand's betrayal of the terms of the treaty, as well as forming a useful alliance against both the Holy Roman Empire and Spain.

Brandon's secret mission was to convince Louis XII to join with England in a combined attack on Ferdinand of Aragon. France and England would invade Navarre and drive Ferdinand out and demand half of Castile on behalf of Katherine of Aragon. Henry VIII believed that after Isabella of Castile's death, Castile should have been divided equally between her daughters Katherine and Juana.[1]

Brandon first met with the French king at Beauvais on 25 October. The king was ill and had to meet Brandon while he was lying in bed. Brandon's letter to Henry shows that Mary was also present, sitting beside her husband.[2]

This Thursday, 25 Oct., my Lord Marquis and he came to Bowoes (Beauvais) where the King and Queen both were, and were brought to their lodging. By the King's request, communicated to him by Cleremond, he went to his Grace alone. Found the King lying in bed, and the Queen sitting by the bedside. And so I diede me rywarynes and knyelled downe by hes byed sede; and soo he brassed me in hes armes, and held me a good wyell, and said that I was hartylle wyecoum, and axsed me, 'How dows men esspysseall good brodar, whom I am so moche bounden to lowf abouf hall the warld?' To which Suffolk replied, that the King his master recommended himself to his entirely beloved brother, and thanked him for the great honor and [love] that he showed to the Queen his sister. The French King answered, that he knew the nobleness and truth so much in Suffolk's master that he reckoned he had of him the greatest jewel ever one prince had of another. Assures Henry that never Queen behaved herself more wisely and honorably, and so say all the noblemen in France; and no man ever set his mind more upon a woman on account of her loving manner. As to the jousts and tournays, my Lord Marquis and the writer both thought if they had answered the challenge it were little honor to win, seeing there were 200 or 300 answerers. The King had promised to introduce them to the Dauphin to be his aids. On the Dauphin's arrival he sent for them, expressed his sense of the honor done him by the King of England, said he would not take them for his aids but for his brethren, and so went to supper; where supped the Duke of Bourbon and my Lord Marquis and I, and 'it he tabylles' (at the tables) young Count Galleas and two others. As they sat at supper they talked of Henry's running, 'of which, I ensure you, he was right glad to hear; and as far as I can see he is not so well content with nothing [as to] hear talking of your grace, and to talk of you [him]self.' The challenge, he said, would be in seven days, which was too soon for them to be ready. We agreed that it was; and thereupon he sent for 'Robart tyete' (*Robertet*) and sent him to the King, who was content to respite it 15 days. After supper the Dauphin brought us to the King, who promised Henry a harness and a courser; 'for he says your grace has mounted him so well, he will seek all Christendom but he will honor your grace well.' B[eauvais], 25 Oct.

P.S.—My lord of Longueville recommends him to the King for a true and faithful servant, as he seems to be indeed. Begs to be remembered to the Queen '[and to] all me nold fyellowes boweth men [and wo]myn; and I bysche yovr grace to [tell my]sstres Blount and mysstres Carru [the] next tyme yt I wreth un to them [or se]nd them tokones thay schall odar [wre]th to me or send me tokones agayen.' By Richmond, the last [time] he went to the King, Suffolk sent a letter of gold (?) and now sends another as a remembrancer, because he has no word whether the King received the first.[3]

Louis is clearly pleased with how Mary was behaving herself, both as his wife and as the future Queen of France. Naturally, no mention of the proposed invasion was provided within the letter, these matters were not to be discussed in an open missive.

It must have been an interesting situation for Mary to have been in, sitting beside her aged husband while the man that she secretly harboured feelings for knelt beside the bed. Louis XII was everything that Brandon was not. He was first and foremost the king of a powerful nation, secondly, he was fabulously wealthy and more than ready to lavish expensive gifts on his beautiful young bride, but he was elderly and gout-ridden. Brandon was thirty, handsome and athletic, a close friend of the King of England, but lacked the financial resources to compete with either Henry or Louis. If there was any tension within the room it goes unrecorded and most likely Mary, being the well-mannered, carefully presented woman that she was, would not have let even the faintest hint of her feelings be known.

Brandon would continue negotiations over the next few weeks. Initially Louis pretended to be interested in a joint attack against Ferdinand, but he was really only interested in recovering the duchy of Milan for France. Louis welcomed England's support in this campaign, but seemed to be vague in setting an actual date for a meeting with Henry.[4] Despite Brandon's lack of diplomatic experience and also having to organise the jousting events in his spare time, he was eventually able to get the French king to agree to a meeting with the English king. He was able to begin discussing some possible strategies for a joint attack. Louis was impressed with Brandon's efforts:[5] 'No prince christened hath such a servant for peace and war.'[6]

While discussions of war were taking place, Mary, on behalf of her husband, began negotiations with her brother regarding the possible ransom of a Frenchman. One of the duties and expectations of being a queen was that Mary would undertake charitable works and use her position of power to support and be a patron of those of lower status:

My most kind and loving brother,

I heartily recommend me unto you. Pleaseth it your grace to understand that my lord the king hath instantly desired me to write unto yon, that it would please you, for his sake and mine, to send unto my lord Darcy, to deliver François Descars, upon a reasonable ransom, unto you ; and that it would please your grace to pay his ransom for the time, and that be might be delivered unto your grace, you shortly to have the money again, after that word is of his deliverance, or else he not to return as hither. Furthermore, the duke of Bretagne, otherwise called the dauphin, hath divers seasons moved me to write to your grace for the said Francois, forasmuch as he is one of his servants; the which to do I made him promise, and to the duke of Longueville also: for I assure your grace they made me and tbe noblemen of my company great cheer, from Boulogne forth; as the duke of Norfolk, the lord marquis, with other noble men, can inform your grace. These premises considered, I beseech your grace to desire the lord Darcy to deliver, upon as little a ransom as reasonably may be, his said prisoner ; for, as I am credibly informed here, he is but a poor gentleman. Now somewhat I would that my lord the king, (and) the both dukes to whom I am much bound, should think he should be the more favoured for my sake. When this man is delivered, I beseech you to send word by the bringer of this, or some other, what his ransom is, which I pray God may be reasonable and little, who preserve your grace. Amen.

From Abbeville, the 18th day of October, by your very loving sister,

Mary Queen of France.[7]

Two days later on 20 October Mary wrote once more to her brother.

My most kind and loving brother,

I heartily recommend me to you, certifying your grace that, since my departing from you, I have sent you divers letters, and as yet I have had no manner word from your grace, whereof in part I marvel, considering that certain letters be come from your grace hither. I trust, though I be fiir from you, that your grace will not forget me; but that I shall shortly hear from you, whereof I heartily desire you. And whereas I have written unto your grace touching the deliverance of a prisoner which my lord Darcy hath, I beseech you that his ransom might be as favourable, and driven to a small a sum as might be ; assuring your grace that, trusting that favour should be showed him, my lord the king, at the instance of the duke of Bretagne and the duke of Longueville, hath sent this week his letters unto Boulogne, that divers of your subjects, being prisoners there, should be delivered, after the custom of the sea. As for 200 marks, or 250 marks, I hear say they would be content to give, or else to continue still; which, I trust to God and you, shall not be, who preserve your grace. Amen.

Written at Abbeville, the 20th day of October,

By your loving sister,
Mary.
To my most kind and loving brother the King of England.[8]

The results of Mary's requests are unknown, but it would not be the last time that Mary would seek assistance for those of lesser standing than herself. After she became Queen of France Mary wrote to Thomas Wolsey seeking support for her former teacher, John Palsgrave, who had recently been released from Mary's services by Louis. Mary hoped that Wolsey could help to keep Palsgrave in France, finding him work in Paris.

My lord,
    I heartily recommend me unto you, desiring you for my sake to be good lord to my servant John Palsgrave, and provide for him some living that he may continue at school. If he had been retained in my service, I would have done for him gladly myself, but since he was put out of my service, I willed him to come to Paris, partly because I trust verily that you will provide for him (that) he may be able to continue, and also because I intend myself somewhat to do for him. Howbeit, because my estate is not yet made, I wot not how much. I shall be glad to help him that he shall not need to come home. Praying you heartily not to forget him. Commending you, my lord, to God who have you in his keeping.
At Paris, the 13th day of November.
Mary Queen of France.[9]

Four days later Mary also wrote to her brother on behalf of Mr Vincent Knight, imploring her brother to help this man who had been a faithful and dutiful servant to the king. She pleaded most graciously for Knight to be released from prison and his money restored to him for he had been imprisoned for not paying his bills, yet it was not his fault since he was owed money by the Privy Council and they had not paid him.

My very dear lord and brother,
    I recommend myself most humbly to your good grace, praying you to accept my recommendations in behalf of a poor

honest man, Mr. Vincent Knight, who has always dwelt and remained in your kingdom since he came in with our late dearest lord and father, whom God absolve. The poor man has made several voyages over here during the wars, by command of your privy-council, which had promised him a benefice. This they have not granted, but, in lieu of it, have had him put into prison in your city of Tournay, whilst you were there, where he remained seven weeks, and was then taken prisoner to England; where he has been in your prison of the Fleet, without any veritable cause, for the space of forty-four weeks, and has lost and spent all his property in prison, as we have been duly advertised by some of our especial servants in England. My dearest lord and brother, I pray you earnestly, both for my sake, as a reward of the services he has done you, and that he may more eagerly supplicate God for you and me, to do him some good, and, if it please you, to command the bishop of York to have his money restored to him and to be gracious to him. By so doing you will bestow great charity and alms. Praying our Lord God to give you, my most honoured lord and brother, a good and long life.

From Paris, the 17th day of November.

By your good sister,

Mary.

To my very dear lord and brother the King of England.[10]

As well as doing so during her time in France, Mary would also provide patronage and support in the latter years of her life. While residing at Westhorpe Hall in Suffolk she would be greatly loved by the people of the country, who would often petition her and Mary would attempt to assist as far as she was able.[11]

While the journey from Abbeville to Paris was taken slowly owing to Louis XII's poor health, the French king was not complaining at the opportunity to spend more time with his new wife. While the king was ill Mary would sit beside him, singing or playing the lute in an attempt to entertain him and keep him happy. Louis was so smitten with his new bride that he 'could not bear her to leave his side'.[12] The English ambassadors wrote to Henry of how well behaved and dutiful Mary was towards her new husband and Henry wrote back to the French king:

We have heard how she conducts herself towards you, in all humility and reverence, so that you are well content with her, and we have conceived very great joy, pleasure, and comfort, in hearing and understanding this. And our will, pleasure, and intention is, that in so acting, she should preserve from good to better, if she wish and desire to have our love and fraternal benevolence; and thus we gave her advice and counsel, before her departure from us, and we make no doubt that you will, day by day, find her more and more all that she ought to be with you, and that she will do everything which will be to your will, pleasure, and contentment.[13]

Naturally, Henry VIII took full credit for the way Mary was conducting herself. The reality was that Mary was simply doing what she had been brought up to do. She was a woman in an age when a wife served her husband as dutifully as she should. While behaving as the dutiful, faithful, loving wife Mary knew she could manipulate her husband and those around her. This would become even more evident after Louis's death.

Mary continued her acts of kindness on the journey to Paris. Whatever town the court stopped at she would use her prerogative as queen to release any prisoners in confinement.[14] French custom dictated that an uncrowned queen was not allowed to enter Paris and thus Mary's coronation would have to take place at the cathedral of St Denis. The court arrived at St Denis on 31 October.[15]

Mary was crowned Queen of France on Sunday, 5 November 1514. Early in morning the English Ambassadors were informed by Monsieur de Montmorency that they needed to make their way to the cathedral of St Denis so they could take their seats before other, less important people arrived. At ten o'clock there was a great blast of trumpets signalling Mary's arrival. A few moments later the French members of nobility arrived including the Ducs d'Alençon, Bourbon, Longueville and Albany, the Comte de Vendôme and the Comte de Saint-Pol.[16] After them came Mary. There are no accounts of what Mary wore for her coronation; for such a momentous occasion it surely must have been a gown of the most dazzling design and material. Mary was led by the hand through the cathedral by Francis d'Angoulême to a cushion in front of the high altar. Mary knelt and the Cardinal de Brie stepped forward anointing Mary with the sacred oil before placing the royal sceptre in her right hand and the rod of justice in her left. The Cardinal then placed a ring on Mary's finger and the matrimonial crown of France on her head. After this Francis stepped forward and helped Mary to her feet before guiding her to the chair of state beneath a canopy on the left side of the altar. The crown was so heavy that Francis had to move to stand behind where Mary sat so that he could hold the crown symbolically above the new queen's head. High Mass was then sung by Cardinal de Brie before Mary once more approached the altar. She made an offering before receiving the sacrament. Once this was done the ceremony was officially over and Mary left the cathedral of St Denis with her ladies and other nobles to return to her apartments where she was joined by Louis XII, who had been secretly watching the coronation.[17]

While Mary's coronation had been a relatively low key affair, her entrance into Paris would be one of the grandest spectacles ever held. At seven o'clock the following morning, Louis XII left St Denis early so that he could await the arrival of his wife and new queen. Mary left shortly after nine o'clock.[18] The French queen rode in an open carriage covered with a cloth of gold. She wore a magnificent gown of gold brocade covered in pearls and a jewelled necklace.[19] At eighteen, dressed in cloth of gold, her breathtaking jewellery sparkling, Mary must have looked like a goddess. Francis d'Angoulême rode by Mary's side, the pair it is reported, often speaking to one another. It must have been over the last few days that Mary began to acquaint herself with her son-in-law and gain an opinion of him; it would be a relationship which she would rely on heavily after the death of her husband. Behind Mary rode her ladies, as well as Louis' daughters, Claude and Renée.[20]

Paris was bedecked to welcome the new queen. Tapestries hung along the streets and the entire town was decorated with lilies and roses. On her journey there Mary was greeted by a number of tableaux. The first was at St Denis. Here an enormous ship had been built, complete with real sailors who climbed the rigging. There was even wind blowing into the sails. The ship held images of Ceres, Bacchus and at the helm the Greek hero, Paris. These symbolised the corn, wine and general commerce of the city.

Mary was presented with a carefully written programme of the tableaux illuminated with gold leaf. A choir sung her praises,[21]

> Noble Lady, welcome to France,
> Through you we now shall live in joy and pleasure,
> Frenchmen and Englishmen live at their ease,
> Praise to God, who sends us such a blessing!

> Most illustrious, magnanimous Princess, Paris reveres and honours you
> And presents this ship to your nobility,
> Which is under the King's governance.
> Grains, wines, and sweet liqueurs are therein,
> Which the winds propel by divine ordinance.
> All men of good will
> Receive you as Queen of France.

> To Mary, who has replaced war
> By peace, friendship, and alliance,
> Between the Kings of France and England.[22]

Mary progressed to the second tableau, which was a beautiful marble fountain in front of a background of celestial blue. The three Graces danced in the surrounding garden while lilies of France and English roses grew out of the fountain. A further poem celebrating the joining of the lily and the rose was read.

The third tableau displayed Solomon and the Queen of Sheba representing the wisdom of Louis XII. The fourth tableau was at the Church of the Holy Innocents. A two-tiered scaffold had been erected at the front of the church and a person dressed as God the Father held a large heart and a bouquet of red roses over figures of Louis and Mary, now both dressed in gold and ermine.

The fifth tableau was the most spectacular. A grand walled city had been constructed enclosing a garden in which grew a rose bush. By a great feat of design a magnificent rose bud grew upwards out of the bush towards a balcony where a lily was growing before a golden throne, covered in a beautiful pavilion. When the rosebud reached the lily, it opened to reveal a young woman. The woman then recited a poem comparing Mary to love. This entire scene was watched by four Virtues and from outside the constructed walls, Peace, who had vanquished the evil of Discord.

Continuing her journey Mary was presented with the sixth tableau at the Chastellet de Paris. Here the virtues of Justice and Truth sat on thrones beneath a grant replica of the French crown. Surrounding them the god and goddesses Phoebus, Diana, Minerva, Stella Maris and Concord sat in a meadow listening contentedly to a long speech comparing Louis to the sun and Mary to the moon.

Late in the afternoon Mary finally reached the seventh and final tableau at the Palace Royale. Here the Angel of the Annunciation, Gabriel, spoke to the Virgin Mary who sat under the coat of arms of France, which was supported by a porcupine and a lion. The lion represented England, the porcupine the French Order of the Porcupine established in 1394 by Louis de France, Duke of Orléans. At the foot of the stage, shepherds and shepherdesses sang a song celebrating Mary in heaven and Mary on earth.

As the peace between God and man,
By the intervention of the Virgin Mary,
Once was made, so now we,
The French burghers, are relieved of our burdens;
Because Mary has married with us.
Through her, justice and peace join
In the fields of France and the countryside of England;
Since the bonds of love hold arms in restraint,
We have acquired for ourselves, equally,
Mary in heaven and Mary on earth.[23]

After this final tableau Mary and her entourage travelled to Notre Dame where she was greeted by all the learned men of the city: doctors, lawyers and members of the Church. As Mary entered the great cathedral bells were rung and the organ began to play. As she made her way to the high altar the clergy sung the *Te Deum*. A Mass was conducted and Mary was formally welcomed to the city by the Archbishop of Paris. Mary returned to her litter and she and all those who accompanied her returned to the Palace Royale at around six o'clock.[24]

The banquet was held in the Grande Salle, a spectacular room 222 feet long and 84 feet wide. The room had been built with supporting Doric columns and the walls were lined with effigies of all the French kings. Tapestries hung about the walls and large sideboards covered with gold and silver plate surrounded each pillar showing the wealth of the French king. Musicians played light music while Mary and her guests ate.

Seated at a marble table, Mary was joined by her daughter-in-law Claude, Louise of Savoy, (Francis' mother) and Louise's daughter, Marguerite of Navarre. For Mary this must have been a rather tense situation. Unless Mary bore her husband a son it would be Francis who inherited the French crown. Louise of Savoy was a fierce woman, devoted to her son as well as being politically astute and an extremely clever diplomat. Louise would have been very much aware of how tenuous her son's claim to the throne had become with Mary's marriage to Louis. The subject of their conversation remains unknown; both knew the implications of this marriage.

The banquet consisted of a mixture of culinary and mechanical extravaganzas including a phoenix beating its wings until it was consumed by fire, a cock and a hare jousting and an image of St George on horseback leading a damsel.[25] After the dishes were served Mary thanked the heralds and musicians and gave them an alms dish and plate worth around 200 crowns. After everyone had eaten, a number of 'pastimes and diversions'[26] were provided. It is reported that Mary fell asleep before the banquet was over, utterly exhausted from the rigours of the day and that she had to be carried to her rooms. Louis had retired some time earlier.

The next day, 7 November, Mary attended Mass before travelling to the Hôtel des Tournelles where she joined her husband until the grand tournaments to celebrate her marriage and coronation started.[27] On 11 November Mary met with the merchants of the city, who presented her with a magnificent gift of gold and silver plate worth at least 6,000 francs. They also requested that she attend a banquet in her honour at a time of her choosing. Through her maître d'hôtel, Mary thanked the merchants and assured them of her love for the city and that she would attend the banquet as soon as she had consulted with the king.

On 15 November Mary wrote once more to her brother regarding her current position,

> My most kind and loving brother,
> I recommend me unto your grace as heartily as I can, and I thank your grace for your kind letters, and for your good counsel, the which I trust to our Lord God I shall follow every day more and more. How lovingly the king my husband dealeth with me, the lord chamberlain, with other of your ambassadors, can clearly inform your grace, whom I beseech your grace heartily to thank for their great labours and pains that they have taken as here for me; for I trust they have made a substantial and a perfect end. As touching mine almoner, I thank your grace for him, Of his demeanour here your grace shall be informed better than I can write; as knoweth our Lord Jesu, who preserve your grace. Amen.
> From Paris, the 15th day of November, by your loving sister, Mary.
> To the King my brother.[28]

Mary's letter starts by thanking her brother for his council, wishing to always follow his words. How much counsel Henry VIII was actually providing his sister remains unknown. It is most likely that he was passing messages through his ambassadors, yet Henry was days, if not weeks, away by messenger and Mary, now more than ever, was relying on her own wit and skills. Her letter shows that she appears to be content with her new life. The elderly and frail Louis was proving to be a loving and kind husband and Mary seems happy with him.

A series of tournaments to take place at Abbeville after the wedding in Mary's honour had been organised by Francis. It had soon been realised that the tournament would be far grander than first expected so the arrangements were postponed in order that the event could be held in a more lavish setting. Francis desired to have a tournament that would rival anything produced by the English king and one which would showcase his own great skills at the joust.

While the jousts were, in part, to celebrate Mary's wedding, it could not be overlooked that there was an underlying tension between England and France, each country wishing to outdo the another and be crowned the champion of the event through the endeavours of their champions. Henry VIII had ordered his represntatives to spare no expense and part of Charles Brandon's mission was to support Francis in organising the jousting events. He was an extraordinarily skilled jouster and excelled at hand-to-hand combat, so took to the task with great enthusiasm.

The tournaments began on Monday 13 November. Due to poor weather the events took place intermittently until the 23rd, with only five full days of actual jousting and fighting. A large stage had been built in the Parc des Tournelles in which spectators could sit and watch. As guests of honour, Mary and Louis presided. It is reported that Louis had to lie on a couch to watch and that Louis' daughter, Claude, sat by his side.

Representing the English team, Sir Edmund Howard, Sir Edward Neville, Sir Giles Capell, Sir Thomas Cheyney, Sir William Sidney, Sir Henry Guildford, Thomas Grey Marquis of Dorset and Charles Brandon, Duke of Suffolk, were chosen. Dorset and Brandon would lead the group. Henry paid some of the contestants to cover the costs of their horses and armour. Brandon chose to take over his own horses and armour having been granted £1,000 by the king to equip himself.

Francis led the French team, accompanied by nine other equally skilled men. The tournament itself was a complicated affair. A number of courses were run by each participant, on horseback with spears, and on foot with lances and swords. There were hand-to-hand contests in which a great melée of men were divided into teams. In total there were approximately 305 participants.

The tournament began with a formal announcement from the heralds:

By the high and most puissant prince, the Duke of Valois and Bretagne, for the Joyous advent of the queen to the said Paris; my said lord had had published through the kingdoms of France and England, by Mountjoy, first and sovereign king-at-arms of the French, and by the order of the most Christian king our sovereign lord, to let all princes, nobles, and gentlemen know, the five enterprises proposed, attached and signified by five shields;

viz. the silver shield, the golden shield, the black shield, the tawny shield, and the grey shield; the enterprises are declared according to the roll which my said lord gave to the said Mountjoy, who has published them as aforesaid; wherefore through the said publication, many princes, lords and gentlemen, have touched (the shields), as hereafter may be seen.[29]

We have seen the different coloured shields earlier, at the tourney held when Mary and Louis first met. After the announcement came the introduction of each knight who came out and rode once around the lists before making a second lap to present himself to the king and queen. The French sought to outdo the English in both competition and dress. Francis was reported to have worn a different suit of armour each day. The first day he wore silver and gold, then the next crimson and yellow velvet over his armour and on the third day he wore the Tudor colours of green and white to compliment Mary. The French Duke of Bourbon and Earl of St Polle were also gorgeously dressed in tawny velvet and cloth of silver and purple velvet respectively. The English simply wore the red cross of St George on their armour; their victories would be on the jousting field, not the catwalk.[30]

With the formalities over, the events could officially start. Naturally, all eyes were on Francis and Brandon, both considered to be the best jousters of their respective teams, and official champions of their respective kings. On the first day, the Duc d'Alençon, Francis' brother-in-law, distinguished himself by running ten consecutive courses. He could have done more but he suffered a minor hand injury. Despite d'Alençon's efforts, it was Brandon who received the honours for the first day. He ran at least fifteen courses in which he was the challenger for thirteen, the more demanding role. It was reported that several horses were killed and one Frenchman lost his life.[31]

On the second day, Brandon continued to display his great skill. In three consecutive rounds he managed to unhorse his opponent, one of the most difficult feats of the joust. Dorset was also reported to have performed well, breaking many spears. On the fourth day Brandon ran six courses, almost all run consecutively, an achievement which must have been exhausting.[32] After this, things got a little rough. Dorset wrote:

> My Lord of Suffolk and he ran three days, and lost nothing. One Frenchman was slain at the tilt, and divers horses. [On Saturday the 18th] the tournay and course in the field began as roughly as ever I saw; for there was divers times both horse and man overthrown, horses slain, and one Frenchman hurt that he is not like to live. My Lord of Suffolk and I ran but the first day thereat, but put our ayds thereto, because there was no noblemen to be put unto us, but poor men of arms and Scots, many of them were hurt on both sides, and no great hurt, and of our Englishmen none overthrown nor greatly hurt but a little of their hands. The Dolphyn himself was a little hurt on his hand. [On Tuesday, the 21st] the fighting on foot began, to the which they brought an Almayn that never came into the field before, and put him to my Lord of Suffolk to have put us to shame if they could, but advantage they gat none of us, but rather the contrary. I forbear to write more of our chances, because I am party therein. I ende[d] without any manner hurt; my Lord of Suffolk is a little hurt in his hand.[33]

Despite the toughness of the events it would appear from Dorset's letter that it was the English who were faring better. On Tuesday 21 November, the fighting on foot began. Due to a hand injury Francis was no longer able to compete. He wished to highlight the poor skill of the Englishmen and decided to put Dorset and Brandon into battle against all challengers. Both men appeared to have fared well and it was reported that Francis was furious.[34]

In an attempt to outshine and bring Brandon down, Francis brought in an enormous German of great strength and skill. He was reported to be taller and stronger than any Frenchman and was disguised so that no one would know he was German. Brandon found himself against an unexpected opponent. However, he was a skilled fighter. He not only had his personal pride, but that of his country to uphold. After unhorsing his German opponent Brandon struck him with the butt end of his spear causing the German to stagger, but the fighting continued. After lifting their visors to draw breath, Brandon and the German continued to fight with blunt-edged swords. Despite such a fierce opponent Brandon was able to defeat the German with his superior skill and managed to take him by the neck and pummel him about the head until blood came out of his nose. The defeated German was quickly whisked away so that no one would discover his true identity.[35] Brandon and the Englishmen were the clear winners of the magnificent tournament. Brandon's only injury was a sore hand, which had been made a little worse after his battle against the German. Louis was reported to have been pleased that Francis did not fare well and stated that Suffolk and Dorset 'did shame all France' and deserved the great praise they received.[36]

After the tournament Brandon wrote to Henry regarding his diplomatic mission, the only mention of how he performed at the jousting in a single line in which he stated 'my lord, at the writing of this letter the jousts were done; and blessed be God all our Englishmen sped well, as I am sure ye shall hear by other.'[37]

With the tournament over and the English as victors, all that remained was Mary's ceremonial appearance as Queen of France, which was held at the Hôtel de Ville on 24 November. Mary arrived on horseback, with the Dukes of Bourbon and Suffolk and other noblemen riding before her. By her side was Francis and following her came Claude and other ladies of Mary's court. So many French men and women came to praise the new queen that Mary and Louis were unable to enter via the front door as it was blocked by the throng. At first it was suggested that Mary's personal guard of English archers should push a way through but Mary would not have this in case someone was hurt. Instead, the couple entered through a porter's door and up a narrow staircase to the banqueting hall.[38]

After the main courses a magnificent dessert was prepared just for Mary, who enjoyed it so much she ordered that some be taken to her stepdaughter, Renée, who was four years old and Louis' youngest child. This action greatly delighted the dignitaries and observers. Those at the banquet all tried to outdo one another with tributes to their new queen. They also boasted that no French king had been killed in battle since Clovis, nor had any been killed by his own people or cast out of France. While clearly words of flattery, there was a subtlety here, the tributes clearly comparing the stability of the French monarchy to that of the turbulent reigns of the English kings of the previous century. Mary pretended not to notice and did not evince any objection.[39]

On 27 November 1514, Mary, Louis and the court left for Saint-Germain-en-Laye for three weeks, where they stayed in Louis' country palace. At this time the majority of the English dignitaries began to return home. Brandon remained for some time, continuing with his secret mission to convince Louis to go to war with England against Spain. With no firm promise, Brandon returned to England in time for Christmas.[40]

In the following weeks Mary conducted herself as cordially and as dutifully as she had thus far. Brandon wrote to Cardinal Wolsey explaining that Mary frequently sought the council of Louis' most trusted advisers asking

> ...how she might best order herself to content the King, whereof she was most desirous; and I her should lack no good will; and because she knew well they were the men that the King loved and trusted, and knew best his mind, therefore she was utterly determined to love them and trust them, and to be ordered by their Council in all causes, for she knew well that those that the King loved must love her best, and she them.[41]

Mary may have realised that her time with her husband was drawing to a close and devoted herself to Louis, who was now struggling with his gout. Louis frequently requested Mary to be at his side, either singing, playing the lute or simply providing companionship. In fact the only time that Mary left her husband was when he asked her to visit members of the nobility. She gave all of herself in order to please her husband and it was evident to those who saw him that the French king was deeply in love with her.[42] On 28 December Louis wrote to Henry of his love for his wife:

> My good Brother, Cousin, and Comrade, with all my heart 1 commend myself unto you very affectionately. I have by this bearer, your Officer of Arms, received the letters written by you to me on the ninth of this month, and have heard by the said bearer of the joy you had in hearing from my Cousin, the Duke of Suffolk, of my news, and the content which I have in the Queen,

my wife, your good sister, who has so conducted herself towards me, and continues so to do daily, that I know not how I can sufficiently praise and express my delight in her. More and more I love, honour and hold her dear; therefore you may be certain that she is, and ever will continue to be, treated in such a manner as shall content her, and you likewise.

And as touching the reception and good cheer which my Cousin of Suffolk has told you I have made him, there is no need, my good Brother, Cousin, and Comrade, to give me thanks; for I beseech you to believe that besides what I know of the place he holds about you and the love you bear him, his virtues, honesty, and good qualities merit that he should be honoured and received as much for what he is, as for your own honour; so I have made him the best cheer that was in my power.

Howbeit as touching the secret matters which my Cousin of Suffolk has spoken to me, and on which I have made such reply as he has declared to you by my ambassadors whom I have dispatched and sent to you, you have little more to hear; therefore I entreat you very affectionately after you have heard them to take resolution thereon, and to advertise me of the same as early as it be possible, that I may dispose and order myself accordingly in following what you command me in your said letters. I will keep things in suspense without taking any conclusion thereon, advising you that in good or evil fortune I will live with you, and not only preserve the good friendship and alliance which is made and sworn betwixt us, but keep the said inviolably, watching rather to augment and increase than to diminish it, and hoping that you, on your part, will do likewise. Praying God, my good Brother, Cousin, and Comrade, that He may have you in His holy keeping.

Your loyal Brother, Cousin, and good Comrade,
Louis.[43]

This was his last letter to the English king.

Toward the end of December Louis, Mary and the court returned to the Hôtel des Tournelles in Paris. Before Mary's arrival in France Louis' doctors had put the king on a strict diet. He had been instructed to wake early, eat his main meal at ten o'clock, refrain from too much excitement and exercise frequently. Yet on Mary's arrival Louis turned a blind eye to such advice and participated in many rich banquets held in Mary's honour.[44]

In the last days of Louis' life Mary sat by her husband's side attempting to comfort him. She spoke frequently with her husband and her son-in-law Francis, who seemed to show little concern for his father-in-law and more concern for Mary's health. By this stage Francis could feel the French crown within his grasp; his concern was that if Mary were pregnant and that child be born a boy; it would be this child, not Francis, who would claim the French throne.[45]

Robert de la Marck, Seigneur de Fleuranges, Marshal of France wrote:

> The King left the palace and took lodgings at Tournelles in Paris because it had the best climate, and also he did not feel very strong, because he had desired to be a pleasing companion with his wife; but he deceived himself, as he was not the man for it; inasmuch as he had for a long time been very sick, particularly with gout, and for five or six years he had thought that he would die of it… because he was given up by the doctors and he lived on a very strict diet which he had broken when he was with his wife; and the doctors told him that if he continued he would die from his pleasure.[46]

Unfair rumours have been attached to Mary claiming that she brought about the death of the French king. Her youth and vigour had inspired something within Louis and he abandoned all advice provided by his doctors and thrust himself into being a valiant, vigorous husband for his wife. While there was some truth to this, the blame surely should not be placed on Mary's shoulders. De la Marck's statements regarding Louis show that the French king had been suffering from gout for five or six years and that even the king believed it would be the cause of his death. Perhaps male pride took over and Louis wished to be a 'pleasing companion with his wife' or die trying. Knowing he was nearing the end of his days, maybe Louis decided he would prefer to have fun as opposed to listening to his doctors. However much the French king wished to live, his health was already on the decline before he married Mary.

He rallied on his wedding and during the following weeks, but not even a beautiful young wife could stay the grim reaper's hand.

King Louis XII of France died on 1 January 1515.[47] The Doge and Senate wrote to Sebastian Giustiniani on 13 January stating that 'the news of the demise of the King of France was true, he having died in Paris on the night of the 1st.'[48] Louise of Savoy, (Francis' mother) wrote in her diary that *le premier jour de janvier mon fils fut Roy de France*.[49] (The first day of January my son became the King of France).

Francis, now the uncrowned king, wrote of his father-in-law's passing that he died '*entre neuf et dix heurs du soir*'[50] (between nine and ten o'clock in the evening). Another account has the king passing at '*environ dix heurs du soir*' (about ten o'clock in the evening). Louise of Savoy gives the time at '*environ onze heurs de nuit*' (about eleven hours at night). A Latin chronicler wrote that the king passed '*entre la dixieme et la onzieme heurs de nuit*' (between the tenth and eleventh hour of night). We know that Mary was not at her husband's side when he passed because reports state that when she was told of the king's death, she fainted. Mary had been married for eighty-two days.[51]

As was customary for a dowager queen, Mary removed herself from court and retired to the Hôtel de Cluny in the Rue des Mathurins St Jaques. The building had been built at the turn of the fifteenth century in a U shape, with the U opening on to a spacious garden.[52] Mary would not have been able to see much of the outside world. As a widow of a king of France, Mary wore a gown of white, giving rise to her name '*La Reine Blanche*'[53] (The White Queen) and shut herself away in '*la Chambre de la Reine Blanche*' (the Chamber of the White Queen).

The customary period for a dowager queen to shut herself away from the world was forty days in order to establish if she was pregnant. Mary's rooms were darkened, windows covered with heavy curtains and lit only by wax candles. Many of her ladies were dismissed, replaced by women bound to Louise of Savoy, Francis' mother.[54] This must have been a very stressful time for Mary. Young, full of energy, Mary was used to a life of entertainment and being in the public eye. She enjoyed banquets, tournaments and other forms of entertainment and sought guidance from those around her. Suddenly all of that had been taken from her and she found herself with only a few ladies, some of whom she did not know, shut off from the world in a darkened room. It is interesting to examine Mary's frame of mind during this period of exclusion. She wrote numerous letters to her brother. These letters will be examined in the next chapter.

Despite the tension and mistrust of the French servants around her, Mary rallied within herself and soon dismissed the Frenchwomen who had been assigned to her and recalled her English servants. One of these women may have been Anne Boleyn, with whom Mary would have numerous dealings later in life. At least for now, in seclusion and waiting out the alloted time, Mary had the companionship of her trusted English ladies.

During the time of Mary's seclusion Louis XII's body was disembowelled, embalmed and laid out in the Great Hall at Tournelles, with the crown, robes and sceptre of a king. People came from far and wide to have one last look at the French king. Louis' funeral procession passed through the streets of Paris lined with people wearing black. The following day Louis XII was buried at Notre Dame Cathedral next to his second wife, Anne of Brittany, mother of his daughter, Claude, now the uncrowned Queen of France since she was the wife of Francis, the man Louis had named as his successor should there be no male heir.[55] If Mary were to be pregnant with a boy, Salic law dictating that only males may inherit the French throne, then it would be Mary's son and not Louis XII's son-in-law, Francis who would inherit the throne.

It is impossible to know just when the dowager queen knew she was not pregnant. It may have been as early as the time of Louis' death. On 14 January Sir Robert Wingfield wrote to Henry VIII 'if the Queen of France be with child, she be kept from danger. If she be a maid, as I think verily she is, to obtain possession of her person.' That is, if she is pregnant, protect her; if not, bring her home.

On 24 January the Venetian ambassador reported that Francis I visited Mary at the Hôtel de Cluny. 'The King went every day to visit the Queen widow, who was sorrowful, lamenting much the death of her husband. The present King meant her to have great power in France, as if she were Queen regnant.'[56] It may have been at this time that Mary informed Francis that she was not pregnant and that he was the heir to the throne.

On 10 February when Sir Richard Wingfield, Nicholas West and Charles Brandon visited Mary they reported that 'there is no truth in the rumour that the French Queen, that now is, is with child. Her physicians do not believe it; and also at our [being there] we saw no great appearance thereof; [and when] we showed her that your grace was right g[lad and] joyous that she was with child, she answered [that] it was not so as yet.'[57] For Mary her time at the Hôtel de Cluny was to mourn her late husband rather than to see if she was actually with child.

King Francis I of France was crowned on 28 January at the ancient city of Rheims, where many of France's previous kings had been crowned. After his coronation the new king returned to Paris to make his grand entry. On 13 February 1515 Francis I entered Paris as France's anointed king. By this time Mary's seclusion at Cluny was over and she watched the grand procession from an upstairs window. In the evening she had the honour of riding to a banquet held in the king's honour with the new French queen, Mary's stepdaughter, Claude.[58]

8

The White Queen

⚜

'There was never princess so much beholden to her sovereign
and brother as she is to your grace; and therefore, as touching
consent to any marriage in these parts, she trusteth that your
grace knoweth her mind therein.'

The letters that pass from Mary over the next few months to her
brother Henry and to Thomas Wolsey are a fascinating insight into
the mind of Mary Tudor during the first months of her widowhood.
They also show, quite simply, just how clever she was. In a time
when women were seen as lesser human beings both physically and
intellectually, Mary was able to convince her brother into accepting
her sudden marriage to a man far beneath her station, having
married without his permission and thus defying him. All the while
Mary was able to obfuscate so that her brother saved face as king
and used her grace and wits to maintain her brother's love.

Having been notified of King Louis XII's death Thomas Wolsey
wrote urgently to Mary:

Having been informed of the danger of the King her husband,
"and that [in] likelihood or this time he is departed to the mercy
of God," offers his consolation and advice "how your grace shall
demean [yourself], being in this heaviness and among strangers,
far from [your] most loving brother and other your assured
friends and servants. Touching your consolation I most heartily

beseech your grace, with thanksgiving to God, to take wisely and patiently such visitation of Almighty God, against whose ordinance no earthy creature may be, and not by extremity of sorrow to hurt your noble person."

Wolsey assures her that Henry will not forsake her; and begs her, for the old service the writer has done her, to do nothing without the advice of his grace, however she should be persuaded to the contrary, and to let nothing pass her mouth

...whereby any person in these parts may have [you] at any advantage. And if any motions of marriage or other [offers] fortune to be made unto you, in no wise give hearing to them. And thus doing ye shall not fail to have the King fast and loving to you, to aitain to your desire [and come] home again into England with as much honor as [queen ever] had. And for my part, to the effusion of my [blood and spen]dyng of my goods, I shall never forsake nor leav[e you].[1]

Wolsey makes the effort to acknowledge the difficult situation Mary finds herself, alone in a foreign country with no man to support her. He reminds Mary that her brother will not forsake her and that she should not do anything rash and specifically not accept any offers of marriage without consulting Henry. If Mary follows this advice she will continue to find her brother loving towards her and that he will bring her back to England with all the honours due to a dowager queen.

Although this letter promises Henry's love and devotion towards his sister, it is a warning. If she does do something rash – such as marrying without his permission – she may lose her brother's love. It is interesting that Wolsey should insert some mention of remarriage so soon after Louis XII's death. Was he aware that Mary had feelings for Charles Brandon? Or was he simply trying to cover all bases should an unexpected proposal arise? Mary was clearly able to read between the lines of Wolsey's letter and was not about to accept being spoken to in such a manner. She replied on 10 January:

My own good Lord, I recommend me to you and thank you for your kind and loving letter, desiring you of your good countenance and good lessons that you hath given to me, for to remember me to the King, my brother, for such causes and business as I have for to do; for as now I have none other to put my trust in but the King, my brother, and you. And as it shall please the King, my brother, and his Council I will be ordered. And so I pray you, my lord, to show his Grace, seeing that the King, my husband, is departed to God, of whose soul God pardon. And whereas you advise me that I should make no promise, My Lord, I trust the King, my brother and you will not reckon in me such childhood. I trust I have so ordered myself since I came hither, that I trust it hath been to the honour of the King, my brother, and me, and so I trust to continue. If there be any thing that I may do for you, I would be glad for to do it in these parts. I shall be glad to do it for you. No more to you at this time but Jesus preserve you.

By your loving friend, MARY QUEEN OF FRANCE.[2]

On 14 January Henry VIII wrote to Francis I sending him his condolences and informing the new king that he would be sending three of his men to acknowledge Francis' accession to the throne and begin negotiations for Mary's return to England.[3] The three men Henry VIII selected were Sir Richard Wingfield, Nicholas West and Charles Brandon, Duke of Suffolk.[4] Upon learning that one of the three men coming to negotiate her return to England was Charles Brandon, Mary may have already begun to turn her mind towards marriage.

Brandon had used family influence and his own close friendship with Henry VIII to climb the social ladder. His grandfather was Sir William Brandon of Wangford and Southwark (c.1425-1491).[5] William Brandon rose from relative obscurity under the service of John de Mowbray, Duke of Norfolk. Before the duke died in 1476 he granted Sir William a seat in the local Parliament and arranged his marriage to Elizabeth Wingfield (d. 28 April 1497).[6] William had a long list of positions including Marshal of the King's Bench, Member of Parliament for Shoreham, Knight of the Shire of Suffolk and Collector of Customs at King's Lynn and Great Yarmouth, Norfolk. William Brandon was also present at the Battle of Tewkesbury, one of the decisive battles in English history where Prince Edward, Henry VI's son, was killed and the Lancastrian forces were defeated. William Brandon was knighted for his efforts. William was also present at the coronation of Richard III, brother of the late Yorkist king Edward IV.[7]

Sir William and Elizabeth Wingfield had three sons, Robert Brandon, William and Thomas and seven daughters. William Brandon Junior was born around 1456 making him about twenty eight years of age when his son Charles was born.

During the time of the Wars of the Roses William Brandon and his brother Thomas had become deeply dissatisfied with King Richard III and chose to head to Brittany to join forces with Henry Tudor and support his claim to the throne. It is believed that at this time William's wife Elizabeth (née Bruyn) was pregnant with their son Charles.

Elizabeth Bruyn of South Ockendon was the daughter and co-heiress of Sir Henry Bruyn. Elizabeth was first married to Thomas Tyrell Esquire who had died in 1473. Sir Henry had died in 1466 leaving Elizabeth a portion of his wealth. Elizabeth and William Brandon married sometime between 1473 and 1476.[8] William died in 1485 and Elizabeth went on to marry William Mallory Esquire. Elizabeth lived until March 1493/4, dying when her son Charles was approximately nine or ten years of age.[9]

William Brandon would not see his son again. Returning to England with Henry Tudor and his men he died in August 1485 at the Battle of Bosworth Field. Henry Tudor was surrounded by a group of his most trusted knights, one of those being Sir William Brandon who proudly held Henry's standard. Richard III charged at Henry's standard bearer with his lance, the lance piercing through Brandon and breaking in half.[10] History records that William Brandon 'hevyd on high' Henry Tudor's standard, 'and vamisyd it, tyll with deathe's dent he was tryken downe'.[11]

It is assumed that after the death of his father, and Henry Tudor taking the throne as King Henry VII, Elizabeth Bruyn returned to England with the young Charles. The exact date remains unknown. It has been suggested that on their return young Charles went to live with his grandfather, Sir William Brandon of Wangford and

Southwark, or possibly his uncle, Thomas Brandon, who had fled England with his brother.[12]

In September 1486 Thomas Brandon became an Esquire of the Body to Henry VII, a position that required him to be close to the king's person; in the spring of 1487 he was commanding a naval force. Six years later he was serving in the French campaign and was knighted after the Battle of Blackheath in 1497. Thomas Brandon was an active member of court and even sat on the King's Council on several occasions as well as acting as a diplomat. He was involved with Henry VII's horses and hawks and in 1499 was appointed as Master of the Horse, having complete control over the care and maintenance of the king's horses, a position that once more brought him into close proximity to the king. Thomas Brandon must have been extremely good at his duties as he was reappointed as Master of the Horse by Henry VIII in 1509.[13]

Charles Brandon is first recorded as participating in the 1501 jousts celebrating the marriage of Prince Arthur to Princess Katherine of Aragon. In 1503 Brandon was waiting on Henry VII at his table and circa 1507, when Brandon was around twenty-three years of age, he too was appointed as an Esquire of the Body, just as his uncle had been.[14] More importantly, in 1505/06 Brandon was part of the King's Spears, a group of men active in in jousting and courtly displays.[15]

With the death of Arthur in 1502, Henry was kept close to the king and under a close watch because he was now the sole heir to the throne.[16] Without having a great deal of freedom[17] it is quite possible that Henry lived out many of his fantasies and desires through Charles Brandon. He was able to watch the older, strong, fit man joust and participate at the lists while Henry was forbidden to participate to avoid injury. He was also able to gossip about romantic interests and women with the muscular and very handsome Charles Brandon, who was becoming quite a ladies' man at court.[18]

Brandon first attracted the attention of Anne Browne, daughter of Sir Anthony Browne, around 1505/06. He confessed to Walter Devereux that 'he was in love and resorted muche to the company of Anne Browne.'[19] Brandon proposed marriage to Anne and the couple slept together, conceiving a daughter who would be named after her mother. Soon Brandon saw better prospects for himself with Anne's aunt and he broke off the 'engagement' and proposed to Margaret Neville, Dame Mortimer, an older widow of some wealth. On 7 February 1507 Brandon had licence of Dame Margaret's lands and began to sell them off in quick succession, profiting over £1,000. (Around £484,000).[20] With the land sold Brandon was looking to annul his marriage to Dame Margaret on the grounds of consanguinity, due to his previous relationship with the Dame's niece and being related to the grandmother of Dame Margaret's first husband.[21]

In 1508 Brandon returned to Anne Browne and the couple married in secret at Stepney church. They later repeated the marriage ceremony publicly at St Michael's Cornhill. In 1510 Anne gave birth to the couple's second daughter, Mary. Anne died shortly after in 1510 and Brandon was left a widower at the age of twenty seven, with two young daughters.[22]

Brandon was selected to be one of the six challengers in the grand tournament held to celebrate the king and queen's coronation. For a man of twenty three/four years of age and who was only an Esquire of the Body and a member of the King's Spears, this was a huge honour and only the beginning of things to come.

After Henry VIII's coronation in 1509 Brandon remained an Esquire of the Body.[23] This position meant that Brandon was responsible for such activities as dressing the king each morning and tending to some of his personal needs. It is easy to imagine both Brandon and Henry spending their days hunting, playing card games, gambling, playing tennis, taking part in archery, practising in the tiltyard, observing and pursuing beautiful women at court. Both Henry VIII and Brandon had a natural talent for all things athletic so it is easy to see how through these endless days of activity and close proximity that Brandon formed a close bond with the king, which would endure thoughout his entire life.[24]

In January 1511 Brandon was named a Justice of the Peace for Surrey[25] and in April 1512 he was granted for life the office of Ranger of the New Forest. In May he was also made Keeper of Wanstead in Essex.[26] Then on 6 October he was given the post of Master of The Horse that had once been held by his uncle. This gave him an annual income of £60 13s (£29,000)[27] from the

Chamber and an additional £40 (£19,000)[28] from the Exchequer.[29] This role gave him responsibility for the king's horses including all those used for hunting and jousting.[30]

In the autumn of that year Henry decided to invade France with an army of 30,000 men.[31] Brandon raised 1,831 men, mostly from Wales. He was also appointed High Marshal and Lieutenant of the Army, with responsibility for military discipline (including dispensing the death penalty), selecting camp sites and creating knights. This was an extraordinarily responsible position for Brandon since at the time he was a mere knight; ostensibly he had power over the Duke of Buckingham, the earls and more experienced knights and men.[32] He also had the honour of leading the Vanguard of the King's Ward, consisting of approximately 3,000 men.

The English army took the city of Thérouanne in Artois in August 1513 without a great deal of difficulty and went on to besiege Tournai. Brandon led the assault on one of the city gates and the city surrendered on 24 September 1513. When Henry was handed the keys to Tournai he gave them to Brandon, who then led his men into the city. This in itself was an extraordinary honour for a man who had only been knighted on 30 March 1513 – a mere six months before. In addition to this great honour Brandon was rewarded with the castle of Mortain.[33]

After this there were several weeks of celebration, during which Brandon was to cause one of the greatest scandals of the age. Henry VIII and his men met with Margaret of Austria, Duchess of Savoy and daughter of Maximilian I, Holy Roman Emperor. Twice widowed and vowing to never remarry, Margaret was the Regent of the Habsburg Netherlands. She was an extremely well educated and influential woman. During these lavish celebrations it was reported that King Henry VIII suggested a marriage between his best friend Brandon and Margaret of Austria. The Duchess, unwilling to marry again, deflected any suggestion of marriage saying that it would deeply offend her father.[34] To suggest a marriage to someone who was only a knight was to insult the Regent of the Netherlands and her father, the Holy Roman Emperor. (Even though Brandon was only a knight of the realm, he had been elected as a Knight of the Garter on 23 April of that year.)[35]

Brandon was contracted to marry Elizabeth Grey, Viscountess Lisle, in 1513. Elizabeth Grey was the daughter of John Grey, 2nd Baron Lisle.[36] When her stepfather, Sir Thomas Knyvet, died in August 1512 she became the ward of Brandon.[37] Brandon had organised the purchase of Elizabeth's wardship for the sum of £1,400[38] (a staggering £677,000 in today's currency),[39] from Sir John Hussey, the Chancellor of the Court of Wards, and he could take seven years to pay it off. While this was a huge sum to lay out, Brandon would receive an income of approximately £800 (£387,000)[40] a year from Elizabeth's lands and Brandon would hold Elizabeth's wardship until she came of age. On 15 May Brandon was created Viscount Lisle and received a number of grants to accompany his new position.[41]

On Candlemas Eve, 1 February 1514, Charles Brandon, Viscount Lisle, was formally invested as the Duke of Suffolk. The ceremony took place at Lambeth and was conducted by the king. Brandon was thirty, still handsome, one of the best jousters in all of England and possibly Europe and a beloved friend of the king. He had climbed the social ladder at court to become a duke, the highest post anyone could hold. He was still nowhere near Mary's station.

The king's friend, Charles Brandon, now Duke of Suffolk, was tasked with bringing Mary, now Dowager Queen of France, back to England. He was instructed to acquire as much of Mary's jewels, plate and coin as he could.[42] Interestingly, there was a rumour at the time that just before Brandon left England, Henry instructed him not to act foolishly and marry Mary while in France, but to wait until both had returned to England.[43] Who might have started this rumour remains unknown. It could have been that Henry did intend to fulfil the promise he made to his sister and knowing of her affection for Brandon would allow her to marry him, but not until they returned home. However, it is more likely that Henry agreed to the marriage at face value, but when Mary returned home he would was going to renege on his promise to Mary that she could choose her own husband and would seek a more diplomatic and advantageous marriage for her elsewhere.

Shortly before Brandon arrived in Paris, two friars from England met with Mary. Their mission was to turn Mary's mind against

Brandon. They told Mary that the council would never consent to her marrying Brandon and in addition that both Brandon and Thomas Wolsey had performed witchcraft in order to manipulate the English king to their will. They also stated that Brandon had used witchcraft to create a disease in the leg of Henry's Groom of the Stool, William Compton.

When Brandon heard about such damaging allegations he immediately informed Thomas Wolsey. Brandon believed that the friars did not come up with such allegations on their own and that someone had coached them, namely the Duke of Norfolk. It was known that while both Norfolk and Brandon appeared to get along, there was a simmering dislike and strong rivalry between the pair.[44]

What is most interesting are not the allegations against Brandon, but the fact that the friars told Mary that the council would not consent to a marriage between her and Brandon. Clearly it was known that Brandon held feelings for Mary and she for him. Spanish humanist scholar, Juan Luis Vives, warned against women marrying for love: 'The 'miserable yonge woman who is entangled by love would be better to have broken a legge of [her] bodie.' He added that 'love causes global devastation: 'murther', 'slaughter', 'distruction of cities, of countreys, and nacions'.[45] Mary saw things differently.

As mentioned earlier, in January 1515 Mary had written to her brother to remind him of the promise he made her, should her husband Louis XII die before she produced an heir.

[In my] most kind and [loving wist I] recommend me unto your grace. I would be very glad to hear that your grace were in good health and p[eace], the which should be a great comfort to me, and" that it will please your grace to send more oft time to me than you do, for as now I am all out of comfort, saving that all my trust is in your grace, and so shall be during my life. Sir, I pray your grace that it will please your grace to be so good lord and brother to me that you will send hither as soon as you may possibly to me. Sir, I beseech your grace that you will keep all the promises that you promised me when I took my leave of you by the w[ater s]ide. Sir, your grace knoweth well that I did marry for your pl[easure a]t this time, and now I trust

that you will suffer me to [marry as] me l[iketh fo]r to do ; for, sir, I k[now that yo]u shall have _s that they _ for I assure your grace that [my mi]nd is not there where they would have me, and I trust [your grace] will not do so to me that has always been so glad to fulfil your mind as I have been: wherefore I beseech your grace for to be good lord and brother to me; for, sir, an if your grace will have gran[ted] me married in any place, [sav]ing whereas my mind is, I will be there, whereas your grace nor no other shall have any joy of me: for, I promise your grace, you shall hear that I will be in some religious house, the which I think your grace would be very sorry of, and all your realm. Also, sir, I know well that the King, that is [my so]n, will send to your grace by his uncle the duke of _ for to ma[rry me here, but I tru]st you[r grace ... I sha]ll never be merry at my heart, (for an ever that I d[o marry while I live). I trow your grace knoweth as well as I do, and did before I came hither, and so I trust your grace will be contented, unless I would never marry while I live, but be there where never [no] man nor woman shall have joy of me; wherefore I beseech your grace to be good lord to him and to me both, for I know well that he hath m[et ma]ny hindrances to your grace of him and me both. Wherefore, an your grace be good lord to us both, I will not care for all the world else, but beseech your grace to be good lord and brother to me, as you have been here aforetime, f[or in you] is all the trust that I have in this world after God. No m[ore from m]e at this [time].
God send your grace [long life an]d your heart's de[sires].
By your humble and loving sister, Mary Queen of France.
To the King my brother this be delivered, in haste.[46]

For a newly widowed woman, Mary's letter to her brother was blatant in her desires. After a formal greeting she reminds her brother in no uncertain terms of his promise by the waterside before she left for France that if Louis XII should die she would be allowed to marry for a second time a man of her choosing. For a woman who was subject to her brother's rule this was a bold reminder. Mary also reminds her brother that she only married Louis to fulfil Henry's wishes and that if she wanted she could remove herself to a religious house – which would be a sore loss for Henry as his sister would no longer be to be married off for future alliances. Within the first few weeks of Mary's widowhood the young Dowager Queen of France was clearly determined to take the direction of her life into her own hands. With Charles Brandon en route for France, Mary did not have long to wait.

Brandon, West and Wingfield were in France by 27 January and finally arrived in Paris on 31 January 1515.[47] On the same day Brandon met with Mary and reported that the dowager queen was eager to return home and see her brother.[48] Brandon was to face two major difficulties in the negotiations to see Mary returned to England. The first was regarding her jewellery. If the late king had given the jewellery to Mary as queen then they were to stay in France, since the jewels belonged to France. However, if they were given to Mary as personal presents, then she would be entitled to take them with her to England.[49] The second difficulty was that the new king, Francis I, was reluctant to let Mary leave.

At eighteen years of age Mary was young, beautiful and now that she was a widow she was once more a useful political tool. While she stayed in France, Francis I could exploit Mary as a bargaining tool for his own purposes. He could organise a marriage between Mary and a French nobleman or even arrange a marriage with a member of the nobility from another country to secure an alliance against England. There were no lack of eligible men throughout Europe who would wish to have the hand in marriage of Mary and also to make an alliance with France. These men included Anthony the Good, Duke of Lorraine; Charles III, Duke of Savoy; John, the son of the Portugese king Emmanuel the Fortunate; and William, Duke of Bavaria.[50]

It was also suggested that Francis I was concerned that should Mary return to England, Henry would turn away from the treaty with France and seek a renewal of the English treaty with the Holy Roman Empire, seeking a new marriage between Mary and Prince Charles of Castile, to whom she had been betrothed before her marriage to Louis. In addition, while Mary was in France, Francis I could retain Mary's jewels and would not have to pay her travelling expenses back to England.[51] A rumour also circulated that the French king even wished to divorce his current wife, Queen

Claude, so he could marry Mary.[52] However, this appears to be unsubstantiated.

In January Mary wrote:

Mine own good and most kind brother,

I recommend me unto your grace, and thank you for the good and kind letters that you have sent me, the which has been the greatest comfort might be unto me in this world, desiring your grace so for to continue, for there is nothing so great a store to me as for to see you, the which I would very fain have the time for to come, as I trust it shall be, or else I would be very sorry, for I think every day a thousand till I may see you. Sir, whereas your grace sends me word that I will not give no credence to them for no suit nor for no other words that shall be given me; sir, I promise your grace that I never made them no promise, nor no other for them, nor never will until that I know your grace's mind for nobody alive; for your grace is all the comfort that I have in this world; and I trust your grace will not fail, for I have nothing in this world that I care for but to have the good and kind mind that your grace had ever toward me, which I beseech your grace to continue, for therein is my trust that I have in this world. Sir, as for the letter that your grace did send me by Master Clinton, whereas you send me word that I should provide myself and make me ready for to come to your grace; sir, an it were to-morrow I would be ready: and, as for my lord of Suffolk, and Sir Richard Wingfield, and Doctor West, there be two or three that came from the King my son [Francis I] for to have brought them to him by the way as they came hitherward, and so hindered them coming hitherward that th—, as I trust shall conclude in a day or two, and then let me know your mind, for an when I do, I will do thereafter. Sir, I beseech your grace for to be good lord to Mr. John, your surgeon, for my sake, and that you will not be miscontented with him for his long tarrying here with me, for I bore him an hand that your grace were contented that he should be here with me awhile ; and so I pray your grace to give him leave for to tarry here awhile with me, for because I am very ill-diseased with the toothache, and the mother withal, that sometimes I wot not what for to do; but if I might see your grace

I were healed. No more to you at this time, but I pray God to send your grace good life and long. By your loving sister, Mary.[53]

By modern standards Mary's letter may sound outré, laden with compliments for her brother. Mary was probably preparing the ground for revealing her secret marriage. It is interesting to note that Mary writes of a toothache that is bothering her as well as 'the mother', which may be referring to a female issue such as menstruation cramps. Mary suffered from toothache on and off throughout her life and at this time it may have been aggravated by the stress and uncertainty she was currently experiencing. If 'the mother' did refer to menstruation it is most likely that during her time in the Hôtel de Cluny Mary's period started and she would have known that she was not with child.

Faced with such uncertainty about her future, Mary Tudor took matters into her own hands. Shortly after Brandon's arrival in Paris Mary proposed marriage and the duke accepted. It is unknown if Brandon's acceptance to the marriage was a spontaneous decision or if he thought about it for several days. What is known is that the couple married without Henry's permission and without the knowledge of the King of France.

While the exact date of the marriage is unknown it can be determined that the couple married before approximately ten witnesses[54] at the Chapel in Cluny, between between 31 January, when Brandon arrived in Paris, and 3 February.[55] We know this because in a letter dated the 3rd Brandon wrote to Wolsey regarding a meeting he had with Francis I. During the meeting Francis told Brandon that he knew of the secret wedding because Mary had already informed him.

My very good lord,

I recommend me unto you and so it is, I need not write yon of none thing [but only of] a matter secret, for all other matters you shall perceive by the letters sent to the king, the one from me, and the other from my fellows and me. My lord, so it was that the same day that the French king gave us audience, his grace called me unto him, and had me into his bed-chamber, and said unto me ' My Lord of Suffolk, so it is that there is a bruit in this my realm, that you are come to marry with the queen, your master's sister;' and when I heard him say I answered and said that I trusted his grace would not reckon no great folly in me, to come into a strange realm and to many a queen of the realm, without the knowledge, and without authority from the king my master to him, and that they both might be content; but I said I assured his grace that I had no such tiling, and that it was never intended on the king my masters behalf, nor on mine — and then he said it was not so; for then (since) that I would not be plain with him he would be plain with me, and showed me that the queen herself had broken her mind onto him, and that he had promised her his faith and truth, and by the truth of a king, that he would help her, and to d[o] what was possibly in him to help her to obtain her heart's desire. And because that you shall not th[ink that I do] bear you this in hand, and that [she has not spo] ke her mind, I will s[hew, you some word]s that you had to her [grace,] and so showed me a ware word, the which none alive could tell them but she; and when that then I was abashed, and he saw that, and said, because for (that) you shall say that yon have found a kind prince and a loving, and because you shall not think m[e] other here I give you, in your hand, my faith and truth, by the word of a King, that I shall never fail unto you, but to help and advance this Marriage betwixt her and you, 'with as good a will as (I) would for mine own [self]'. And when he had done this, I could do none less than thank his grace for the great goodness that his grace intended to show unto the queen and me, and by it I showed his grace that I was like to be undone, if this matter should come to the knowledge of the king my master: and then he said, 'Let me alone for that; I and the queen shall so instance your master that I trust that he would be content; and because I would gladly put your heart at rest, I will, when I come to Paris, speak with the queen, and she and I both will write letters to the king your master, with our own hands, in the best manner that can be devised.

My lord, these were his proper words; [as I] do advertise you; not intending to hide [this or] any other matter from yon; praying yon, with all the haste possible, send me your best [council that yo]u shall think best that I shall [do in this mat]ter; and if you shall think good [to advertise hi]s grace of this letter, I pray yon [also to give mi]ne assurances to his highness, that I had [rather, an I dared, have written] unto him myself.

My lord, after mine opinion, I find myself much [bound] to God, considering that he that I feared most is contented to be the doer of this act himself, and to instance the king my master in the same [where] his grace shall be marvellously discharged [as well] against his council, as all the other noble men of his realm. And thus mine own good lord, I bid yon most heartily farewell, trusting to hear from yon in all the haste [possible]. My cousin Wingfield has put me in remembrance of your affairs which be not forgotten, as you shall well know, by my next letters; and of one thing be you assured, that the amity going forth between the two princes, that we both shall be as well entreated of the king here as ever any two in England. By your's assured, written at some haste 10 leagues from Paris, the third day of February.

To my Lord of York. Charles Suffolk.[56]

Shortly after the marriage Brandon wrote a frantic letter to Henry realising the magnitude of what he had done. It does not appear that Henry received the letter straight away; instead it may have rested in the hands of Thomas Wolsey until he considered the time was right to break the news of the illicit marriage to the king.

Sir, one thing I insure your grace, that it shall never be said that ever I did offend [your] grace in word, deed or thought, but for this [matter] touching the Queen, your sister, the which I ca[n no] lynggar nor wolnot hide fro your grace. Sir, so it is that when I came to Paris the Queen was in hand with me the first day I [came], and said she must be short with me and [open] to me her pleasure and mind; and so she b[egan] and show how good lady [she] was to me, and if I would be ordered by her she would never have none but me. ... She showed me she had wyerelle und[erstood] as well by Friar Langglay and Friar Fr ... dar that and yewar sche cam in Ynggyll [and she sho]uld newar have me; and ther for sche ... wr that and I wold not marre her ... have me nor never come to [England] When I heard her say so I showed ...

plied that but to prove me with, and she ... would not you knew well that my coming ... it was showed her ... and I axsed her wat [it] was; and she said that the best in France had [said] unto her that, and she went into England, she should go into Flanders. To the which she said that she had rather to be torn in pieces than ever she should come there, and with that wept. Sir, I never saw woman so weep; and when I saw [that] I showed unto her grace that there was none such thing [upon] my faith, with the best words I could: but in none ways I could make her to believe it. And when I saw that, I showed her grace that, and her grace would be content to write unto your grace and to obtain your good will, I would be content; or else I durst not, because I had made unto your grace such a promise. Whereunto, in conclusion, she said, 'If the King my brother is content and the French King both, the tone by his letters and the todar by his words, that I should have [y]ou, I will have the time after my desire, or else I may well think that the words of ... in these parts and of them in England [be] true and that is that you are come to tyes me home (?) [to the in]tent that I may be married into Fland[ers], which I will never, to die for it; and so [I posse]ssed the French King ar you cam (?); and th[at if] you will not be content to follow [my] end, look never after this d[ay to have] the proffer again.' And, Sir, I ... in that case and I thought ... but rather to put me ... than to lyes all, and so I gra ... an too; and so she and I was ma[rried] ... and but ten persons, of the which [neither Sir Richard] Wyngfyld nor Master Dyne (Dean) was not [present] on my faith; for she would that I should [not take] them on council, for she said and I did [so] ... she thought they would give mo couns[el] to the contrary; and therefore they know not of it, nor that the writing of this letter, on my faith and truth. Has written word by word, as near as he can, how everything was, and begs the King to forgive him and defend him against his enemies, who will think to put him out of favor.[57]

Mary's marriage put a stop to any possible union that the French king may have had in mind for her in an attempt to create a French alliance with another country. The marriage also ensured Henry could not organise the same for England. At a stroke Mary had pulled herself out of the political chess game – she had chosen her own path.

Mary was playing the role of the weaker sex perfectly. Brandon wrote that she wept and that if he did not marry her then she could only believe that he had come to France to take her home to England so that a marriage alliance could be organised with Charles, Prince of Castile. Brandon's letter showed that a marriage with Flanders was something Mary was adamantly against. Mary used her tears to persuade Brandon into marrying her. This is not to say that there were not true feelings between the pair. The mere fact that Henry made Brandon promise not to marry Mary in France was a strong indicator that the king believed there was affection between the two. Also the arrival of the two friars before Brandon's arrival in France, warning Mary that the council would never let her marry Brandon, points to the fact that the possibility of a marriage was known by more than just Henry. It is quite possible that it was widely known that both had strong feelings towards one another.

What is certain from Brandon's hurried and frantic letter is that Mary was determined to have him for her second husband. She played on the idea that she was not as smart as a man and weak in mind and body. Brandon could have said no, he could have stuck to the promise he had made to Henry before leaving for France, but he did not. He married Mary before ten witnesses, and Mary made sure that Sir Richard Wingfield and Nicholas West were not present for fear that they would talk Brandon out of the marriage. In doing so, Brandon put his fate not in Henry's hands but in the hands of his new wife, Mary Tudor, a princess of England and the Dowager Queen of France.

Wolsey wrote back to Brandon stating that he had received the letter and that he was glad to hear that Brandon was showing some discretion regarding the marriage. He was also glad to hear that he had the French king's consent and that he would bring the matter before Henry himself. He reassures Brandon that they are friends and that he hopes to bring the matter to a successful conclusion.[58]

My Lord,
   In my most hearty manner I recommend me unto your good Lordship, and have received your letter written with your own

hands, dated at Paris the 3ʳᵈ day of this month, and as joyous
I am, as any creature living, to hear as well of your honorable
entertainment with the French king, and of his loving mind
towards you for your marriage with the French queen, our
master's sister, as also of his kind offer made unto you, that
both you and the said French queen shall effectually write unto
the King's grace for the obtaining of his good will and favour
unto the same. The contents of which your letter I have at
good leisure declared unto the King's highness, and his grace
marvellously rejoiced to hear of your good speed in the same,
and how substantially and discretely ye ordered and handled
yourself in your words and your communication with the said
French king, when he first secretly brake with you of the said
marriage. And, therefore, my Lord, the King and I think it good
that ye procure and solicit the speedy sending unto his grace
of the letters from the said French king touching this matter,
assuring you that the King continueth firmly in his good mind
and purpose towards you, for the accomplishment of the said
marriage, albeit that there be daily on every side practices made
to the hindrance of the same, which I have withstanded hitherto,
and doubt not so to do till ye shall have achieved your intended
purpose; and ye shall say, by that time that ye know all, that to
have had of me a fast friend. The king's grace sends unto you at
this time not only his especial letters of thanks unto the French
king for the loving and kind entertainment of you and the other
ambassadors with you, and for his favourable audience given
unto you and them, but also other letters of thanks to the queen,
his wife, and to other personages specified in your letter jointly
sent with the other ambassadors to the king's grace. And his
highness is of no less mind and affection than the French king
is for the continuance of good peace and amity betwixt them.
And his grace will favourably hear such ambassadors as the said
French king shall send hither to commune and treat upon the
same; and upon the overture of their charges ye shall be with all
diligence made privy thereto. The Lady Suffolk [Lady Margaret
de la Pole] is departed out of this present life; and over this,
my Lord, the king's grace hath granted unto you all such lands
as be come into his hands by the decease of the said Lady of

Suffolk; and also by my pursuit hath given unto you the lordship of Claxton, which his highness had of my Lord Admiral for 1,000 marks, which he did owe to his grace. And finally, my Lord, whereas ye desired at your departing to have an harness [suit of armour] made for you, the king hath willed me to write unto you, that he saith that it is impossible to make a perfect headpiece for you, unless that the manner of the making of your sight were assuredly known. And because I am no cunning clerk to describe the plainness of such a thing, inasmuch as ye shall perceive by this my writing what the matter meaneth, ye may make answer to the king's (grace) upon the same, like as ye shall think good. And whereas ye write that the French king is of no less good will towards me than his predecessor was, I pray you to thank his grace for the same, and to offer him my poor service, which, next my master, shall have mine heart for the good will and mind which he beareth to you ; beseeching you to have my affairs recommended, and that I may have some end in the same, one way or other. And thus for lack of more leisure I bid you most heartily farewell, beseeching you to have me recommended to the queen's grace.

From my house beside Westminster.[59]

Earlier, on 4 February, Sir Richard Wingfield, West and Brandon had visited Mary and had written to the king of their visit:

Came to Paris on Sunday, 4 Feb. Visited Queen Mary on Monday before noon, and according to their instructions made overtures to her, at length, of the King's wish that she should not consent to any motion of marriage in these parts nor determine to stay there. She thanked the King for sending to her 'in her heaviness' my Lord of Suffolk and others, as well to comfort her as for obtaining of her dower. She said she were an unkind sister if she should not follow your mind and pleasure in every behalf, for there was never princess so much beholden to her sovereign and brother as she is to your grace; and therefore, as touching consent to any marriage in these parts, she trusteth that your grace knoweth her mind therein; and albeit she has been sore pressed in that matter as well by the King [that now is?] as other,

yet she never consented, nor never wolde do, [but rather] suffer
the extremity of death. And as touching her [stay] here, she never
was nor is minded thereto, for she [counts] every day an hundred
till she may see your grace.[60]

By 4 February Mary and Brandon were already married, although
Wingfield and West were unaware. Mary is playing the role of a
dutiful sister perfectly, despite the fact that she has already secretly
married. She admits that it would be wrong for her not to follow
her brother's wishes and that she is bound to her brother. She does
point out that when it comes to marriage, her brother knows her
wishes.

Knowing that Mary is already married, we can see her next words
have a double meaning – 'and albeit she has been sore pressed in
that matter as well by the King [that now is?] as other, yet she never
consented, nor never wolde do, [but rather] suffer the extremity of
death.' This may be referring to the fact that she knows that her
brother wishes to make another marriage for her, possibly to form
an alliance with Flanders. Mary declares she would rather face
death than marry against her heart.

On the same day Brandon wrote a letter to Wolsey:

Had been in hand with the Queen touching the matter she broke
to the French King, as mentioned in his last. She had showed him
that the French King made such business, that she was 'soo wyrre
and soo afyerd' he should go about to undo Suffolk, she thought
it best to break the matter to him, and said, 'Sir, I beseech you that
you will let me alone and speak no more to me of the matter; and
if you will promise me by your faith and truth, and as you are a
true prince, that you will keep it counsel and help me, I will tell
you all my whole mind. And he gave her his faith in her hand that
he would keep it counsel, and that he would help her to the best
of his power.' Having told him her mind, and said she could not
think 'but the King her brother w[ould be disp]lysed (?)' with her,
she besought him to get the King['s consent]. He said he would do
that was in him possible, and write to the King her brother with
his own hand; which agrees with what Francis himself told him, as
mentioned in his last letter. Now that Wolsey knows all, beseeches

his good offices as all his trust is in him, and requests [an answer?] in all possible haste. 'Also, my lord, I pray you that you will look to the _ ; for I insure you that, and it be made to the honor [of our] master, as I am sure the French King will do none otherwise, it shall be the greatest honor and wealth to the King my master and the realm of England that ever came to it. Will write to Wolsey what their mind is as soon as he can perceive it, before they send it, and begs Wolsey to do the same to him, if he hear it first. Paris, 8 Feb.[61]

Once more Mary outmanoeuvred those around her. She was well aware that she needed to have Francis on her side should she continue to maintain her brother's love towards her. Mary convinced Francis to write to Henry on her behalf by promising him that she will tell him everything on her mind. Francis may have believed that he was getting the upper hand in this deal; he would be able to manipulate Mary into telling him her brother's wishes for her future and in return, all he had to do was write a letter supporting Mary's marriage. It is Mary who is winning the battle of wits here, as she is able to feed whatever information she desires to Francis and in return, he will support the marriage and help to convince Henry to accept Mary and Brandon back in England.

Francis I did write to Henry informing him of the marriage:

...in this town of Mon ... has been to visit the queen his 'belle-mère,' Henry's sister, as he used to do, to know if he could show her any attention. On his asking whether she contemplated a second marriage, she confessed the great esteem she had for the Duke of Suffolk, 'que davant t[out] autre ele desyreroyt aveque [la] bonne voulonté et lamye ... maryage dele et de luy se fys[t],' and prayed him not only to give his own consent, but to write to Henry in Suffolk's favor, which he now does.[62]

Aware that now there was no doubt Henry knew of the secret marriage, Mary wrote to her brother personally:

Pleaseth it your grace, the French king, on Tuesday night last past, came to visit me, and had with me many diverse discoursing, among the which he demanded me whether I had ever made any promise of marriage in any place, assuring me upon his honour, and upon the word of a prince, that in case I would be plain with him in that affair, that he would do for me therein to the best of his power, whether it were in his realm or out of the same. Whereunto I answered, that I would disclose unto him the secret of my heart in humility, as unto the prince of the world after your grace in whom I had most trust, and so declared unto him the good mind which for divers considerations I bear to my lord of Suffolk, asking him not only to grant me his favour and consent thereunto, but also that he would of his own hand write unto your grace, and to pray you to bear your like favour unto me, and to be content with the same; the which he granted me to do, and so hath done, according as shall appear unto your grace by his said letters. And, sir, I most humbly beseech you to take this answer which I have made unto the French king in good part, the which I did only to be discharged of the extreme pain and annoyance I was in, by reason of such suit as the French king made unto me not according with mine honour, the which he hath clearly left off. Also, sir, I feared greatly lest, in case that I had kept the matter from his knowledge, that he might have not well entreated my said lord of Suffolk, and the rather for to have returned to his former malfantasy and suits. Wherefore, sir, since it hath pleased the said king to desire and pray you of your favour and consent, I most humbly and heartily beseech you that it may like your grace to bear your favour and consent to the same, and to advertise the said king by your writing of your own hand of your pleasure, and in that he hath acted after mine opinion in his letter of request, it shall be to your great honour ... to content with all your council, and with all the other nobles of the realm, and agree thereto for your grace and for all the world; and therefore I eftsoon require you, for all the love that, it liked your grace to bear me, that you do not refuse but grant me your favour and consent in form before rehearsed, the which if you shall deny me, I am well assured to lead as desolate a life as ever had creature, the which I know well shall be mine end. Always praying your grace to have compassion of me, my most loving and sovereign lord and brother, whereunto I have entreated you, beseeching God always to preserve your most royal estate.

I most humbly beseech your grace to consider, in case that you make difficulty to condescend to the promises as I wish, the French king will take new courage to renew his suits to me; assuring you that I had rather to be out of the world than it so should happen; and how he shall entreat my lord of Suffolk, God knoweth, with many other inconvenience, which might ensue of the same, the which I pray our Lord that I may never have life to see.

By your loving sister and true servant,

MARY QUEEN OF FRANCE.[63]

Mary deflects any blame for the marriage from Brandon onto the French king himself. She says the reason she married Brandon was because Francis was pressurising her, possibly for a marriage to himself, even though he was already married to Queen Claude; or perhaps more likely, 'such suit as the French king made unto me not according with mine honour' means an alliance between France and another country forged through her marriage into the European nobility. This possibility would have alarmed Henry as it would create a diplomatic crisis if France used an English princess to align with another country against England. Already there had been talk that France may align with Castile and this would be of great concern for England. Consider the diplomatic complexity should an English princess, now Dowager Queen of France, marry Prince Charles to become Princess of Castile. Her husband would become king of all Spain and possibly come to the imperial throne when his grandfather, the Holy Roman Emperor, Maximilian, died, despite the queen being a princess of Castile.[64] Cleverly, Mary convinced Henry that the reason she had married Brandon was to prevent being used as a means for France to create such an alliance to England's disadvantage. In her letter Mary once more placed herself in the position of a helpless pawn rather than the cunning woman that she truly was.

Frustratingly no official reply from Henry VIII exists, but Wolsey wrote to Suffolk on the king's behalf:

The King, by advice of the Council, is writing to Suffolk and the other ambassadors in answer to their letters dated Paris, 18 Feb. After consulting with the Council [on Sunday last], the King

Mary Tudor by Joannas Corvus. Painted in 1529/1530 when Mary was aged 34 years. The inscription upon the frame reads: 'maria soror illustrissio regi henrico VIII ac gallorum regina coniunxque illustri principi carolo duct suffociae. Ano aetatis suae xxxiiii', 'Mary the sister of the illustrious King Henry VIII, and wife of the illustrious Prince Charles, Duke of Suffolk, age 34.' (Courtesy of Lisby under Creative Commons 2.0)

Bust of King Henry VII of England by Pietro Torrigiano. (Courtesy of the Metropolitan Museum of Art)

Above: The marriage of Henry VII and Elizabeth of York, as depicted by H. Cook after Jan Gossart. (Courtesy of the Metropolitan Museum of Art)

Henry VIII by Wenceslaus Hollar. (Courtesy of the Metropolitan Museum of Art)

Armor garniture, probably of Henry VIII. The decorations are attributed to Holbein and it was made at the royal workshops of Greenwich, perhaps in 1527. (Courtesy of the Metropolitan Museum of Art)

Bust of King Louis XII, husband of Mary Tudor. (Courtesy of the Metropolitan Museum of Art)

Marriage tapestry of Louis XII and Mary Tudor. Located at Hever Castle, the tapestry covers the left hand wall of Anne Boleyn's Books of Hours room. (Courtesy of Hever Castle & Gardens)

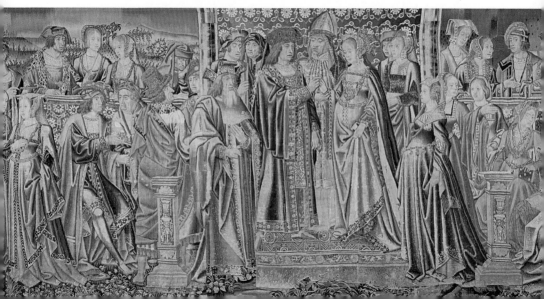

King Francis I, successor of Louis XII, in a painting by Joos van Cleve. Had Mary been pregnant, he might never have taken the throne. (Courtesy of the Metropolitan Museum of Art)

The capture of King Francis I at the Battle of Pavia in a drawing by Dirck Volckertsz Coornhert. (Courtesy of the Rijksmuseum)

A miniature of a scene from the Triumphs of Emperor Charles V: the Emperor enthroned among his enemies (from left: Suleiman the Magnificent, Pope Clement VII, Francis I, the dukes of Cleves and Saxony, and the landgrave of Hesse). (Courtesy of the British Library)

Portrait commonly attributed
to Mary Tudor but most likely
Queen Isabella of Castile.
(Courtesy of David Baldwin)

Sketch of Mary Tudor from
early 1515 at the Hotel Cluny.
Mary wore white, the traditional
French colour for mourning.
Sketched shortly after the death
of King Louis XII, possibly by
Jean Perreal. (Public domain)

LA ROYNE MARIE

Charles Brandon, Duke of Suffolk. Master of the Brandon Portrait. Painter unknown. (Illustration from *Burlington Magazine*, 1937)

Wedding portrait of Mary Tudor and Charles Brandon. Painter unknown. (Courtesy of Woburn Abbey)

Above: Frances Grey. (Courtesy of Feuerrabe under Creative Commons 2.0)

Left: The young Edward VI, son and heir of Henry VIII, by Hans Holbein. (Courtesy of the Metropolitan Museum of Art)

Illuminated P of the Michelmas Term of 1554 showing the marriage of Mary I and Philip II on the front of document KB27/1172 held at The National Archives, Kew. Queen Mary is positioned seated on the right, the traditional position of an anointed king.

Above: St Mary's Church, Bury St Edmunds. Burial place of Mary Tudor. (Courtesy of Nathen Amin)

Left: Mary Tudor's grave at St. Mary's Church, Bury St Edmunds. (Courtesy of Nathen Amin)

Above left and right: A lock of Mary Tudor's hair encased in a delicate ring. Cut when her body was moved from the Abbey at Bury St Edmunds to St Mary's Church, Bury St Edmunds on 6 September 1784. Photos from the collection of Geoffrey Munn.

Right: Inscription on the inside of the leather box detailing the provenance of the ring containing a lock of Mary Tudor's hair. Photo from the collection of Geoffrey Munn.

This ring was given by me to the Lady Katharin Manners, eldt. daut. to John 7th. Duke of Rutland on Xmas Day, 1897. It contains a lock of the hair of her ancestress the Lady Mary Tudor, daur. of King Henry VII, who mard. 1stly Louis XIIK ing of France & 2dly Charles Brandon Duke of Suffolk Her descent by the latter marriage the Lady Frances Brandon, daut. of Charles Brandon 6th Duke of Suffolk, became the wife of John Manners Marquess of Granby, eldt. son of John 3d. Duke of Rutland. Mary Tudor died on 25 June 1533 & was burd. 22d. July at the Monastery of St. Edmondsbury. On the dissolution of that house, her coffin was removed to the Parish Church. On 6th Sept. 1784, her tomb & its leaden coffin were opened. Her hair, nearly 2 feet long, was found in perfect condition, & this lock was then cut off. The Inscription inside the ring is a copy of that on the coffin Another lock, enclosd. in a locket was exhibd. in the Tudor Exhibition New Gallery London, 1890 See Cat. 186

Francis Pierrepont Barnard.
St Mary's Abbey,   Windermere.

A stained-glass window by Clayton and Bell in St Mary's Church, Bury St Edmunds, that depicts events in Mary Tudor's life. The top windows, from left to right, show Mary's marriage to Louis XII; her entry into Paris; her mourning for her late husband; Erasmus and Sir Thomas More visiting the royal children at Eltham; her betrothal to the future Charles VI; and her departure from Dover in 1514. The bottom row, from left to right, show Mary's marriage to Charles Brandon, their reconciliation with Henry VIII and her funeral at St Edmunds. (Courtesy of David Baldwin)

called Wolsey apart and bid him write to Suffolk to use all efforts
to obtain from the French King his plate of gold and jewels.
Doubts not he will succeed if he insist upon it. He would be glad
to allow Suffolk to return with the Queen, but not until he has
completed her business. Advises him, therefore, "substantially to
handle that matter and to stick thereunto; for I assure you the
hope that the King hath to obtain the said plate and jewels is
the thing that most stayeth his grace constantly to assent that ye
should marry his sister; the lack whereof, I fear me, might make
him cold and remiss and cause some alteration, whereof all men
here, except his grace and myself, would be right glad.' Encloses
copy of the letter the King has written with his own hand to the
French King. Could not induce him by any persuasion to write
otherwise; 'for his grace thinketh that if he should make plain
grant at the first instance of the French King he would think that
his grace was agreed to the said marriage before your coming
thither, and so consequently the French King might think that ye
had not been plain with him.'[65]

Henry wants Mary's dowry returned, or as much of it as possible.
Henry could not appear to have willingly accepted the illicit
marriage because his permission was not sought. He needs to be
seen to punish both Brandon and Mary for their actions. Ultimately
Henry was manipulating Brandon into getting what he wanted.
In return for all Mary's gold, plate and jewels of her dowry that
Brandon secured, Henry would agree to let the couple return home
to England and remain married.

From Brandon's next letter dated 5 March it would appear that
neither Mary nor Brandon had heard from the king. They were
waiting, hoping to have gained the king's favour so that they may
return home. It is unknown if Mary wrote any letters to Henry
between 15 February, when she informed him that the French king
knew of her marriage to Brandon, and Brandon's next frantic letter
to Henry on 5 March. If any were written these have not survived.

My Lord, I am obliged to you next God and my master, and
therefore I will hide none thing from you, trusting that you will
help me now as you have always done. Me Lord, so it is that

when I came to Paris I heard many things which put me in great fear, and so did the Queen both; and the Queen would never let me be in rest till I had granted her to be married; and so to be plain with you, I have married her heartily, and have lain with her, insomuch I fear me lest she be with child. My Lord, I am not in a little sorrow if the King should know it, and that his grace should be displeased with me; for I ensure you that I had rather died than he should be miscontent ... let me not be undone now, the which I fear me shall be, without the help of you. Me Lord, think not that ever you shall make any friend that shall be more obliged to you; and therefore me own good Lord ... help me Lord, they marry as well in Lent as out of Lent, with licence of any bishop. Now my Lord, you know all, and in you is all my trust, beseeching you now of your assured help, and that I may have answer from you of this and of the other writings as shortly as may be possible, for I ensure you that I have as heavy a heart as any man living, and shall have until I may hear good news from you.[66]

Clearly Brandon has become distressed at not having heard from the king personally with regard to the marriage to Mary. Brandon's whole existence, his very being was reliant on the king and to earn his disfavour could be devastating. Interestingly both Brandon and Mary now lay the blame for the marriage squarely on Mary. Whether this was decided by Brandon or Mary, or the two of them, this is a very clever ploy, as it would almost impossible for Henry to punish his sister with imprisonment or harsh treatment.

In a second letter Brandon adds, perhaps at Mary's suggestion, that a diamond with a great pearl belonging to Mary should be sent to the king and that Henry can have whatever plate, gold and jewels of her dowry he desires. This 'diamond with a great pearl' appears to be the fabulous Mirror of Naples that Louis XII had given her. Obviously, Mary and Brandon knew that one way back to the king's heart was through the trappings of kingship:

As touching the Queen's matter and his, thinks that a diamond with a great pearl, hereby sent from the Queen, should be delivered to the King, with a promise that whenever she obtains the residue he shall have the choice of them according to her former writing. 'Me lord, sche and I bowth rymyttys thes mattar holly to your dyskraseun, trestyng that in hall hast posebbyll wye schall her from you sum good tydynges tocheng howar afyeres.' 5 March.[67]

Francis I was reported to have been 'sore displeased at the loss of the diamond called "the Mirror of Naples".'[68] Henry declared that it was 'but a small thing and her own by right'[69] – that the jewel had been given to Mary as a personal gift rather than a gift to the Queen of France. If the jewel had been given to Mary as queen, then it would belong to the next queen. At the end of the day there was little Francis could do. He offered Henry 30,000 crowns for the return of the jewel but Henry laughed at this, saying it was worth twice as much.[70] Henry is reported to have worn the Mirror of Naples on his hat at his famous meeting with Francis in 1520 at the Field of Cloth of Gold.[71] After this, the Mirror of Naples disappears from history.

Thomas Wolsey passed on the letter to Henry and the king made a great show of being greatly displeased and deeply disappointed in the man he believed to be a close friend and loyal servant: not simply because Brandon had committed treason by marrying the king's sister, but also because he had broken his promise and a man's word was of great importance.[72] Wolsey wrote back to Brandon:

My Lord, With sorrowful heart I write unto you, signifying unto the same that I have to my no little discomfort and inward heaviness perceived by your letters, dated at Paris the 5th day of this instant month, how that you be secretly married unto the King's sister, and have accompanied together as man and wife. And albeit ye by your said letters desired me in no wise to disclose the same to the King's grace, yet seeing the same toucheth not only his honor, your promise made to his grace, and also my truth towards the same, I could no less do but incontinent upon the sight of your said letters, declare and show the contents thereof to his highness, which at the first hearing could scantly believe the same to be true : but after I had showed to his grace that by your own writing I had knowledge thereof, his grace, giving credence thereunto, took the same grievously and displeasantly, not only for that ye durst presume to marry his sister without his knowledge, but also for breaking of your promise made to his grace in his hand, I being present, at Eltham; having also such an assured affiance in your truth, that for all the world, and to have been torn with wild horses, ye would not have broken your oath, promise, and assurance, made to his grace, which doth well perceive that he is deceived of the constant and assured trust that he thought to have found in you, and so his grace would I should expressly write unto you. And for my part, no man can be more sorry than I am that ye have so done, being so encumbered therewith that I cannot devise nor study the remedy thereof, considering that ye have failed to him which hath brought you up of low degree to be of this great honor; and that ye were the man in all the world to be loved and trusted best, and was content that with good order and saving of his honor ye should have in marriage his said sister. Cursed be the blind affection and council that hath brought you hereunto! Fearing that such sudden and unadvised dealing shall have sudden repentance. Nevertheless, in this great perplexity, I see no other remedy but first to make your humble pursuits by your own writing, causing also the French king, the queen, with other your friends, to write: with this also that shall follow, which I assure you I write unto you of mine own head without knowledge to any person living, being in great doubt whether the same shall make your peace or no; notwithstanding, if any remedy be, it shall be by that way. It shall be well done that, with all diligence possible, ye and the queen bind yourself by obligation to pay yearly to the King during the queen's life 4,000 of her dower; and so ye and she shall have remaining of the said dower 6,000 and above to live withal yearly. Over and besides this ye must bind yourself to give unto the King the plate of gold and jewels which the late French king had. And whereas the queen shall have full restitution of her dote, ye shall not only give entirely the said dote to the King, but also cause the French king to be bound to pay to the king the 200,000 crowns, which his grace is bounden to pay to the queen, in the full contentation of the said dote de novissimis denariis, and the said French king to acquit the king for the payment thereof; like as the king hath more at the large declared his pleasure to you, by his letters lately sent unto you. This is the way to make your peace; whereat if ye deeply consider what danger ye be and shall be in, having the king's displeasure, I doubt not both the queen and you will not stick, but with all effectual diligence endeavour yourselves to recover the king's favor, as well by this means as by other substantial true ways, which by mine advise ye shall use, and none other, towards his grace, whom by corbobyll drifts and ways you cannot abuse. Now I have told you my opinion, hardily follow the same, and trust not too much to your own wit, nor follow the council of them that hath not more deeply considered the dangers of this matter than they have hitherto done. And as touching the overtures made by the French king for Tournay, and also for a new confederation with the king and him, like as I have lately written to you, I would not advise you to wade any further in these matters, for it is to be thought that the French king intendeth to make his hand by favoring you in the attaining to the said marriage; which when he shall perceive that by your means he cannot get such things as he desireth, peradventure he shall show some change and alteration in the queen's affairs, whereof great inconvenience might ensue. Look wisely therefore upon the same, and consider you have enough to do in redressing your own causes; and think it will be hard to induce the king to give you a commission of trust, which hath so lightly regarded the same towards his grace. Thus I have as a friend declared my mind unto you, and never trust to use nor have me in anything contrary to truth, my master's honor, profits, wealth, and surety; to the advancement and furtherance whereof no creature living is more bounden; as our Lord knoweth, who send you grace to look well and deeply upon your acts and doings; for ye put yourself in the greatest danger that ever man was in.[73]

Now both Francis and Mary had written to the king informing him of the marriage. Therefore while on the surface this letter shows a king furious with his sister and friend, when the letter is explored deeper it shows a king only after two things – saving face and money. It was vitally important that the king looked to be in control of all things at all times. Mary's marriage to Brandon showed the king as having no control over his sister or his courtiers. It was vital that Henry appeared, at least on the surface, to be furious over the sudden marriage. He needed to show that while he had no idea what was happening he was not willing to let it simply go unpunished, no matter how much he may love his sister and dear friend. Therefore he showed his great displeasure by punishing the pair and by making them pay a hefty fine for their betrayal. He also demanded Mary's entire dowry and that Brandon should convince Francis to pay 200,000 crowns as previously promised.

In addition to Brandon's previously heartfelt plea to the king, Mary wrote another letter to her brother:

Pleaseth it your grace, to my greatest discomfort, sorrow, and disconsolation, but lately I have been advertised of the great and high displeasure which your highness beareth unto me and my lord of Suffolk for the marriage between us. Sir, I will not in any wise deny but that I have offended your grace, for the which I do put myself most humbly in your clemency and mercy. Nevertheless, to the intent that your highness should not think that I had simply, carnally, or of any sensual appetite done the same, I having no regard to fall in your grace's displeasure, I assure your grace that I had never done against your ordinance and consent, but by the reason of the great despair wherein I was put by the two friars .... which hath certified me in case I come to England your council would never consent to the marriage between the said lord and me, with many other sayings concerning the same promise, so that I verily thought that the said friars would never have offered to have made me like overture unless they might have had charge from some of your council, the which put me in such consternation, fear, and doubt of the obtaining of the thing which I desired most in this world, that I rather chose to put me in your mercy accomplishing the marriage than to put me in the order of your council knowing them to be otherwise minded. Whereupon, sir, I put my lord of Suffolk in choice whether he would accomplish the marriage within four days, or else that he should never have enjoyed me; whereby I know well that I constrained him to break such promises as he made your grace, as well for fear of losing of me as also that

I ascertained him that by their consent I would never come into England. And now that your grace knoweth the both offences, of the which I have been the only occasion, I most humbly and as your most sorrowful sister require you to have compassion upon us both and to pardon our offences, and that it will please your grace to write to me and to my lord of Suffolk some comfortable words, for it should be greatest comfort for us both.

By your loving and most humble sister, MARY.[74]

Mary is tactically clever to shift the reason for the marriage from knowing her brother would not consent, to focusing on the two friars that came to warn her that the Council who would never agree to such a marriage. Henry, as king, could naturally never be blamed for anything, he was after all appointed by God; however the Council was a different matter and it was they who had sent the two messengers. Mary shifts the focus from Henry to the Council. It was not for fear of Henry's reprisal that Mary kept the marriage secret, but of what the Council would say and do when they heard.

Mary also shifts the blame for the marriage from Brandon to herself stating that she suggested the marriage to Brandon and that if he did not marry her within four days he could never 'enjoy' her. She confesses that it was she who made Brandon break his promise to the king and it was not Brandon's decision. Mary also alludes to the fact that the Council would never have let her return to England, which the king has tasked Brandon to arrange, and thus if they did not marry he would never be able to complete his task. Whether there is any truth in all this will never be known. Charles Brandon, as with Henry, had grown up aiming to achieve the knightly ideals of chivalry. The opportunity of rescuing a real princess in distress didn't come along every day. Perhaps this in itself was enough for Mary convince Brandon to marry her and thus see her returned safely to England.

On 6 March Mary wrote to Henry from Paris, in the hope that he will 'continue his favor to her and her friends, and send for her with all convenient speed'.[75]

Once again it is frustrating that the copy of Henry's letter to his sister does not survive. From the tone of Mary's short reply we can speculate that whatever the content of Henry's letter, it ended with a resolution and love between the siblings, with the king once again having showed his favour towards his younger sister.

With the crisis of her sudden marriage to Brandon now seemingly settled, Mary wrote a public letter to her brother giving up her dowry to him:

> Be it known to all manner persons that I, Mary Queen of France, sister unto the King of England, Henry the VIIIth, freely give unto the said King my brother all such plate and vessel of clean gold as the late King Loys of France, the XIIth of that name, gave unto me the said Mary his wife; and also, by these presents I do freely give unto my said brother, King of England, the choice of such special jewels as my said late husband King of France gave me: to the performance whereof I bind me by this my bill, whereto with mine howne hand and signed with my name, and to the same have set my sawlle, the ix[th] day of February, the year of our Lord fifteen hundred and fourteen. By your loving sister, Mary Queen of France.[76]

Suddenly the tone of Mary's letters had changed. Instead of signing off as Mary, she was now Mary Queen of France. No matter how many jewels or gold her brother took from her, Mary would always be the Dowager Queen of France and that was something she would not let her brother forget.

Ultimately the price Mary had to pay for being headstrong, being her own woman and following her heart, was simply her dowry – which of course was not hers to begin with. Mary was able to manipulate the men around her, to convince them of her loyalty and to gain her heart's desire by playing the weak female. She wept, she feared for her life; she worried and played her role perfectly, all the while manoeuvring the men to her purpose; a marriage of her own choosing.

At the end of March Mary was still in France. The decision was made that Mary and Brandon should marry in a more public ceremony. The reason behind this may be the fact that Mary thought herself to be pregnant, as Brandon had suggested in a previous letter. If this was the case then it would be of vital importance that the child be born in wedlock. The pair married for a second time on March 31.[77] Of the more public wedding, Louise of Savoy, Francis' mother, reported, '*que presque immédiatement après le mort de ce monarque elle donna sa main á un homme de basse condition*'[78] (that almost immediately after the death of the monarch she gave her hand to a man of low condition). Certainly it did not go unnoticed that Mary, now a Dowager Queen of France, had married a duke, a man beneath her station.

On the same day Francis wrote to Henry regarding Mary's marriage and her great desire to return to England:

> Had received Henry's letter thanking him for the great affection he had shown to his sister Mary, 'ma belle mère,' and to 'mon cousin' the Duke of Suffolk, and informing him that the said Queen has lately written with her own hand desiring above all things to return to England, which Henry also desires and prays Francis to allow. 'Et apres son retour a v[ous] communiqué oveques ele et sen ... intensyon que aryes a ma contem[plation] et pour honneur et faveur de m[on d]yt cousyn de Sufort de tant plu[s ...] commande. Mon frere, quant ... er mersys que me fayte ... e jay en vers ... de mon dyt cousyn ... nen estre nul besoyn ... que je y veus contyneur de ... eus et pour lonneur et a ... vous et au regart de son alee de ... et la este est et sera touryours en ... verte quant le tans se trouvera [con]venable.' Thanks Henry for his assurance that he would hold Suffolk 'pour recommandé' on his account. Queen Mary has again told him that she is more and more desirous that the marriage between her and Suffolk should take effect, and has this day desired him again to write to urge Henry to consent to it, which he not only does in this letter, but has written more at length to his ambassador, Mons. de la Guysche, instructing him what to say to Henry on the subject.[79]

More than ever Mary was now in limbo. She and Brandon could not return to England without her brother's formal consent. Yet now that Mary was no longer able to be married off or used by Francis there was little room for her at the French court. It is clear from Francis I's letter that Mary desperately wanted to return home.

Brandon too appeared desperate to return home because he wrote to Wolsey in haste wishing to know what jewels and plate they could give to Henry to satisfy him.[80] Henry was a man who liked costly items, be it castles and palaces, fine clothing, or gold and jewels, and he was smart enough not to pass up an opportunity to get them. While Mary had been able to convince her brother to agree to her marriage, Henry was able to use his sister's precarious position in France to gain as much of her wealth as possible before allowing her to return home.

The inventory of the jewellery Mary was allowed to retain as Dowager Queen of France is an impressive document:

... of silver graven with the arms of England ... weighing 15¾ oz. at 3s. 4d. the oz., 51s. 3d. ... Queen's baldric weighing 2¾ oz. 76s.; [mak]ing of the same, 13s. 4d. Fine gold for the garnishing of the Queen's frontlet, 14 oz.½ dwt., at 40s. per oz. Silvering for the garnishing of 4 carving [knives], 65s. 10d. A case for 'the King's collar of garters,' 4s. '[Mak]yng new of a gilt pot to a macher [Mr.] Compton hath in his keeping weighing [more than] the old pot by 2 oz., 6s. 8d.'; making and gilting the same pot, 46s. To Henry for mending the collar of diamonds, 20s.; &c. Total 175*l.* 18*s.* Paid to Rob. Amadas and Henry Holtweler [by Sir Hen.] Wyat, for device on baldric, 4 roses set with diamonds ... , 9l. 5s. 2d. Delivered to the same a double A, set with fair diamond and a fair large table balais. with a [lar]ge pearl, weighing together with the gold 1¾ [oz., to wh]iche there must be made an M of a goodly [size], 47s. 2½d., Delivered to them a bracelet to mend, 2 triangle diamonds, to diamonde called a dake and [a rou ?]nde peal, and 4 table diamond, a fair [diam] onde taken out of a cross and 9 fair pearls, to make a device for her neck; also 8 pearls and 9 rubies, all orient taken [out of t]he M, and 12 pearls taken out of the K, to set in [a bra]sslet, and 6 roses of rubies and 14 small pearls [for ano]ther bracelet; also 9 fair rubies set in colettes. Total, 72l. 7s. 2d. 'Rest clear to the said Amadas, 102l. 14s. 4d.'

To Wm. Holland. New making of 2 pots broken [and a] collar of the Queen's, 8l. Making of a chafing dish, weighing 35 oz., at 4d. the oz. New making of 4 bowls of the Queen's broken, 20s.

8d. New making of an ale pot, of a broken ga ... pot, parcel gilt
21s. 9d.; &c. Total, 19l. 15s. 9d.

To John Twyselton, goldsmith. For 25 ozs. of [cra]mpe rings
of gold, at 40s. the oz. For 140 ozs. of crampe rings of silver, [at]
4s. the oz. For mending of a chafing dish, [with the] head and
the ring broken off, 3s. For mending of a great pot, 12d. Total,
78l. 4s.

Grand total, 200l. 14s. 1d.; 'which sum, John Heron, we will
that ye content and pay upon the sight thereof.' Signed: Henry R.[81]

There was still much haggling over the other costs to be paid, such
as for Mary's transport to and from France as well as the payment
of her servants.[82] On 14 April the official order was given that
Francis should pay Mary 20,000 gold crowns for her travelling
expenses in two 10,000-crown sums over two years.[83] In addition,
Francis was to pay 200,000 gold crowns as return of Mary's
dowry.[84] While the issue of Mary's dowry was finally sorted there
were other diplomatic matters that needed attending to.

While Mary and Brandon's secret marriage was being dealt with
quietly by Wolsey, the matter of peace between England and France
was also being negotiated. On 7 August 1514, an alliance of peace
had been made between Henry and Louis XII.[85] Part of that peace
treaty was Mary's marriage to Louis.[86] With Louis now dead and
Francis king, a new peace treaty needed to be negotiated – hence
Mary's subtle reminders to her brother that Francis could have used
her to form an alliance with another country against England. On
5 April 1515 a peace treaty between the two countries was signed:

Treaty of peace between France and England, arranged by
John de Selva and Peter de la Guiche, on behalf of Francis I., and
Thomas Abp. of York, Thomas Duke of Norfolk, Richard Bp. of
Winchester and John Yonge, on behalf of Henry VIII., during the
life of the two princes. Permission to be granted to the Venetians
and Florentines for free resort into both countries: neither parties
to maintain those disaffected to either: prisoners to be released
– injuries redressed – mutual defence against invasion – England
to lend France 5,000 archers – France to lend England 5,000
lances. Lists of confederates included. Arrangements for Scotland.

Conservators of the peace on the part of France, sc., De Piennes for Picardy, the Duke of Alençon for Normandy, Lord Rieux for Britanny, Lautrec for Aquitaine, Bourbon for Languedoc, De la Tremoille for Burgundy, Dorval for Champagne: for England, the Chancellor, the Treasurer, the Privy Seal, &c. London, 5 April 1515. Signed by the French commissioners.[87]

Despite the newly married couple attempting to keep their marriage relatively low key it would soon become clear that those back in England were well aware of what had happened. Sebastian Giustiniani and Pietro Pasqualigo, Venetian Ambassadors in England, wrote home: 'On the preceding day (20th April), the peace with France had been formally proclaimed. News expected hourly of the departure from Paris for England of the Queen Dowager Mary, who they understood was married to the Duke of Suffolk.'[88]

Finally, on 16 April Mary and Brandon left Paris for Calais. They stopped for a time at Montreuil. It was over two months since Henry had been informed of the secret marriage, but neither Mary nor Brandon had been granted permission to return home. On the 22nd he wrote a desperate letter to Henry pledging his loyalty and service. He believed that the English Council was out to destroy him and metaphorically threw himself at Henry's feet promising to endure any punishment that the king considers appropriate:

Most gracious Sovereign Lord, So it is that I am informed divers ways that all your whole council, my Lord of York excepted, with many other, are clearly determined to tympe your grace that I may either be put to death or put in prison, and so to be destroyed. Alas, Sir, I may say that I have a hard fortune, seeing that there was never none of them in trouble but I was glad to help them to my power, and that your grace knows best. And now that I am in this none little trouble and sorrow, now they are ready to help to destroy me. But, Sir, I can no more but God forgive them whatsoever comes to me; for I am determined. For, Sir, your grace is he that is my sovereign lord and master, and he that hath brought me up out of nought; and I am your subject and servant, and he that hath offended your grace in breaking my promise that I made your grace touching the queen your sister; for the which I, with most humble heart, will yield myself into your grace's hands to do with my poor body your gracious pleasure, not fearing the malice of them; for I know your grace of such nature that it cannot lie in their powers to cause you to destroy me for their malice. But what punishment I have I shall thank God and your grace of it, and think that I have well deserved it, both to God and your grace; as knows our Lord, who send your grace your most honourable heart's desire with long life, and me most sorrowful wretch your gracious favour, what sorrows soever I endure therefor. At Mottryll, the 22nd day of April, by your most humble subject and servant, CHARLES SUFFOLKE.[89]

Mary and Charles travelled from Montreuil to the area held by the English around Calais where they had to await permission from Henry to return home.[90] From Calais Mary wrote one last letter to her brother. This time she sought the advice and assistance of Thomas Wolsey in composing it. Mary dictated the letter to Wolsey's secretary Turk. Turk then travelled across the Channel to give the letter to Wolsey who made multiple corrections before sending the letter and Turk back to Mary. Unfortunately, the final copy of the letter does not exist, but it is most likely that Mary followed Wolsey's advice and stuck close to the suggested corrections:

My most dear and entirely beloved brother,

In most humble manner I recommend me to your grace

Dearest brother, I doubt not but that you have in your good remembrance that whereas for the good of peace and for the furtherance of your affairs you moved me to marry with my lord and late hus-band, king Louis of France, whose soul God pardon. Though I understood that he was very aged and sickly, yet for the advancement of the said peace, and for the furtherance of your causes, I was contented to conform myself to your said motion, so that if I should fortune to survive the said late king I might with your good will marry myself at my liberty without your displeasure. Whereunto, good brother, you condescended and granted, as you well know, promising unto me that in such case you would never provoke or move me but as mine own heart and mind should be best pleased; and that wheresoever I should dispose myself, you would wholly be contented with the same. And upon that, your good comfort and faithful promise, I assented to the said marriage, which else I would never have granted to, as at the same time I shewed unto you more at large. Now that God hath called my said late husband to his mercy, and that I am at my liberty, dearest brother, remembering the great virtues which I have seen and perceived here-tofore in my lord of Suffolk, to whom I have always been of good mind, as you well know, I have affixed and clearly determined myself to marry with him; and the same [I] assure you hath proceeded only of mine own mind, ithout any request or labour of my said lord of Suffolk, or of any other person. And to be plain with your grace, I have so bound myself unto him that for no cause earthly I will or may vary or change from the same.* Wherefore my good and most kind brother, I now beseech your grace to take this matter in good part, and to give unto me and to my said lord of Suffolk your good will herein. Ascertaining you, that upon the trust and comfort which I have, for that you have always honourably regarded your promise, I am now come out of the realm of France, and have put myself within your jurisdiction in this your town of Calais, where I intend to remain till such time as I shall have answer from you of your good and loving mind herein; which I would not have done but upon the faithful trust that I have in your said promise. Humbly beseeching your grace, for the great and tender love which ever hath been and shall be between you and me, to bear your gracious mind and shew yourself to be agreeable thereunto, and to certify me by your most loving letters of the same, till which time I will make mine abode here, and no farther enter your realm. And to the intent it may please you the rather to condescend to this my most hearty desire. I am contented and expressly promise and bind me to you, by these presents, to give you all the whole dote [dowry] which was delivered with me, and also all such plate of gold and jewels as I shall have of my said late husband's. Over and besides this I shall, rather than fail, give you as much yearly part of my dower, to as great a sum as shall stand with your will and pleasure; and of all the premises I promise, upon knowledge of your good mind, to make unto you sufficient bonds. Trusting, verily, that in fulfilling of your said promise to me made, you will shew your brotherly love, affection, and good mind to me in this behalf, which to hear of I abide with most desire ; and not to be miscontented with my said lord of Suffolk, whom of mine inward good mind and affection to him I have in manner enforced to be agreeable to the same, without any request by him made; as knoweth our Lord, whom I beseech to have your grace in his merciful governance.

[*This section was originally: 'So it is, brother, as you well know, I have always borne good mind towards my lord of Suffolk; and him, as the case doth now reqnire with me, I can love before all other, and upon him I have perfectly set my mind – settled and determined; and upon the good comfort of your said promise the matter is so far forth that for no cause earthly I will vary or change from the same. And of me and of mine own towardness and mind only hath it proceeded.']⁹¹

For the last time Mary reminded her brother of the promise he had made. In this letter she also added that Henry promised not to try and persuade her out of a second marriage, but in fact that he would support her decision. Mary reminded her brother that she had long 'held her heart' towards Brandon and that it was her decision alone to marry him and she was not persuaded or forced by Brandon or anyone else.

Mary reminded Henry that by staying in Calais she was now in English territory and under England's laws and thus placed herself at her brother's feet, once more his dutiful servant. She accepted his laws and begged him to allow her and Brandon to return to England. As an incentive, Mary reminded her brother of the promise she had made to give him her entire dowry as well as yearly payments of whatever sum he desired. Finishing her letter Mary also asked her brother to be kind to her husband knowing that Brandon's status relied on royal patronage. Such a humble request demonstrated Mary's true understanding of the way that both men and women positioned themselves at court and how in the end a person's very existence came down to the king's favour.

In reality, Mary had her brother over a barrel. She was a Dowager Queen of France and the king's dearly beloved sister. What would the people of England think of their king if he refused to allow his own sister to return to England? Henry always had his image and reputation to think of and Mary was well aware of this. By promising her full dowry to Henry as well as the payment of a yearly fine, Mary was able to soothe Henry's battered pride and make it appear that the king was punishing her and Brandon. In return, Mary was able to marry the man she loved and return home.

Luckily the newlyweds did not have to wait long and shortly after, they landed at Dover on 2 May. About a mile-and-a-half from Birling Manor, they were met by Henry and a great retinue.[92] The king warmly greeted his sister 'rejoicing greatly in her honourable return, and great prosperity'.[93] An ironic greeting, in that it was not Mary who was prospering, but her brother, who now possessed all her dowry. Henry also accepted Mary's explanation that it was she who was responsible for the marriage, not Brandon.

Having gained the king's acceptance of their marriage Brandon and Mary were formally married at Greenwich on 13 May in the presence of Henry and Queen Katherine of Aragon.[94] Andrea Badoer and Sebastian Giustiniani, the Venetian ambassadors in the English court wrote:

On the 13th instant the espousals (le sponsalitie) of Queen Mary to the Duke of Suffolk at length took place; there were no public demonstrations, because the kingdom did not approve of the marriage. Wishing to ascertain whether this marriage had been concluded with the King's consent, were assured by great personages that it had first been arranged between the bride and bridegroom, after which they asked the consent of King Henry, who, however, had maintained his former friendship for the Duke, which would appear incredible, but is affirmed by the nobility at the Court. Have, therefore, abstained from paying any compliments either to the King or to the bride and bridegroom, but have determined to visit his Majesty in a day or two, and congratulate him on his sister's arrival. Should they understand that the great personages of the Court intend to make public mention of the event, and that it was celebrated, they would then offer congratulations in the Signory's name on the marriage, but not seeing it solemnized as becoming, would keep silence, to avoid giving offence.[95]

Despite the king consenting to the marriage, not all in England were happy with the unconventional union:

Against this marriage many men grudged, and said that it was a great loss to the realm that she was not married to the Prince of Castile; but the wisest sort was content, considering that if she had been married again out of this realm, she should have carried much riches with her; and now she brought every year into the realm nine or ten thousand marks. But whatsoever the rude people said, the Duke behaved himself so that he had both the favour of the king and of the people, his wit and demeanour was such.[96]

Mary and Brandon were required to return Mary's entire dowry. Brandon was instructed to relinquish his wardship of Lady de Lisle and all rights to her inheritance and property. In addition to this the couple had to pay £24,000 (£11,610,000)[97] in yearly instalments of £1,000 (£484,000).[98] This is a a massive sum, but records showed that six years after the marriage, by 1521, Mary and Brandon had only repaid £1,324[99] (£641,000).[100] The king was more interested in making a show rather than actually enforcing regular repayments.

No matter what the common people thought, Mary Tudor was now married to a man she loved. With such a dramatic, romantic marriage it is unsurprising that ballads and poems were written about it. The following is a ballad entitled 'The Song of an English Knight'. Written in the the sixteenth century, most likely after the death of Mary's granddaughter, Lady Jane Grey, it highlights Brandon's romantic wooing of the French queen. (Thomas Wyatt it is not.)

Eighth Henry ruling in this land,
He had a sister fair,
That was the widow'd queen of France,
Enrich'd with virtues rare:
And being come to England's court,
She oft beheld a knight,
Charles Brandon nam'd, in whose fair eyes,
She chiefly took delight.

And noting in her princely mind,
His gallant sweet behaviour,
She daily drew him by degrees,
Still more and more in favour:
Which he perceiving courteous knight,
Found fitting time and place,
And thus in amorous fort began,
His love suit to her grace:

I am at love fair queen, said he,
Sweet let your love incline,
That by your grace Charles Brandon may,
On earth be made divine:
If worthless I might worthy be
To have so good a lot,
To please your highness in true love
My fancy doubteth not.

Or if that gentry might convey
So great a grace to me,
I can maintain the same by birth,
Being come of good degree.
If wealth you think be all my want,
Your highness hath great store,
And my supplement shall be love,
What can you wish for more?

It hath been known when hearty love
Did tie the true love knot,

Though now if gold and silver want,
The marriage proveth not.
The goodly queen hereat did blush,
But made a dumb reply;
Which he imagin'd what she meant,
And kiss'd her reverently.

Brandon (quoth she) I greater am,
Than would I were for thee,
But can as little master love,
As them of low degree:
My father was a king, and so
A king my husband was,
My brother is the like, and he
Will say I do transgress.

But let him say what pleaseth him,
His liking I'll forego,
And chuse a love to please myself,
Though all the world say no:
If plowmen make their marriages,
As best contents their mind,
Why should not princes of estate
The like contentment find?

But tell me, Brandon, am I not
More forward than beseems?
Yet blame me not for love, I love,
Where best my fancy deems.
And long may live (quoth he) to love,
Nor longer live may I,
Than when I love your royal grace,
And then disgraced die.

But if I do deserve your love,
My mind desires dispatch,
For many are the eyes in court,
That on your beauty watch;

But am not I sweet lady, now
More forward than behoves?
Yet for my heart, forgive my tongue,
That speaks for him that loves.

The queen and this brave gentleman
Together both did wed,
And after sought the king's good-will,
And of their wishes sped:
For Brandon soon was made a duke,
And graced so in court,
Then who but he did flaunt it forth
Amongst the noblest sort.

And so from princely Brandon's line,
And Mary's did proceed
The noble race of Suffolk's house,
As after did succeed:
From whose high blood the lady Jane,
Lord Guilford Dudley's wife,
Came by descent who with her lord,
In London lost her life.[101]

9

As Wife and Mother

❧

'The beautiful Lady Mary, the King's sister, late Queen of France,
now consort of the Duke of Suffolk.'

It has been proposed that Mary spent much of her early married life
at Suffolk Place on her return to England. Suffolk Place was a large
mansion fronting on to the High Street at Southwark. The front
was ornamented with turrets and cupolas and had beautiful stucco
work. The building was constructed around a courtyard. Suffolk
House also went by the names Duke's Palace and Brandon's House.
An inventory dated 18 December 1535 details all the gold and
silver plate contained in Suffolk House. The total came to the sum
of £1,457 (£580,000).[1] Many years later when the king obtained
Suffolk House, he renamed it Southwark Place and eventually
turned it into a mint.[2]

The immediate issue that the newlyweds faced was financial
stability. With Mary's entire dowry, her plate and coin handed
to Henry, and regular payments owed, this meant money was
a constant issue. Mary's only source of income was £4,000
(£1,518,000) a year for her dowry payments, paid by King Francis
I. While considered a great deal of money, the major problem was
obtaining the payments. Throughout the following years England
would go to war with France and during that time payments were
stopped. Therefore Mary's dower payments could not be relied on.

While Brandon's financial situation throughout the late 1510s and 1520s is difficult to assess, it was not much better than Mary's. Between 1515 and 1519 Brandon's income was around £3,000 (£1,139,000) a year, and on his marriage to Mary Tudor he lost the wardship of Elizabeth Lisle and therefore the income from her lands. This reduced his income to approximately £1,500 (£570,000) a year. Without regular income in 1515–1516 Brandon was forced to borrow £12,000 from the Crown and an additional £3,000 against the Welsh revenues to which he continued to have access to through his post as Chamberlain.[3] The couple also had to draw on Brandon's Welsh holdings, as well as the £40 a year (£19,000) he was granted on his creation as Duke of Suffolk. Brandon had been granted a stewardship of Crown lands worth around £6 13s 4d a year as well as around £500-worth of land and possessions.[4] Brandon held various offices that would have brought in income from other areas, but this is hard to calculate and certainly would not have amounted to any more than £1,500 (£570,000) a year. Brandon had to draw on the De La Pole estates in Suffolk that had been granted to him by the king in February 1515. Richard De La Pole had been a constant thorn in Henry's side as he had a distant claim to the English throne.[5]

Brandon received sporadic payments for his French pension although the exact sum cannot be calculated. In total, the Brandons' financial income would have been around £7,000 per annum (£2,657,000) if all promised payments were received.[6] This was not enough and Brandon had to beg Wolsey to ask the king for a loan of £12,000[7] (£5,800,000). Henry helped the couple by cancelling £5,000 of their debts to the Crown, yet this did little to ease their financial stress.

The war with France in the 1520s of course affected both Mary and Brandon's French pensions. The payments did come intermittently throughout this period, but Brandon was constantly chasing both pensions. Brandon wrote that his wife's payments 'restith much of her honour and profit, and mine also'.[8] Brandon was heavily reliant on Mary's dower payments for his own financial dealings.

In 1525 under a new scheme created by Thomas Wolsey, the Council in the Marches was incorporated into the Council of

Princess Mary and Brandon lost his position as Chamberlain. Brandon's position was granted to his deputy. Brandon was compensated with the castle of Ewelme, although it was not so much the loss of income, but the loss of military status that affected the duke. No longer could he be the one to call on the people in the North to march to war.[9] In addition to this loss and all their financial difficulties, Brandon and Mary still had to make payments of £1,000 (£380,000) a year to the king as a fine for their marriage although, as previously, these payments were not regularly enforced.[10]

Mary and her husband, like many at court, were living beyond their means. As Dowager Queen of France and sister to the king, Mary had to be seen to maintain a high standard of living. She had to have the clothing and servants suitable for her position and all of this cost money. In 1524 Brandon had fifty-one servants who earned 26s 8d each a year. His physician, Master Leonard, was the highest paid member of the Brandon household earning £20 (£7,600) a year.[11] In total Brandon was spending around £1,000 a year just on his own servants. In 1526 Mary had at least fifty of her own servants – forty-three men and seven women, including two knights, an esquire and a Frenchman. The total wages for these servants was £327 (£124,000), although it is most likely that lesser ranking servants were not included in this total. Therefore the wages of servants would have been much higher.[12] While this is not a staggering number of servants compared to the king or queen, it did put financial pressure on the couple to see everyone clothed, fed and paid accordingly. Mary had to pay her own servants from her French pension.[13]

A more pressing problem than relative poverty was still, of course, the reaction of the king. Both Mary and Brandon knew that theirs was truly a dangerous liaison. To marry without the king's permission amounted to treason, for which Brandon could have lost his life. Both relied heavily on Henry showing them favour and in order to gain it they needed to be at court. For a few months after their public marriage at Greenwich the couple retired from court, keeping a low profile, perhaps to spend some time together or maybe to let tensions cool. Yet both knew they could not be away for long and soon Mary and her husband were back at court in the public eye.

On 15 November Thomas Wolsey was granted his Cardinal's hat. The following Sunday a grand ceremony was held at Westminster Abbey. Afterwards Mary and Brandon attended a banquet at York Place, Wolsey's chief residence. Mary had the honour of sitting at the head table with her brother and Queen Katherine. As the Dowager Queen of France and sister to the king, Mary was the second highest ranking woman in England.[14]

In February 1516 Brandon resumed his normal position at court, attending council meetings (although sporadically) and participating in regular jousting events. It is assumed that Mary would have also attended court with her husband, perhaps even visiting her long-time friend Queen Katherine, who was pregnant again. Katherine of Aragon gave birth to a daughter named Mary, after her aunt, on 18 February 1516. For the little princess's christening Mary gave her niece a pomander made of gold; an expensive gift not suitable for a baby, but for her to use when she was older.[15]

Despite thinking that she may pregnant in March 1515, Mary did not give birth to her first child until 11 March 1516. Mary gave birth to a healthy baby boy at Bath Place, London, a residence belonging to Cardinal Wolsey, between ten and eleven o'clock at night.[16] There is some question as to why Mary gave birth at Bath Place rather than Suffolk Place. It may be that her labour came on her unexpectedly and she did not have enough time for her lying in, when she would have removed herself from the world for several weeks before giving birth. Or it may simply be that owing to the duke's good relationship with Wolsey and all the Cardinal had done for them in seeing their favour was restored with the king that Bath Place was offered to Mary for the birth of her first child. Brandon now had a son and male heir, who had a claim to the throne through his mother.

The baby boy was christened Henry after his godfather, the king. The christening ceremony took place in the hall at Suffolk Place in great splendour. The hall was decorated with wall hangings of red and white Tudor roses, torches were lit and the christening font was warmed. The christening was performed by John Fisher, Bishop of Rochester, and former chaplain to Mary's late grandmother, Lady Margaret Beaufort. He was assisted by Thomas Ruthall of Durham.

The king attended the ceremony, as did Cardinal Thomas Wolsey, the Duke of Norfolk and other important members of the court. As custom dictated for a male child, two godfathers were chosen, Henry and Cardinal Wolsey, plus one godmother, Catherine of York, the Dowager Countess of Devon, the sixth daughter of King Edward IV.[17] For Charles Brandon it was a great honour to have the king stand as godfather to his son and heir.

After the ceremony Lady Anne Grey carried little Henry to his nursery and Sir Humphrey Banaster, Mary's vice chamberlain, carried his train. Afterwards spices and wine were served by the Duke of Norfolk and presents were given in celebration. The king gave the young Brandon a salt cellar and a cup of solid gold and the queen gave two silver-gilt pots. Mary was not in attendance since she had not yet been churched – the act of attending church for the mother to be seen as once more clean and therefore allowed back into society. The christening's pomp signified the importance of the birth of the king's nephew, as well as Brandon's favour with the king.[18]

While not openly discussed there were many rumblings regarding the birth. Mary's son, under the rule of primogeniture, had a distinct claim to the throne.[19] There were those at court who grumbled about an upstart like Brandon, without a royal lineage, having a son who was in line for the throne through his wife. However, there was little they could do. Henry was the first of four children that Mary would have with her second husband.

Considering his chequered marital history, Brandon worked hard to ensure the legitimacy of both his children and his marriage to Mary Tudor. He appealed to Pope Clement VII to issue a papal bull confirming the legitimacy of his marriage and therefore, his children. It was not until 20 August 1529 that a bull was finally issued:

...that Suffolk in the days of Henry VII had married Margaret Mortymer alias Brandon, of London diocese, on the strength of a dispensation which was not valid, and with her had cohabited although he had previously contracted marriage with Ann Browne, and was related to the said Margaret in the second and third degrees of affinity. Besides, the said Anne and Margaret were related in the second and third degrees of consanguinity, and Suffolk's grandmother was the sister of the father of a former husband of Margaret's (ac etiam ex eo avia tua et genitor olim conjugis dictæ Margaretæ frater et soror fuerant). For these causes, feeling that he could not continue to cohabit with Margaret Mortymer without sin, he caused his marriage with her to be declared null by the official of the archdeacon of London, to whom the cognisance of such causes of old belongs. After this sentence Suffolk married the said Anne, and had some daughters by her, and after her death he married Mary queen dowager of France. The bull ratifies this sentence, and supplies all defects both of law and fact, and visits with ecclesiastical censure all who call it in question.[20]

Less than two months after the christening, on 3 May 1516, Margaret Tudor, Mary's elder sister, arrived in London. Margaret had last been in England in 1503 when she left to marry King James IV of Scotland. Over the next thirteen years, until 1516, Margaret had a volatile marital life, which resulted in her leaving Scotland and coming to stay with her brother for a time. James IV had been killed at the Battle of Flodden fighting the English in 1513. After her husband's death Margaret had become regent to their one-year-old son King James V. In haste and without consulting the Scottish Council, Margaret married Archibald Douglas, sixth Earl of Angus. At the same time the Duke of Albany and cousin of the late King James IV arrived in Scotland as a possible successor to the young James V. Margaret found herself trapped between her husband and the council. She fled Scotland for England while heavily pregnant. At Harbottle Castle in Northumberland she gave birth to a daughter, also named Margaret, on 8 October. Margaret became ill for some time, so she rested before she finally travelled to London.[21]

In London Margaret was greeted by her brother and sister. This was the first time that Mary had seen her sister in thirteen years. When Margaret had left for Scotland Mary was just seven years of age. She was now aged twenty-one, a dowager queen, a mother and still extremely beautiful. It must have been an interesting meeting for the sisters, both having time to exchange stories of their lives, their hardships and the experience of motherhood.

On 19 and 20 May 1516 a spectacular jousting event was organised for Margaret, Dowager Queen of Scotland and the court's entertainment. Henry, Brandon, Carew and Essex were to be one team, Kingston, Capell, Sedley and Howard on the other. On the first day both Brandon and Henry scored well – the king scoring slightly better. On the second Brandon continued to gain high scores and he ended the day with the highest total. The king had not done as well, even though his opponents were not on par with his skills.[22] Frustrated the king vowed, 'never to joust again except it be with as good a man as himself'.[23] Soon after, Brandon became the king's opponent rather than being on the same team, so Henry saw Brandon as a worthy opponent. It can be assumed that Mary was a spectator to such magnificent jousts, perhaps sitting with Queen Katherine and her sister Margaret as they watched their husbands joust – three queens together.

After this Mary and Brandon were away from court. In June 1516 they visited Butley Priory. Butley was in Suffolk, a short distance from Westhorpe Hall, and had an establishment of about seventy-five people. Its annual income was around £400 and it was frequently visited by member of the nobility. Mary and Brandon's visit was recorded in detail by one of the Priory members.[24] (Mary would visit Butley Priory many times after 1516, her last visit coming in 1530 where she stayed for almost two months between September 20 and November 16.)[25]

This year, 1516, June 13th, the most excellent Lady Mary, Queen of France, the most beautiful and beloved sister of our most invincible King Henry VIII, and wife of the most excellent Charles Brandon Duke, of Suffolk, was received, with as much honour as we religiously could. First, a stool was placed with a silken covering and two silken cushions, opposite the gates of our cemetery: then the prior and convent, in silken copes, preceded by the cross bearer, taper bearer, and incense bearer, marched to the said stool; where, when the prelate had arrived, he first knelt down with his servants, then sprinkled holy water over her chaplain, then over himself, and lastly, over the said queen. Then he censed her, and last of all gave the kiss of peace to the said chaplain; the chaplain wearing all the time his prelatical mitre on his head. This ended, the precentor began the antiphone 'Regina coeli' with which he entered the church. even to the high altar.[26]

Brandon was soon concerned about what those around the king were saying about him. He was probably most worried that the Duke of Norfolk had free access to the king and could be whispering against about him. Brandon wrote to Wolsey on 14 July 1516, 'Though he is far off by the King's commandment, his heart is always with him.'[27]

Nevertheless, Henry had decided to visit Brandon and Mary's manor at Donnington later in the year. Mary wrote a humble letter to her brother on 9 September informing Henry of Brandon's great joy at hearing the news. Ever mindful of the reaction to her unsanctioned marriage – even at this late stage – by the man historian John Matusiak called 'England's Nero', she took every opportunity to remind him of her great affection:

My most dearest and right entirely beloved lord and brother, In my most humble wise, I recommend me unto your grace showing unto your grace; that I do perceive; by my lord my husband; that you are pleased and contented that he shall resort unto your presence at such time as your grace shall be at his manor of Donnington; whereby I see well he is marvellously rejoiced, and much comforted that it hath liked your grace so to be pleased; for the which your special goodness to him, showed in that behalf, and for sundry and many other your kindness, as well to me as to him showed and given in divers causes, I most humbly thank your grace; assuring you that for the same I account myself as much bounden unto your grace, as ever sister was to brother; and according thereunto, I shall, to the best of my power, during my life, endeavour myself, as far as in me shall be possible, to do the thing that shall stand with your pleasure; and if it had been time convenient and your grace had been therewith pleased, I would most gladly have accompanied my said lord in this journey. But I trust that both I and my said lord shall see you, according as your grace wrote in your last letters unto my said lord, which is the thing that I desire more to obtain than all the honour of the world. And thus, I beseech our Lord to send unto you, my most dearest and entirely beloved brother and lord, long and prosperous life, with the full accomplishment of all your honourable desires; most humbly praying your grace that I may be humbly recommended unto my most dearest and best beloved sister, the queen's grace, and to the Queen of Scots, my well beloved sister, trusting that she be ascertained from your grace of the prosperous estate and health of my dearly beloved nephews the princes, to whom I pray God send long life,

From Letheringham in Suffolk, the 9th day of September, by the hand of Your loving sister MARY Queen of France.[28]

Brandon need not have worried for as well as the king's visit to his manor at Donnington, Henry also bestowed the wardships of Sir Thomas Knyvett's two sons on him. Knyvett had died on board the ship *Regent* in 1512.[29]

Toward the end of 1516 Mary suffered a bout of ill health. Her husband wrote to Thomas Wolsey regarding his wife's health and their late departure from court.

Sir,

The chief cause of my writing unto your grace at this time is to advertise your grace that the French queen's grace cannot depart from the court so soon as was appointed; for, Sir, it hath pleased God to visit her with an ague, the which has taken her grace, every third day, four times very sharp; but by the grace of God she shall shortly recover; for Sir the king's grace's physicians takes marvellous good heed unto her grace, and also specially his grace comforts her, so like a good and loving sovereign lord and brother, that it takes away a great part of her pain.[30]

Brandon refers to Mary suffering from an ague, the symptoms being fever and shivering, which is sometimes related to malaria.[31] There are no other reports of Mary suffering from malaria yet whatever the illness it appeared that she was in great pain. It is interesting to note that Henry, terrified of illness, attended his sister and provided her with comfort. Certainly this shows the king's deep love for his sister and his concern over her health.

Having returned to health, in March 1517 Mary and Brandon hosted Queen Katherine of Aragon while the queen was on pilgrimage to the shrine of Our Lady at Austin Priory, Walsingham. It was not uncommon for women to go on pilgrimage to Walsingham to pray to the Virgin Mary for a healthy child, preferably a son, as well as a safe delivery. In July of the same year Mary would also go on pilgrimage to Our Lady. Mary and Brandon met Queen Katherine at Pickenham Wade in Norfolk and accompanied her to Austin Priory. Afterwards, they entertained Katherine grandly; however an incident occurred which caused both Mary and Brandon to worry that it would cause Henry's hostility.[32]

My very good lord,

In my most heartiest manner I commend me unto your good lordship, evermore thanking you for the good mind that you have borne unto me, beseeching of your good continuance in the same. So it is, my lord, according to your advice, I met with the queen, my mistress, on Friday last past at Pickenham Wood, and as my duty was, awaited upon her grace to Walsingham, and also, according to your advice, the French queen did meet with the said queen, my mistress and hers, at the next place that was convenient, nigh unto our lodging, and such poor cheer as we could make her grace, we did, with as good heart and mind as her own servants, according to our duties. Furthermore, my lord, as yesterday Monday the 16th day of March, Mistress Jerningham came to the French queen my wife, at dinner time, before the queen my mistress's coming thither, and after that she had been with the said queen my wife, she took her daughter in law aside with her, and called young Berkeley unto them – and there privily ensured the said Berkeley unto the Lady Anne Gray, one of the queen my wife's ladies and mine; which is no little displeasure unto me, seeing he is the king's ward, and that it pleased his grace to put him to my rule and guiding. I had liever have spent a thousand pounds than any such pageants should have been done within the queen's house and mine. My lord I heartily desire and pray your good lordship, that if any misinformations be made unto the king's grace hereof, that it will please you to you, his grace hereof as I have written unto you lest his grace should give credence unto some other light informations herein; which I would abide by upon my honour; and that it will please you to stay the matter unto my coming to London. Also, that it would please your lordship so to order this matter, that it may be an example to all other, how they should make any such mysteries, within any nobleman or woman's house hereafter, and in especially with one of the king's wards. And thus fare you well, my very good lord and I beseech Jesu to send you long life and good health. From the manor of Rising the 17th day of March By your assured CHARLES SUFFOLK.[33]

It would appear that Anne Jerningham had taken advantage of the queen's visit to Mary and Brandon's home and sought to arrange a marriage between one of Mary's ladies-in-waiting, Lady Anne Grey, to John Berkeley. Berkeley was the son and heir of Maurice Berkeley and a ward of the king who had been placed in Brandon's care. Both Brandon and Mary were deeply worried that Henry would take offence at this marriage being arranged without his consent. Another marriage without the king's consent looks at the very least foolhardy![34] Luckily, Henry saw no fault.[34] Their response to this incident showed that Mary and Brandon were well aware that their position was still potentially dangerous.

The following letter written shortly afterwards speaks of the forthcoming jousting events held every year as part of the May Day celebrations. Brandon had heard that the king wished him to participate and he greatly desired Mary to join him at court. He wanted Mary to be once more in her brother's company, a thing which she also wished for, as well as to be able to participate in the court festivities. It may also be that Brandon did not wish to be separated from his wife and to have her cheering him on while he jousted:

Sire,

In the most humble wise I recommend me to your grace; and, Sire, so was it at the last time I was with your grace, I went through, with my lord cardinal, for such debts as the queen your sister and I am in, to your grace; for the which it was thought by your grace's council learned that, the queen your sister and I both must confer divers things, before your judges, according unto the law; and, Sire, I beseech your grace that she may come up, to the intent that she may do all such acts, according as be devised, or shall be devised, most for your grace's surety; to the intent, whatsoever shall happen of me, that your grace may be in surety, and that it shall not be said but it is her deed and free will, the which your grace shall well perceive that it is done with good mind and heart; and, Sire, the coming up of her to see your grace shall rejoice her more than the value of that, if it should be given to her.

Sire, it is so that I have heard, by my Lord Morley and others, that your grace intends to have some pastime this May, and that your grace's pleasure is that I shall give mine attendance on your grace, the which I shall be as glad to do as any poor servant or subject that your grace has living. Howbeit, Sire, I am somewhat unprovided of such things as belong to that business; wherefore, if it may stand with your grace's pleasure, I would bring up the queen your sister against Easter, to both plays, and then to remain, till she and I may know your grace's further pleasure, to the which she and I shall obey with humble heart, according to her duty and mine, as knows God, who preserve your grace in long life, with as much health and honour as your most noble heart can desire, which is both her and my daily prayer.

By your most humble subject and servant CHARLES SUFFOLK.[35]

Despite their worries, Mary and Brandon were soon recalled to court. On 16 May 1517 Margaret Tudor returned to Scotland. Henry and Wolsey had negotiated a treaty that allowed Margaret to return home and visit her son, James V. Mary was now seven months pregnant with her second child and she would never see her sister again.[36]

Mary had one more engagement to attend before she gave birth to her second child. By mid-1517 the political winds were changing from an alliance with France to one with Spain and the Holy Roman Empire. At the beginning of July, Prince Charles, Mary's former fiancé, sent ambassadors to meet with Henry and discuss a possible alliance. Henry always wanting to impress and spent to do so. When the ambassadors entered London Henry VIII sent four hundred horsemen, prelates, knights, and barons to meet them. The following Sunday they were escorted to court where they met

Henry dressed in stiff brocade in the Hungarian fashion with a collar of great ostentation around his neck. Queen Katherine of Aragon, Mary, Norfolk, Buckingham, the Marquis of Dorset and other barons were also present. They were all wearing cloth of gold with costly necklaces and chains, 'everything glittered with gold.'[37]

Mary was almost nine months pregnant. Why did she not remove herself from court for her 'lying in'? Considering the events that followed it may be that Mary did not realise that she was so far along with her second child. Not long after attending court Mary had set out on a pilgrimage to Walsingham, most likely to pray for the safe delivery of her child, when her labour came on quite suddenly. She was forced to stay with the Bishop Nicholas West of Sly, at Hatfield, and on 16 July 1517 between two and three o'clock in the morning she gave birth to a healthy baby girl. The little girl was named Frances, as she was born on St Francis Day. Her name also allowed Mary and Brandon to pay tribute to King Francis I, who had supported them in their marriage several years earlier.[38]

Due to the suddenness of the labour and birth, and that it was a baby girl, Frances' christening was a low key event compared to her brother's and was held in the local parish church. As custom dictated, Frances had two godmothers and one godfather. Queen Katherine and her daughter Princess Mary were the godmothers. Since both were unable to attend, Lady Elizabeth Boleyn was sent to stand in for the queen and lady Elizabeth Grey stood for the princess. Frances' godfather was the Abbot of St Albans.[39]

Mary removed herself from court for a time after the birth and lived at the couple's country home of Westhorpe Hall. Built between 1515 and 1523, Westhorpe Hall was situated in East Anglia and would become the family's main country residence. It was a moated brick court house of considerable size with terracotta plaques and battlements. It had beautifully decorated chimneys, a cloistered chapel that had a magnificent stained glass window,[40] oak-panelled rooms and a striking statue of Hercules. The surrounding parks were well stocked with deer for hunting and the gardens were designed in the French fashion. Brandon stated that the building costs for Westhorpe Hall were £12,000 (£3,865,000). Much of this would have come from Mary's intermittently received French pension.

Westhorpe Hall was demolished in the 1760s. Martin, a historian at Thetford described it:

> ...went to see the dismal ruins of Westhorpe Hall, formerly the seat of Charles Brandon, Duke of Suffolk. The workmen are now pulling it down as fast as may be, in a very careless and injudicious manner. The coping bricks, battlements and many other ornamental pieces, are made of earth, and burnt hard, as fresh as when first built. They might, with care, have been taken down whole, but all the fine chimneys and ornaments were pulled down with ropes, and crushed to pieces in a most shameful manner. There was a monstrous figure of Hercules sitting cross legged with his club, and a lion beside him, but all shattered in pieces. The painted glass is likely to share the same fate. The timber is fresh and sound, and the building, which was very lofty, stood as when it was first built. It is a pity that care is not taken to preserve some few of our ancient fabrics. To demolish every piece of old architecture is quite barbaric.[41]

In March 1518 Mary was ill again. Brandon wrote to Wolsey to excuse himself from attending court and the council because of Mary's poor health.

> My lord,
>
> Whereas I, of a certain space, have not given mine attendance upon your lordship in the king's council, according to my duty, I beseech your lordship to pardon me thereof. The cause why, hath been that the said French queen hath had, and yet hath, divers physicians with her, for her old disease in her side, and as yet cannot be perfectly restored to her health. And, albeit I have been two times at London, only to the intent to have waited upon your lordship, yet her grace, at either time, hath so sent for me, that I might not otherwise do but return home again. Nevertheless, her grace is now in such good amendment, that upon Tuesday or Wednesday next coming, I intend, by God's grace to wait upon your lordship. From Croydon the 16th day of March.[42]

Brandon's letter shows his concern for his wife and that in her pain, Mary sought comfort from her husband. The court physician, Master Peter, was sent to to Mary and it appeared that for a time Mary felt better but it did not last. Brandon's second letter to Wolsey evinces genuine distress. Mary desperately wanted to come to London, so much so that she cried regularly. Seeing his wife so upset prompted Brandon to write this second letter in the hope that if Mary did come to London and see her brother, her health might improve.

> My lord,
>
> So it is that the French queen has been sick, and so upon that, she sent for Master Peter, to whom she had a great mind unto, and so since, she is worse than she was before; insomuch that now she has taken such a phantasy that she thinks that she should not do well, with out she should come up to London for remedy; insomuch that she weeps every day, and takes so on that I am afraid it should do her harm; and for the eschewing thereof, I intend, with all diligence possible, to bring her up; and, my lord, I insure you it is need, for her disease sheweth that it must ask great counsel, as you shall know at her coming up.
>
> My lord, now since it is so far that she must needs come up, I beseech you, as her and my only trust is in you that you, will be so good lord unto her and me, as to be means unto the king's grace, that she may have a lodging in the court; an it be but one chamber, because it shall not be said that she is now in worse favour than she was at her departing. My lord, all her trust and mine is in you, and therefore she nor I will make none further labour for this matter.[43]

Mary also decided to write to her brother:

> My most dearest and best beloved brother,
>
> I humbly recommend me to your grace. Sire, so it is that I have been very sick, and ill at ease, for the which I was fain to send for Master Peter the physician, for to have holpen me of the disease that I have. Howbeit I am rather worse than better. Wherefore

I trust surely to come upto London with my lord; for and if I should tarry here, I am sure I should never aspear the sickness that I have. Wherefore, Sire, I would be the gladlier a great deal to come thither, because I would be glad to see your grace, the which I do think long for to do; for I have been a great while out of your sight, and now I trust I shall not be so long again; for the sight of your grace is to me the greatest comfort that may be possible. No more to your grace at this time, but I pray God send you your heart's desire, and shortly to the sight of you.

By your loving sister MARY, the French Queen.[44]

Frustratingly Mary's letters give no indication as to what she was suffering from. In his first letter Brandon referred to 'her old disease in her side' suggesting that whatever the problem was may have been recurring. Poor health seems to have plagued Mary throughout her life. In her childhood she suffered from unknown illnesses for which she received medicines, and as she grew she complained of toothaches and issues that may have been related to menstruation or other gynaecological problems. In 1516 Mary suffered from a severe bout of ague as well as constant pains in her side that vexed her so greatly she was reduced to tears. It may have been a combination of these illnesses that would eventually lead to Mary's early death.

10

Concerning France

❧

'The French couldn't stop gazing at her because she looked
more like an angel than a human creature.'

On 23 September 1518 French ambassadors arrived in England
with the hopes of forming a new alliance. In the summer of that
year Mary Tudor, the two-year-old daughter of Henry VIII and
Katherine of Aragon and Mary's namesake, had been betrothed to
the Dauphin, Francis I and Claude's seven-month-old son.[1]

On 2 October at St Paul's, the Treaty of Universal Peace was
signed between France and England.[2] The treaty declared that
neither member of the treaty should attack the other and that if one
party was attacked the other would provide aid. The treaty also
saw the return of Tournai to France for which Henry would be paid
compensation. The remainder of Mary's dowry, worth 323,000
crowns, was to be settled and it was further agreed that regular
payments of Mary's French pension would be made.[3]

After the signing, there was supper and a play. Henry participated,
as he loved to do, as did his sister Mary. They had the main parts:

...twelve male and twelve female maskers, made their appearance
in the richest and most sumptuous array possible, being all
dressed alike. After performing certain dances in their own
fashion, they took off their visors: the two leaders were the King
and Queen Dowager of France, and all the others were lords and

ladies, who seated themselves apart from the tables, and were served with countless dishes of confections and other delicacies. Having gratified their palates, they then regaled their eyes and hands; large bowls, filled with ducats and dice, being placed on the table for such as liked to gamble: shortly after which, the supper tables being removed, dancing commenced, and lasted until after midnight.[4]

It must have been a delight for Mary to be back at court. On 5 October in the queen's chamber at Greenwich, Princess Mary was betrothed to the Dauphin of France by proxy. The French admiral stood in for the infant dauphin and the ambassadors asked the King and Queen of England for their consent to the marriage. Wolsey placed a diamond ring on Princess Mary's tiny finger. Henry stood before his throne while Queen Katherine stood on one side of the throne and Mary on the other. A Mass was held, followed by a magnificent banquet.[5]

As part of the alliance, a meeting between Henry and Francis was to be organised for the following year. Before the organisation for this meeting could begin, the Holy Roman Emperor Maximilian died on 12 January 1519[6] and a new emperor had to be elected. Many names were put forward, including Henry VIII and Francis I. For most of Europe, it was a foregone conclusion that Maximilian's grandson, Prince Charles of Castile, would be elected. It came as no surprise when Charles was elected on 28 July 1519. Due to these political changes in the Hapsburg Empire, the meeting between Francis and Henry was postponed until the middle of 1520.

Mary's whereabouts between the end of 1518 and the end of 1519 are a matter of conjecture. It may have been that she retired from court to give birth to her third child, a daughter named Eleanor, who was born between 1518 and 1521, although there are no records surrounding the circumstances of her birth, or her christening. Eleanor may have been named to honour Charles V's favourite sister. It can be assumed that she was christened as all babies were and that godparents were appointed.[7] We are able to locate Mary in September 1519 at one of her favourite places, Butley Priory. By this time Mary was becoming known as a patroness. On 27 September she wrote to Thomas Wolsey regarding the brother of one of her well-loved servants:

Right reverend father in God,

In my heartiest wise I commend me to you. And whereas it was so that at your last being with my lord and me at Letheringham hall, I did instance you to be good and gracious lord unto my trusty and well-beloved servant Susan Savage, as for concerning the trouble of her brother Antony Savage, in the which premises your grace the same time did promise to shew your gracious favours in all thecauses reasonable of the said Antony; and in trust whereof I have caused the said Susan Savage to inquire and bring forth before your grace her said brother upon your foresaid promise. And for because that I have caused him to be brought before you at this time, therefore I do pray you in my most heartiest manner, that according unto your promise to me made you will be good and gracious lordunto the foresaid Antony in all his foresaid causes. And in so doing your grace shall not only do a meritorious deed to be rewarded of God, but also bind me at all times to be as ready to do your grace or any of yours as far pleasures; as knoweth our Lord; who keep your grace.

From Butley abbey, the 27th day of September.

By your loving friend,

Mary the French Queen.[8]

Anthony Savage and several members of his family had legal troubles regarding local autonomy, corruption, and rights of sanctuary. The previous year in February several of the men of the Savage family had been accused of murder and abuse of authority.[9] Due to Mary's great love of her servant Susan, she sought Thomas Wolsey's intercession. Mary's letter showed that she had previously had a conversation with Wolsey regarding intervening in Savage's legal case. Four months later Mary wrote once more to Wolsey telling him that the legal case against Anthony Savage had cost him everything and he was under such extreme financial strain that he feared it would be the end of him.

Myn especiall good lorde in mynn moost harty wise I commende me vnto you hertely besechyng you to be good lorde unto Anthony Savage. And to have in your remembraunce the promise that ye made unto me at Letheringhamm concernyng thobteynyng of his pardone. Wherin I pray you now to be his good lorde the better for my sake and as this mynn especiall desire. My lorde I write not unto you for that I think you have forgotyn your said promyse herin. But in consideracion of his long and peynefull suyt that he hath hadde and susteyned to his utter undoing wherby he is so farr enpoverisshed that he hath not wherby to lyve nether without somme gracious remedy may be shortly for hym provyded he shall never be. Able to lyve in tyme to come I amm so bolde to desire you of your goodnes to have hym in your good remembraunce. And to have remors and pitie unto hymm in this bihalff And thus the holy goost have you in blissed keping

From henham the xxijth day of January

By yowres Marie the Frenche queen.[10]

While we do not know the exact outcome of Anthony Savage's legal case, it is known that in May 1520 Savage received a pardon. This may have in part due to Mary's pleading letters to Wolsey.

At the beginning of 1520 arrangements were finally being made for the grand meeting between Henry and Francis. On 16 March 1520 Brandon replied to a letter from Wolsey wherein the Cardinal asked him how many horses and people Mary would be taking with her to France. Brandon leaves the details with Wolsey and asks him 'take the peyne to ordre the same as ye shall think shall stonde moost with the kinges pleasur and her honor'.[11]

Unfortunately, the list of those who attended Mary no longer survives, but it is known that Brandon took with him five chaplains, ten gentlemen, fifty-five servants and thirty horses. All of these would have been paid out of Brandon's own pocket and the expense of transporting, feeding and clothing these men appropriately would have been extremely high. Brandon brought along his own armour and throughout the celebrations Brandon participated in multiple jousts.

While the arrangements for the fabulous Field of Cloth of Gold were being organised, Henry was beginning to doubt England's alliance with France. With Maximilian's grandson elected as Charles V, Holy Roman Emperor, the English king was starting to think that a better alliance might be made with Spain. Therefore he sent out an invitation for Charles V to come to England. Charles V was to be crowned on 23 October 1519 and he informed Henry that he would visit England during his journey from Spain to Aachen. Charles was delayed and did not arrive in England until the beginning of May 1520, shortly before Henry was due to leave for his meeting with Francis.[12]

Charles V and his entourage arrived at Dover on Saturday 26 May 1520. Here he was met by Wolsey and invited to stay at Dover Castle. Upon hearing of the Emperor's arrival Henry rode to Dover to visit him. Accompanying Charles V was Germaine de Foix, Dowager Queen of Aragon and the second wife and widow of Ferdinand of Aragon (Queen Katherine's father). The following day Henry and his men escorted Charles V to Canterbury where the court waited to depart for France. Despite the lateness of Charles V's arrival, Henry ensured the Holy Roman Emperor was suitably entertained.[13]

Upon their arrival, the emperor and the king went to Canterbury Cathedral where they were both blessed by the Archbishop of Canterbury. The pair walked to the Archbishop's lodgings, which had been carefully prepared for Charles V's visit. At the top of the stairs Charles was greeted by his aunt, Queen Katherine, who was dressed in a magnificent gown of gold. On seeing her nephew Katherine wept and embraced him warmly.

After breakfast another Mass was held, which Mary attended. Mary and Katherine sat in a second enclosure away from Henry and Charles, so it may be possible that at this time Charles still had not seen the woman to whom he had once been formally engaged. Mary, as always, was extravagantly dressed 'in silver lamé, in plates, joined throughout with gold cords at the extremities of which were fine pearls instead of tags'.[14]

Once Mass was completed Henry and Charles dined together accompanied by Queen Katherine and Mary. Still young, Mary had retained her beauty and must have shone. The chronicler Hall recorded that she had prepared an entirely new wardrobe for Charles V's arrival.[15] 'For these noble meetings of so high princes: and especially the Queen of England and the Lady Dowager of France, made great cost on the apparel of their ladies and gentlemen.'[16] What did Charles think on first seeing the woman to whom he was once engaged? Did he feel as though she had slipped through his fingers? In 1519 Charles was still an eligible bachelor and may have lamented the loss.

After dinner there was dancing and Germaine de Foix, Dowager Queen of Aragon and her ladies were escorted by Mary and 200 Spanish ladies into Canterbury. The following day another Mass was held in which Mary, dressed in a gown of silver lamé, accompanied Germaine de Foix, both women walking behind Queen Katherine.

After Mass another dinner was held, during which Charles V sat at the centre of the table; Henry to his left and Queen Katherine to his right. Mary sat beside her brother and Queen Germaine next to Katherine.[17] After the meal followed an evening of entertainment and dancing. Mary, always enjoying such an opportunity, danced with her brother and her husband. Charles was invited to dance; he politely declined.[18] The romantic view is that Charles refused to dance as he was lamenting the loss of Mary as a wife.

On the Tuesday, Charles, Germaine de Foix and the rest of the Spanish court left Dover, bade farewell by Henry, Katherine and Mary.[19] Another meeting had been organised for shortly after Henry's visit to France. Until that time the whole court had to turn their mind to the departure for France.

The Field of Cloth of Gold was a spectacular event to be held from 7 to 24 June 1520, on a piece of land between the English-held town of Guines and the French town of Ardres. The land was dubbed the Field of Cloth of Gold because of the cloth the English had commissioned for the main tent. The event was organised to celebrate the ratification of the Treaty of London between England and France.[20]

Henry was determined to show the French the riches and greatness of England. To do so he ordered ornate clothing to be designed and made, expensive furnishings to be collected and a magnificent pavilion to be created in which the royal family would reside. While the royal coffers paid for many of these items, other members of the nobility were forced to pay their own expenses. These included furnishings, clothing, horses, and weapons and armour for those participating in the jousts. Such was the expense that many noblemen had to mortgage their houses, sell property and take out loans in order to take part in this extraordinary event.

On 31 May 1520 Henry and his entourage, including Mary and her husband, set sail from Dover accompanied by approximately 5,000 men and women, together with some 3,000 horses.[21] They landed at Calais and rested a time before travelling to Guisnes on 5 June.[22]

On 7 June the French and English kings finally met in a valley between Guines and Ardres. Henry wore cloth of silver decorated with jewels and a hat with white plumes and Francis wore cloth of gold frieze and jewels. The kings rode towards one another and when they met they removed their bonnets, dismounted and embraced one another warmly. They were led to an English pavilion where they could talk.[23] A spectacular pavilion had been set up for the king and Katherine to stay in during the event. The pavilion apparently covered four acres and was made up of wood and canvas tents that could be joined together or separated by hangings to form rooms. Within the pavilion there were private apartments and a chapel.[24] Sketches of the pavilion show that it was made from red cloth decorated with Tudor roses and fleur-de-lis and fringed with gold. The mottos '*Dieu et mon droit*' and '*semper vavat in eterno*' were embroidered on the eaves. On the top of each pavilion pole were models of beasts including greyhounds, dragons, antelope and lions.[25] It is estimated that 6,000 people were hired to build the pavilion and the other tents.[26] Mary and her husband Charles Brandon had the honour of residing in one wing.[27]

The Field of Cloth of Gold event lasted seventeen days and included a range of entertainments including archery, wrestling, jousting, magnificent feasts and of course the exchanging of expensive gifts. Although an outward display of friendship and unity, the events were a chance for each country to try and outdo the other in strength, skill and a show of wealth.

The Duke of Suffolk was one of the stars of the jousts. On Thursday 14 June he ran twenty-four courses, broke eighteen staves and scored three hits. This was a tremendous display of strength, skill and stamina and for his efforts he was rewarded with great prizes.[28] Mary was the star of the grand meeting. As Dowager Queen of France and a princess of England she was the connection between both countries. Mary had a good understanding of the French ways of course. On 11 June Mary proceeded to the tiltyard, carried in a litter of cloth of gold embroidered with lilies and monograms of L and M, signifying Mary's marriage to the late King Louis XII. It is reported that the French were delighted by Mary's beauty, which had not faded despite childbirth and illness.[29]

One evening King Francis dined in the English camp where he was entertained by Queen Katherine. Katherine and Francis sat opposite one another at the head table, each under a cloth of estate. Mary was sat at a table by herself, a few yards from the French king.[30] By having a table to herself, Mary was allowed to shine in her beauty and grace and this isolation underscored her position as the Dowager Queen of France. On the 17th Mary accompanied her brother and dined at the French camp with Queen Claude.[31] On another occasion Mary and Henry entered the French camp accompanied by a party of masqueraders.[32]

When the whole extravaganza finished on 24 June, Francis returned to Abbeville. Instead of returning to England immediately, Henry and his court went to Gravelines where they met Charles V, the Holy Roman Emperor. Once more, a possible alliance between England and Spain was discussed. More discussions were held in which Henry's daughter was offered as a bride for her cousin Charles V, but a formal treaty of friendship was not finally agreed until 25 August 1521, more than two years later.

After the Field of Cloth of Gold we hear nothing of Mary until the beginning of 1522. It may have been that the cost of taking both Brandon's and her entourage and presenting themselves in such splendour had taxed the Brandon household to the limit and that Mary removed herself from court in an attempt to save money. Or perhaps she simply wished to spend time with her growing family while her husband conducted business and represented them both at court.

The theme at court for Shrovetide in March 1522 was 'unrequited love'. To celebrate, a series of jousting events were held. The highlight of the celebrations was a pageant held at Cardinal Wolsey's York Place on the evening of Shrove Tuesday. It is here that we catch another glimpse of Mary. The pageant was entitled the Château Vert (or the green castle). At the beginning of the night the audience were led into a large chamber hung with arras and brightly lit. At one end of the hall was the 'Château Vert'. The castle was built of wood and painted green, consisting of three towers. In the towers were eight beautiful ladies, each representing a quality of chivalry. The women were dressed in white satin with their 'quality' written on their gowns in yellow satin. They wore headdresses of Venetian gold and Milan bonnets. The qualities the women represented were beauty, honour, perseverance, kindness, constancy, bounty, mercy and pity. Mary played the lead role of beauty, Anne Boleyn made her debut at court as perseverance and her sister Mary played kindness.[33] Opposite these eight women were eight men representing the perfect male virtues: nobleness, amorousness, youth, attendance, loyalty, pleasure, gentleness and liberty.

The eight female virtues were protected from assault by eight members of the royal chapel dressed as Indian women representing danger, disdain, jealousy, unkindness, scorn, sharp tongue and off-handedness. A spokesman for the male virtues asked for the women to come down but the negative virtues resisted and the male virtues had to storm the castle by force. Henry led the attack on the castle; the men threw oranges, dates and other fruits thought to bring pleasure. The women were rescued and it may have been that Henry rescued his beautiful sister. After this everyone took off their masks off to reveal who they were and a the feasting began.[34]

After these pageants we hear nothing of Mary until the loss of her firstborn son. Sometime during 1522 the young Henry died. There are no details surrounding the boy's death. At just five or six years of age, the little boy could have died from a number of illnesses or accidents. One can only imagine how devastated Mary must have been over the loss of her son. There are also no records of where Henry was buried. It may have been in a church near his home at Westhorpe.

The only positve development at this time was that Mary was pregnant for the fourth time and sometime during 1522 she gave birth to another son. He too was named Henry, once more after the king, although no further information about his birth, location or christening survives.[35]

As well as having three surviving children Mary had two stepdaughters to care for, Anne and Mary, daughters of Brandon's first wife, Anne Browne. By now Anne was sixteen years of age and Mary was twelve. Both were of marriageable age so Mary and her husband had to turn their attention to finding suitable husbands, and dowries, for both girls. By March 1525 Anne married Edward Grey, Lord Powis.[36] Brandon had purchased Grey's wardship in 1517 for the sum of £1,000[37] (£380,000).[38] Anne had been at the court of Margaret, Duchess of Savoy and Regent of the Netherlands, in order to further her education. However, at the insistence of Mary, Anne was recalled to England.[39] Mary wished her family, including her stepdaughters, to be by her side. Mary appears to be a woman who deeply loved all her children.

Brandon's other daughter by his first wife, Mary, was married to Thomas Stanley, Lord Monteagle, sometime in 1527 or early 1528. As with Edward Grey, Brandon had purchased Thomas Stanley's wardship. Later, Stanley would be appointed as a Knight of the Bath during the coronation of Henry's second wife, Anne Boleyn. He also took part in Anne Boleyn's trial in May 1536, as a member of the jury who found her guilty of treason. Mary Stanley (*née* Brandon) went on to give her husband six children, three sons, William, Francis and Charles, and three daughters, Elizabeth, Anne and Margaret. Mary would serve Henry's third wife Jane Seymour as a lady-in-waiting.[40] During her marriage there was some unspecified allegation from Grey regarding Mary's misbehaviour; if there was any truth in the accusation it remains unknown.[41]

For their son, the second Henry, Mary and Charles Brandon sought a greater marriage. At this point little Henry Brandon was the only legitimate male heir to the English throne and Mary and Brandon needed to find a future wife befitting such a position. In March 1528 Brandon bought from the king the wardship of Katherine Willoughby, daughter and heiress of the late Lord Willoughby de Eresby who had died in October 1526, for an impressive £2,266 13s 4d[42] (£860,000).[43] Katherine had a large inheritance from her father and thus would bring young Henry a large sum of money and extensive lands.

Returning to international relations, in the spring of 1521 France attacked Naverre and an attack was made against Imperial Luxemburg in the name of France. While both attacks were unsuccessful France had broken the Treaty of London and Henry was now forced to make a decision. Would he support France or the Holy Roman Empire?

Over the next few months negotiations took place between England and Spain. On August 25 1521 the secret Treaty of Bruges was signed between Charles V and Thomas Wolsey on behalf of Henry VIII, declaring that Henry would support Charles in the war against France. In May 1523 England officially declared war on France.[44] This created a difficult financial situation for Mary and Brandon. A substantial part of the Brandon income was Mary's dowager pension of £4,000 (£1,518,000)[45] per annum. War with France halted that payment.[46] Brandon was receiving a small pension from Francis and that too stopped.[47] Brandon was ever the opportunist and when Charles V visited England for a second time, he hosted an event at Suffolk Place where Henry and the Emperor dined and hunted. Mary would have ensured the Emperor was wined and dined to the limit of the household budget. Brandon was able to secure a small imperial pension, although this could not make up in full for the grand sum that Mary had lost.[48]

At the end of August 1522 Brandon was appointed Lieutenant-General[49] and sent to Calais at the head of an army of 10,000 men.[50] Brandon was to be paid 100s a day. As a comparison of income with the ordinary members of the army, foot soldiers received 6d a day and those men on horseback, 8d a day.[51] Brandon reached Calais on 24 August. There were difficulties with supplies and plague in the area. Some of the men in Brandon's army became infected.[52] Mary stayed in England, probably at Westhorpe, with her young children and stepdaughters.

The campaign began on 1 October.[53] Brandon's initial target was Boulogne. On 26 September Henry issued orders for Brandon to march straight for Paris.[54] The aim was for a triple attack on the capital. The French Duke of Bourbon, who was rebelling against the French king, would attack from the south; Charles V and his army would attack from the east and Brandon and his men from the north. After receiving Burgundian reinforcements, Brandon's army took the French stronghold of Belle Castle and utterly destroyed it. Between 18 and 20 October they destroyed the riverside crossing at Bray and on the 28th Brandon's army captured Montdidier in northern France.[55] Along the way to Paris other towns surrendered and soon Brandon was within 80 km of the city. Events did not turn out as planned.

Charles V was more interested in securing his Pyrenean frontier and focused much of his effort on the war in Northern Italy. Once Charles had recaptured the port of Fuenterrabia he held back his army. The Duke of Bourbon's revolt fell apart and the aid that Margaret of Austria had promised did not come.[56] Brandon was left at the head of 10,000 men with no reinforcements or method of resupply.

By November, winter was upon the English army. There was heavy rain followed by an intense frost. Many men died from the cold or the plague and Brandon faced the choice of digging in for the winter just outside of Paris or returning to Calais. He chose the latter. By mid-December Brandon and his men were back in Calais waiting for suitable conditions to cross to England. Brandon returned in the New Year. Of the 10,000 men that had left for the campaign in August, fewer than half returned.

Henry VIII openly blamed the Duke of Bourbon for the failure of the attack and no blame was laid on Brandon. Despite the failure to take Paris, Brandon had proved himself as a military commander. He had deferred to his war council, but had also made crucial decisions regarding the invasion that had proved valuable. His military efforts showed the king that Brandon was an effective, skilled and trustworthy commander, which surely improved Brandon's standing.[57]

Soon another chance of war with the old enemy France arose. In February, just outside the Lombard town of Pavia, French troops had been crushed in battle by the imperial army. Francis I had been captured and was now Charles V's prisoner. When Henry heard the news he openly expressed his joy. Outwardly, Mary may have rejoiced at the capture of the French king, England now being aligned with Spain; internally, her feelings may have been a very different matter. With Francis's capture there was little chance that Mary's French pension would ever be paid regularly.

On hearing the news of the French king's capture Henry declared that God had provided this opportunity to once more go to war with France.[58] Yet as much as the king desired war, his coffers were near empty, drained by the French war two years previously.[59] The idea of an 'Amicable Grant' was soon proposed, aiming to bring in around £800,000 (£303,660,000).[60] To bypass Parliament the grant was designed so that people were not levied to pay taxes, but rather to give 'gifts' of money to the king for the purpose of war.[61] A specific amount was required calculated on income.

The clergy were required to pay a third of their income if they earned more than £10 (£3,800)[62] per annum. The common people who earned over £50 (£19,000)[63] a year were required to pay 3s 4d in the pound. People earning £20 and £50[64] per annum needed to pay 2s 8d per pound, and anyone earning less than £20 (£7,600) per annum were ordered to pay 1s per pound.

Between 1522 and 1523 a loan of £250,000 (£94,900,000) had been forced on the common people and as of 1525 it had not been repaid.[65] Now the king was demanding more money. With people struggling financially there were soon rumblings of dissent in Essex, Kent, Norfolk, Warwickshire and Huntingdonshire.[66] The people protested that the levy had not been passed through Parliament and therefore they were not required to hand over their money. The clergy argued that they had not agreed to it in convocation. In Lavenham, Suffolk, around 4,000 people came together to protest against the grant.[67] To counter this Henry VIII sent the dukes of Norfolk and Suffolk to the area to dispel the protest and to deal with any rebels. Several leaders of the protest were arrested and taken to Fleet Prison.

Hearing of the great discontent throughout the country Henry quickly laid the blame on Thomas Wolsey. He claimed that he knew nothing of the grant[68] and in a council meeting he stated 'that his mynd was neuer, to aske any thyng of his commons, whiche might sounde to his dishonor, or to the breche of his lawes'.[69] All talk of the grant and going to war with France was dropped.[70]

The war with France stopped the payments of both Mary's and Brandon's French pensions. In August 1525 Mary wrote to Wolsey asking for assistance in the restoration of her pension (presumably with the non-payments to be included in the total sum):

My lord.
In my most hearty wise I commend me unto you. So it is, divers of my rights and duties concerning my dote in France have been of late time stayed and restrained, in such wise as I nor mine officers there may not have nor receive the same, as they have done in

times past; being to my damages therein, and to their great trouble many ways, as my trusty servant George Hampton, this bearer, shall show unto you, to whom I pray you to give credence in the same. And, my lord, in these and in all others, I evermore have and do put mine only trust and confidence in you, for the redress of the same; entirely desiring you, therefore, that I may have the king's grace's my dearest brother's letters, and yours, into France, to such as my said servant shall desire. And by the same I trust my said causes shall be brought to such good conclusion and order now, that I shall from henceforth enjoy my rights there, in as ample wise as I have done heretofore.

And, so it may stand with your pleasure, I would gladly my said dearest brother's ambassadors, being in France, now by your good means should have the delivery of all these said letters, with their furtherance of the contents of the same, to that they may do. And thus, my lord, I am evermore bold to put you to pains without any recompense, unless my good mind and hearty prayer, whereof you shall be assured during my life to the best of my power; as knoweth our Lord, who have you on his blessed tuition.

At Wingfield castle, the third day of August
Yours assured,
Mary the French Queen.
To mine especial good lord my Lord Cardinal.[71]

Without regular payments coming from France, Brandon was forced to borrow £12,000 (£4,555,000)[72] from the Crown in 1515/1516 and an additional £3,000 (£1,139,000)[73] from the revenues of his offices in Wales.[74]

Mary's son, Henry, was made an earl in a double ceremony with Henry Fitzroy, the king's illegitimate son by Bessie Blount. On 18 June 1525 at Bridewell Palace, Henry Fitzroy was created Earl of Nottingham and given the dukedoms of Richmond and Somerset. The young boy came out and knelt before the king, and once he was created Duke of Richmond and Somerset he took his place on the dais beside his father. Following this Henry Brandon, now only two or three years old, was created Earl of Lincoln.[75] The earldom may have been granted to him as it was closely associated with the De La Poles. The king was distancing not only the title but the people of East Anglia from the rebellious De La Pole family. Whatever the reason behind little Henry Brandon's elevation, it was another demonstration of the king's contentment with his parents.

Just over two months later, on 30 August, the Treaty of More was signed between Cardinal Wolsey and Francis I's mother, Louise of Savoy, who was acting as regent of France during her son's imprisonment. The treaty was signed by Wolsey and Louise of Savoy's ambassadors John Brinon and John Joachim at Wolsey's home, The More. The treaty would see Henry VIII give up some of his territorial claims to France in return for a substantial income as well as all the back payments of Mary's French pension.[76]

Giovanni Gioachino departed England for Calais in October 'to bring 50,000 ducats from France on account of the pensions, and 10,000 ducats for Madame Mary, the King's sister, Queen Dowager of France'.[77] We do not know if Mary ever received this back payment. Her constant financial struggles suggest she either did not receive the pension or only received part payment and that if these sums were paid, they disappeared into the royal coffers to reduce the outstanding loans to the Brandons.

On 14 January 1526 Francis I and Charles V signed the Treaty of Madrid. In the treaty Francis relinquished his claims to Burgundy, Italy and Artois. In return for his freedom he was to send his two sons, Henry and Francis, to be 'guests' of Charles V. In effect the boys were hostages. On 17 March 1526 Francis was finally freed.[78] On hearing the news of the French king's release Mary wrote to Francis on 9 May to congratulate him. Mary reminded Francis of her love and promising that if she could have helped him she would have done so. The declaration that she 'will always have need in my affaires of your good grace' is probably a not particuarly subtle reference to her dowager pension.

My lord, I cannot congratulate you enough on your joyous and greatly desired return to your realm. And above all that it has pleased God to bring you back to health, and in the same proportion to the distress of your capture and the grievous and dangerous illness that you have had, which gave me great pain, the greater has been the joy of your return and the recovery of

your good health, and not only to me, who feel myself obliged to you for so many reasons, but also to the King of England, my lord and brother, and generally to all the princes and lords of this country. And if the ladies are to be placed in that number, they deserve to have good part therein, because there are none of them who have seen you nor any who have heard of the virtues and graces that God has given to you, who have not pitied you and given good and devout prayers. And if it had been possible for me, by bearing part of your troubles, to give you some relief, I would have done it with the best of hearts, such that it is not possible to express. And nonetheless I have thanked the Almighty for the grace that He has given you to deliver you from this anxiety and to bring you back in good health into your kingdom where I find so much honesty and goodness in my lady and my cousin, your good mother, that I do not know how to thank you enough. I will always have need in my affaires of your good grace, to which very humbly I recommend myself, and praying that He will give you very good and long life. Written in our manor of Southwark, London, this 9th day of May.
your good mother and cousin,
Mary.[79]

Mary had faced many struggles since her return to England. She had lost her firstborn son in 1522 at six years of age and had to face the constant struggles for her French pension. Yet she had also experienced many joys. She was the mother of three healthy children, as well as two stepdaughters, and her youngest had been created the Earl of Lincoln – and at this point in her brother's reign, was the only legitimate male heir to the throne. She had regained her brother's favour and love, participated in magnificent events at court as well as returning to France to be present at the spectacular Field of Cloth of Gold. By the end of 1526, Mary was thirty years old and had suffered several serious bouts of ill health. From this time forward Mary slowly slipped into the shadows, preferring to spend her time away from court rather than in the limelight.

11

The Final Years

❧

'The Duchess of Suffolk, the late Queen Dowager of France, is
dead.'

There are few records of the last six years of Mary's life. The
woman who had lived her life for so many years in the spotlight
was now being eclipsed. Events at court were beginning to unravel.

In 1527 the first steps had been taken to acquire an annulment
of Henry VIII's marriage to Katherine of Aragon. The pair had
married on 8 June 1509. By 1527 the couple had been married for
eighteen years and only had one surviving daughter. Henry wanted
a secure future for the Tudors and that meant a male heir. For poor
Katherine there had been multiple pregnancies and all but one had
resulted in miscarriage, stillbirth, or death only weeks after birth.
Henry was desperate for a legitimate son and began to have doubts
about the legitimacy of his marriage. While the story of Henry VIII
and Katherine of Aragon's divorce is far too long to tell here, it
must be mentioned briefly as it frames the final six years of Mary
Tudor's life.

Henry claimed adamantly that he had broken God's holy law. He
referred to the passage in Leviticus, chapter 20 verse 21, which stated
that 'if a man shall take his brother's wife, it is an impurity, he hath
uncovered his brother's nakedness, they shall be childless.'[1] Henry
chose to disregard his daughter's existence and regarded himself
childless because he had no living legitimate sons. He believed that

by taking his brother's widow as his wife he had broken the Word of God. Katherine for her part argued that she was the true Queen of England, that she had never had sexual intercourse with Arthur and she was a true maid when she came to her wedding bed with Henry. Therefore they had not broken any law and God had chosen to bless them with a daughter. Pope Julius II had granted a dispensation for Henry and Katherine's marriage, yet Henry now argued that the Julius II had exceeded his powers and had no authority to grant any dispensation.[2]

Pope Clement VII was unable to grant Henry VIII a divorce, or to renounce the dispensation. Apart from the fact that once a papal dispensation is given, it cannot be withdrawn, there were more pressing events for the Pope. On June 1 1527 Rome had been ransacked by the imperial army, led by the Holy Roman Emperor, Charles V and the Pope had been besieged in Castel Sant'Angelo until June of 1527, when he surrendered and paid a ransom in exchange for his freedom.[3] Charles V was Katherine of Aragon's nephew and Clement VII was in no position to sanction his captor's aunt being removed from her position as Queen of England. The imperial forces finally withdrew in February 1528. Continued pressure from Thomas Wolsey together with the withdrawal of the imperial forces saw the Pope's final release. He finally agreed to send a papal legate to England. Cardinal Campeggio was chosen for this task, but was given secret instructions to stall the hearing for as long as possible.[4] Campeggio was an old man riddled with gout and, frustratingly for Henry and Thomas Wolsey, his journey to England was slow and painful.[5] The Italian Cardinal finally arrived in London on 8 December 1528 where he was lodged overnight at Charles Brandon's house, most likely at Southwark, before being taken to Bath House the next evening.[6] The hearing for Henry VIII's' Great Matter' officially started at Blackfriars on 31 May 1529.[7]

Mary was implacably against the annulment. Part of it may have been that she objected to her brother questioning the authority of the Pope. Mary had been raised a Catholic and seemed to have been traditional in her beliefs, never showing any indication that she was interested in the religious Reformation that was sweeping across Europe. Although little is known about Mary's religious views there is a small insight into her husband's beliefs. Arthur Bulkeley was chaplain to Brandon from around 1530. It is unclear when he left Brandon's services, but Bulkeley was appointed Bishop of Bangor in 1541 and was consecrated on 19 February 1542. He died the following year on 14 March.[8] In addition to having Bulkeley as his personal chaplain, Brandon's chapel was graced with statues of saints and he hired Nicholas Cutler to be the master of six choir boys.[9] Brandon was also known to patronise former monks.[10] Brandon appears to have followed traditional Catholic teachings and therefore it can be assumed that Mary would have attended Mass regularly in the family chapel. In addition, it is known that Mary often visited Butley Priory, one of her favourite places, and attended Mass there.

Mary may have objected to her brother's annulment due to her personal religious views. However, it is also likely that she took offence due to her deep and long friendship with Queen Katherine. Mary and Katherine had known one another since Katherine had arrived in England in 1502. They were sisters-in-law, first through Katherine's short-lived marriage to Arthur and then through her marriage to Henry VIII. The pair would have seen each other regularly at court and many records survive of Katherine and Mary attending banquets, sitting together watching pageants and jousting events as well as enjoying dancing and other displays in one another's company. In addition, in March 1517, Mary and Brandon hosted Queen Katherine while the queen was on pilgrimage to the shrine of Our Lady, at the Austin Priory at Walsingham.[11] The women clearly became close over the years. Mary and Katherine would have shared their joys and triumphs as queens, their fears and concerns over their husbands. They would have bonded over their mutual love for Henry, as brother and husband. They would have shared heartbreak and joy in the birth and loss of their children. For Mary, to see her friend and the woman she felt to be rightly queen, cast aside for another must have been shocking and infuriating. Worse, Henry's eye had turned to Anne Boleyn.

Anne Boleyn had been a lady of Mary's while Mary was married to Louis XII. Although not a great deal is known of Anne's actions at this time, Mary would have been familiar with the girl who was about five years her junior. She met Anne again during the

Shrovetide celebrations and at the pageant Château Vert, which took place at York Place, London, where Mary played the role of beauty and Anne that of perseverance. With Anne becoming a regular feature at court, Mary would have watched as her brother began to pursue Anne and cast Katherine aside.

Meanwhile, in March 1528 Brandon had bought the wardship of Katherine Willoughby from the king with the intent of marrying Katherine to his son Henry.[12] There are no records regarding Mary's thoughts or feelings about this marriage, or of her views on young Katherine. Shortly after purchasing Katherine's wardship the young girl came to live with Mary to be raised and educated. Katherine Willoughby, the daughter and sole heir of William, 11th Baron Willoughby and Maria De Salinas, was born on 22 March 1519. Maria was a lady of waiting to Katherine of Aragon who had come from Spain with her in 1502 to England to marry the late Prince Arthur.[13] A marriage with Katherine would bring Mary and Brandon's son wealth as well as a beautiful wife with a strong family lineage.

To be sent to live with a prominent member of court or someone of importance and to become their ward was common during the Tudor age. For example, Anne Boleyn gained a position within Margaret of Austria, Duchess of Savoy's court to learn the skills required to be an intelligent and dutiful woman.[14] Brandon had sent his oldest daughter Anne to serve Margaret of Austria for a period of time before being recalled on Mary's wishes in 1515.[15] To be taken in as a ward was also helpful to the family as they no longer had to provide not only food and clothing for the child and were not required to pay for the child's education. When Mary Boleyn's husband, William Carey, died in 1528, she was left in a precarious position, with little money and two children to raise. Her son, Henry, became a ward of his aunt Anne Boleyn. It would have been Anne's responsibility to see the boy clothed and educated and this helped to relieve the financial burden for Mary Boleyn.[16]

By being sent to live with the Brandons, Katherine had the opportunity to learn many skills. Katherine would have watched and been guided by Mary in all manners concerning the running of a noble household as well as how to conduct oneself. In the latter years of her life Katherine Willoughby was a frequent letter writer.

Katherine may have learned her epistolary skills, particularly how to request service and favours from others, from Mary.

In 1528 Mary continued her patronage and support of those in her service. In January Mary began to write a series of letters to Anne de Montmorency, the Grand Master of France. She attempted to help her clerk of the closet, Anthoine du Val, obtain a similar position in the service of King Francis I.[17] Mary's first letter was dated 15 January:

Monsieur, the Grand Master,

I am very sorry not to have had the opportunity of [word unknown] you in this country that I might have offered you the reception which at all times is due to you, since I hear that the affairs of the king my son-in-law, your master, are very well conducted through your good means, on which account you receive honour, and I am greatly pleased. Monsieur the Grand master, there is over there [in France] a person named Anthoine du Val, who, from the time of my going to France, served the king my husband, – the deceased prince, of good and blessed memory, whom God absolve, in the office of clerk of the closet; and since his death, has likewise attended me in the same office, in which he has conducted himself very worthily. And since I have heard that, hitherto, he has not been able to gain admission to the same position, in the house of the king my said son-in-law, for which I feel grieved, I determined to make application to you, for this Anthoine da Val; that you will be pleased at this my request, to cause to be given to him the first vacant office of clerk of the closet, in the household of the said lord, and to hasten to him the letters of retaining, placing him speedily in attendance, so that on the occurrence of the vacancy, none may step in but himself. And what moves me to write to you is, that you have the power to do this, and also that I verily believe you will not refuse me as I place confidence in you, as well in this, as in greater affairs; praying you very kindly to let him understand that this present, according to my request, has been of service to him. If I had spoken to you by word of months I should have offered the request to you; commending yon, Monsieur, to God, whom I pray to give yon his grace. Written at Norwich, the 15th day of January.

Mary's request appeared to have been unsuccessful. However, she was determined not to give up on behalf of her servant du Val. She wrote to Anne de Montmorency twice more, on 18 June 1528[18] and 26 December 1528[19] continuing to try and have him secure a position in Francis I's court for du Val. In addition to writing to Montmorency, Mary also wrote to her childhood friend, Jane Popincourt, in an attempt to gain her support. Popincourt had been placed within Mary's household when Mary was a child in order to assist Mary in learning French through conversation. As previously mentioned, Popincourt had been suggested as one of the women to come to France to attend Mary when she was queen but because of her affair with the Duke of Longueville, Louis XII immediately put a stop to this. By 1528 Jane Popincourt was back in France. From Mary's letter it appears that she and Jane had kept in contact over the years and that Jane was more than just a friend; Mary considered her to be family. It is interesting to note that Jane had sent presents for Mary's children, a touching gesture between close friends. Mary implored her friend to help her cause and do all she could to see Anthoine du Val installed as a clerk in the court of Francis I.

Mademoiselle du Poppincourt, my good friend,

I have received the letters which you yon sent me by my secretary Saint Martin with the jetvireship and the head-dresses for my children, for which, and also for the kind remembrance you have had of me, I heartily thank you; perceiving that you do not forget the benefits of the time past, and how we two were brought up together, on which account I always regard you as one of my own relatives, and demean myself more familiarity towards you than towards any other in those parts. Wherefore I am disposed to employ you, that you may, in my name, ask the Grand Master to have in his very good recommendation, Anthoine du Val, who formerly was my clerk of the closet; and that, from regard to me, he will procure for him the like situation, in the establishment of the king my son-in-law, as I wrote to him more fully; and I pray you not to be negligent in this matter, but continually to urge it so that I may obtain my request concerning him; and from time to time, may be advertised by you of his reply. In so doing, you will do me a very great kindness, which I shall never forget; and of this you may be fully assured; as knows our Lord, who have you, my good friend, in his good keeping. Written at London, the 20th day of June. Your good mistress and friend, Mary. Countersigned, De Saint Martin.

To Mademoiselle de Popincourt, my good friend.[20]

Unfortunately, the outcome for Anthoine du Val remains unknown. From Mary's many letters to Anne de Montmorency, the Grand Master of France and to her dear childhood friend Jane Popincourt, it is clear that Mary tried her very best to support her servant.

Mary's last known letter of patronage was written only three months before her death. She wrote to Viscount Lisle, Lord Lieutenant of Calais. In her letter Mary sought assistance for another servant named John Williams, hoping that he would be accepted by Lisle as a soldier at Calais:

Mary the French Queen.

Right trusty and right well-beloved cousin.

We greet you well, desiring you at this our intercession, you will be so good lord unto John Williams, this bearer, as to admit him into the room of a soldier in Calais, with the wages of eightpence by the day; assuring you, cousin, in your so doing you shall shew unto us full good and acceptable pleasure, which we shall right willingly acquit at your desire in time coming, trusting the conditions, Tiaviour (behaviour), and personage of the said John be such as you shall be contented with the same. Praying you, cousin, of your good mind herein, you will advertise us by this bearer in your writing.

At London, the 30th day of March.

To our right trusty and right well-beloved cousin the Viscount Lisle, lord lieutenant of Calais.[21]

Throughout her life Mary used her position and influence as an English princess, a Queen of France and as the lady of her household to aid and support those around her. As a Catholic it was expected that Mary would use her position to aid those of lesser means. However, it does appear that with the vigour and determination that Mary put into supporting those of her household, she was not just following her Catholic duty, but that she had a genuine love of helping and assisting others.

As Mary wrote her letters of support for John Williams, the trial, which Henry VIII hoped so desperately would secure the annulment of his marriage, did not go as planned. Cardinal Campeggio and Wolsey were to lead the trial, and despite Wolsey's strong desire to serve his king, things were not to go the cardinal's way. There were almost two months of to-ing and fro-ing, Henry's hopes relying heavily upon the arguments put forward by Wolsey. On 23 July 1529 Cardinal Campeggio announced that he could not give a final judgement until he had discussed the matter further with Pope Clement VII. He then adjourned the hearing indefinitely.

Needless to say, Henry VIII was furious. All his hopes of having a quick annulment to his marriage to Katherine of Aragon had just been dashed. Brandon, it would seem, was equally furious at the results. He had attended the trial that day, sitting with the king in a gallery above the door. After the king had stormed out in anger Brandon rose and shouted from the gallery, 'By the Mass it was never merry in England whilst we had cardinals amongst us!' Cardinal Wolsey replied 'If I, a simple cardinal, had not been, you should have had at this present time no head upon your shoulders wherein you should have a tongue to make any such report in despite of us!'[22]

Wolsey's retort was sharp and straight to the point. It was Thomas Wolsey who had interceded when Brandon had committed treason by marrying Mary without the king's permission. Brandon did not reply to Wolsey's remark and quickly hurried out in search of his king. Interestingly this is not the first time that animosity between Brandon and Wolsey had arisen. On 4 February of the same year the Spanish Ambassador Mendoza had written to his king stating that he believed Anne Boleyn thought Thomas Wolsey was trying to hinder the trial rather than bring it to the desired outcome. He also noted that he believed Brandon had joined with the Boleyns and the Duke of Norfolk to bring about the fall of Wolsey.[23] Mendoza wrote:

This suspicion [of the lady] has been the cause of her forming an alliance with her father [Viscount Rochford], and with the two

Dukes of Norfolk and Suffolk, to try and see whether they can conjointly ruin (desbaratar) the Cardinal. Hitherto they seem to have made no impression on the King, save that the Cardinal is no longer received at Court as graciously as before, and that now and then King Henry has uttered certain angry words respecting him.[24]

Although this might seem disloyal of Brandon, the duke was no fool. He knew that if he threw his lot in with Wolsey he could be brought down with him, especially since his own rival, the Duke of Norfolk, was against Wolsey. Brandon was smart enough to know that his position relied heavily on the king's good graces and, if the king was against Wolsey, then so too was Brandon. For her part, Mary had permanently removed herself from court, retiring to her home at Westhorpe, refusing to accept Anne Boleyn as anything more than her brother's mistress. Although her removal from court was seen as a protest, it may also have had something to do with Mary's failing health.[25]

In May 1529 rumours had started to spread of negotiations for a possible peace treaty between Francis I and Charles V, which were to be held at Cambrai. Desperate to see England represented, the king sent Brandon and Sir William Fitzwilliam across the Channel. After a short briefing the pair left on 17 May with the offer to provide Francis I English troops and money to go to war against Charles V.[26] On arriving in France, Brandon and Fitzwilliam were entertained at length in an attempt to stop both men from attending the peace talks at Cambrai.[27] It is important to note that once more, Brandon was sent with another, far more secret mission. He was to seek out Francis I's thoughts regarding Wolsey and to see if Francis thought the Cardinal was obstructing Henry's divorce. Francis' reply is interesting and he seems to walk a fine line, as Brandon writes in a letter to his king:

Campeggio, who told Francis he was going to England and afterwards to Spain by commission of the Pope. On which Francis asked him how he could go into Spain, and yet do what the king of England wished for the divorce; and he replied that he did not think that the divorce would take effect, but should be dissembled well enough. Thinking that the King was deceived, he told the bishop of Bath what the Cardinal had said, desiring him to advertise you of it. I then proceeded to inquire of him, promising that what he said should never be revealed, What say you of the cardinal of England in this matter? and he replied, When he was with me, as far as I could perceive, he desired that the divorce might take place, for he loved not the Queen; but I advise my good brother not to put too much trust in any man, whereby he may be deceived, and the best remedy is to look to his own matters himself; – saying further that the cardinal of England had great intelligence with the Pope and with Campeggio, and, as they are not inclined to the divorce, it is the more needful for the King to have regard to his own affairs.[28]

In the end both Brandon and Fitzwilliam were recalled from France as no matter their presence, a peace treaty between Francis I and Charles V was inevitable.[29]

In the end Henry VIII would have the annulment of his marriage, but Thomas Wolsey would not live to see it. On 9 October 1529 Wolsey was charged with praemunire, asserting the power of papal jurisdiction over the supremacy of the English monarch. The Cardinal was stripped of his role as Lord Chancellor. He was sent to Esher, Surrey, then arrested in early November 1530 and died on 29 November on his way to London for his trial.[30]

There are no records of Mary's feelings regarding Wolsey's fall from grace and his death. He had supported her secret marriage to Brandon and guaranteed that they returned from France. Yet he was also instrumental in Mary losing all of her dowry and she and Brandon being forced into debt due to the payment of a large fine. While Mary had written often to Wolsey seeking patronage for members of her household, she was also very much aware that he was beneath her station. In the end Brandon would receive his share of the spoils from Wolsey's fall. He was granted Wolsey's prize mules as well as the manor of Sayes Court in Deptford. He also took in the clerk of Wolsey's kitchen.[31]

Being away from court provided Mary with the opportunity to visit the neighbouring towns and priories. Each Easter, Mary would make an appearance at the Bury St Edmunds Easter fair. Westhorpe Hall was located not too far away and Mary would attend the fair, sitting under a cloth of gold and holding court for the local town. The people of Suffolk greatly respected and adored Mary, never forgetting that she was a Dowager Queen of France and sister to the king. They welcomed her warmly and presented her with gifts and entertainment.[32]

In April 1530 amidst the drama of Henry VIII's Great Matter, Margaret Tudor, daughter of Margaret Tudor, Dowager Queen of Scotland, and her second husband Archibald Douglas, sixth Earl of Angus, came to stay with Mary. In December 1528 Henry VIII and James V of Scotland concluded the Treaty of Berwick. As part of the treaty Douglas pledged his allegiance to England and Henry invited his niece to court. It has been proposed that owing to Mary's hatred of Anne Boleyn she insisted her niece come to stay with her at Westhorpe Hall, rather than at court under the guidance of Anne.

Margaret was fifteen and as niece of the King of England and half-sister to the King of Scotland it was expected that she would live in a style befitting her status. This of course meant money and it must have been yet another financial strain on Mary and her husband to have Margaret and her entourage living with them. Yet despite the financial strain Mary was determined not to have her young niece influenced by Anne Boleyn. It was at Westhorpe Hall that Margaret forged a lifelong friendship with Katherine Willoughby, Brandon's eleven-year-old ward. Margaret grew close to her aunt and it is reported that on Mary's death Margaret was 'bereft'.[33]

Margaret stayed with her aunt for approximately eight months. In December 1530 Henry VIII had Margaret moved to the household of his daughter, Princess Mary, where Margaret was appointed to be the chief lady of Mary's privy chamber.[34] Margaret's aunt Mary probably felt relieved that the Brandon household no longer had to carry the financial burden of her niece's stay.

By 1531 Henry VIII had openly separated from his wife and took Anne Boleyn with him wherever he went. On 6 June 1531 Eustace Chapuys, Ambassador to Charles V, wrote to his master, 'Suffolk and his wife, if they dared, would offer all possible resistance to this marriage; and it is not two days since that he and the treasurer, talking of this matter, agreed that now the time was come when all the world should strive to dismount the King from his folly, for which they see no better means nor colour than the immediate issuing of that happy sentence which is so much delayed. It will find here many supporters, and therefore should be pressed bluntly.'[35] Chapuys was, as Charles V's man, naturally dead set against Anne Boleyn and lost no opportunity to demean her in his despatches. On another occasion Chapuys reported to Charles V that Anne 'had been accused by the Duke of Suffolk of undue familiarity with a gentleman who on a former occasion had been banished on suspicion.'[36] This gentleman was Sir Thomas Wyatt, poet, courtier and long-time friend of the Boleyn family and from his poetry it is quite probable that he had feelings for Anne. However, there is no evidence to suggest that Anne returned these feelings. While there turned out to be no truth in this rumour, Henry was furious with his friend and had banished him from court for a time. In return for this accusation, Anne Boleyn made one of her own, declaring that Brandon was sleeping with his daughter Frances![37] Mary's reaction to the outrageous slur is unrecorded. Brandon unfortunately did not appear to learn his lesson and he spoke with the treasurer of the king's household, Fitzwilliam, hoping to work with him to persuade the king against marrying Anne Boleyn.[38]

In 1532 Mary spoke publicly about her opposition to the marriage and where her loyalties lay, speaking about Anne Boleyn in unfavourable terms. This resulted in a quarrel between some of the Duke of Norfolk's men (the duke being Anne Boleyn's uncle) and Brandon's men. On April 23 Carlo Capello reported:

> At the moment of his arrival at the Court, one of the chief gentlemen in the service of said Duke of Norfolk, with 20 followers, assaulted and killed in the sanctuary of Westminster Sir (D'no) William Peninthum (sic) chief gentleman and kinsman of the Duke of Suffolk. In consequence of this, the whole Court was in an uproar, and had the Duke of Suffolk been there, it is supposed that a serious affray would have taken place. On hearing of what had happened, he (Suffolk) was on his way to remove the assailants by force from the sanctuary, when the King sent the Treasurer [Thomas Cromwell] to him, and made him return, and has adjusted the affair; and this turmoil displeased him. It is said to have been caused by a private quarrel, but I am

assured it was owing to opprobrious language uttered against Madam Anne by his Majesty's sister, the Duchess of Suffolk, Queen Dowager of France.[39]

The murderers were pardoned, but in 1533 the Duke of Norfolk demanded that Brandon relinquish the office of Earl Marshal to Norfolk, which Brandon had held since the death of Norfolk's father in 1524. The king complied with this request, perhaps in order to punish Brandon. Yet he did grant Brandon the warden and Chief Justice of the royal forests south of Trent.[40]

While these dramatic events were unfolding Brandon and Mary managed to find time to organise the wedding of their oldest daughter, Frances. Now legitimised by papal bull, Brandon and Mary Tudor's children were highly prized in the marriage market. Previously, a marriage between the Duke of Norfolk's son Henry Howard, Earl of Surrey, and Frances Brandon had been proposed, but Norfolk turned down the marriage idea on the grounds that Frances' dowry was too meagre. This clearly was another sign that while Brandon was the Duke of Suffolk and a leading man at court, his financial status was still quite parlous. Soon another marriage prospect arrived. In October 1530 Thomas Grey, Marquis of Dorset, had died leaving his son Henry Grey as his heir. Brandon sought the approval of the dowager Marchioness and then bought the wardship of Henry Grey for 4,000 marks. The young couple were married in May at Suffolk Palace in a spectacular wedding attended by the king. It was to be Mary Tudor's last public appearance.[41]

With time ticking, Henry VIII turned from lobbying the Pope to his own Parliament and from October 1529 to April 1536 the Reformation Parliament sat. The Parliament debated the idea that there was only one supreme head in England, the king, and that all matters of Church and State needed to be referred to the monarch and not the Pope. The various laws passed enforced the idea that no foreign power (i.e. the Pope) could dictate law in England and that any laws enforced by the monarch were binding.[42]

The king then went on to accuse the clergy of supporting Thomas Wolsey and in return the clergy offered the king a bribe of £100,000 (£32,210,000)[43] to drop any charges against them. On 7 February 1531 the king demanded that he be known as the

'Supreme Head of the English Church'. Naturally the clergy were against such an idea, but the king was insistent. After some argument the clergy granted the title with one slight alteration. Convocation granted Henry VIII the title of 'Singular protector, supreme lord, and even, so far as the law of Christ allows, supreme head of the English church and clergy'. Henry VIII could now have his annulment because he no longer had to submit to papal authority.

Christmas 1532 came and went with much celebration at court. Rather than giving presents at Christmas, courtiers would present gifts to the king on New Year's Day. For the king to accept a gift and give one in return was a sign of the king's favour. On New Year's 1532 Mary gave her brother a gift of writing tables and a gold whistle, while Brandon gave the king a gold pomander. In return Henry gave his sister and brother-in-law several pieces of silver gilt. The same day Anne Boleyn gave the king an exotic set of richly decorated Pyrenean boar spears, while Henry gave Anne hangings of cloth of gold and cloth of silver and embroidered crimson satin for her room and bed. Katherine of Aragon sent the king a gold cup which Henry VIII refused.[44] The following year in 1533 Mary's present to her brother was unrecorded. Henry gave her more plate. It would be the last New Year's presents that would be exchanged between brother and sister.[45]

On 25 January 1533, just before dawn, Henry married his second wife Anne Boleyn at Whitehall Palace. Unfortunately, records do not state exactly who was in attendance. If Brandon did attend the wedding then he would have been sworn to absolute secrecy as at the time many still believed that Henry was still legally married to his first wife Katherine of Aragon.

It was left to the Dukes of Norfolk and Suffolk to carry the news to Katherine of Aragon. They met with the queen on 9 April 1533 at her residence at Ampthill and informed her that she was no longer Queen of England, and from that day forward she had to style herself as the dowager Princess of Wales. Katherine took the news with grace, but refused either to use the new title or to believe that Henry's marriage to Anne was valid.[46] On 3 July Katherine was given the papers stating that her marriage to Henry had been annulled and that the king was lawfully married to Anne Boleyn. As the king could not have two wives, it was essential that Katherine now style herself as the Dowager Princess of Wales.[47] Katherine declared that she did not recognise any judgement made except that of Pope Clement VII.[48]

In December Brandon was once more sent to try and convince Katherine that she was no longer to style herself Queen of England and, in addition, she must be moved from her present lodgings to Somersham. It is reported that Brandon wished some mischief would befall to him so that he did not have to go.[49] The duke was not looking forward to the task ahead, already having experienced first-hand the outrage that Katherine of Aragon had expressed at being informed she was no longer queen. It would be unrealistic to think that Brandon had not spoken with his wife about Katherine's treatment. It must have been distressing for Mary to hear that her beloved sister-in-law was relegated to Dowager Princess of Wales and no longer recognised as Queen.

When Brandon arrived and informed Katherine of her forthcoming move, Katherine stated she would rather be hewn into pieces than be called dowager princess and that she absolutely refused to go to Somersham. She then slammed the door in Brandon's face. The duke was left standing outside imploring Katherine to see reason and to accept her new position. Brandon then questioned Katherine's servants and they too refused to refer to her as Dowager Princess and insisted that Katherine was the queen. Five days passed, during which time Brandon's men removed the furniture and hangings from the house as well as dismissing most of Katherine's servants. All the while he continued to try to persuade Katherine to leave, but she insisted that the only way she would go was if he broke down the door; an action Brandon clearly would not undertake for fear of the possible ramifications.[50] Brandon was at a complete loss and wrote to Henry explaining the situation, even going so far as to say that he thought the only way they could transport Katherine was if they bound her with ropes! He requested the king's guidance as to what he should do.[51] Brandon had to wait until 31 December when he received instructions from the king that he should leave Katherine where she was and return to court.

The whole situation was an uncomfortable one for Brandon and while he thought Katherine was being stubborn, he was also well aware of her failing health and the ever-deteriorating living conditions she was forced to endure. There is little doubt that personally Brandon shared his wife's views regarding Katherine and her cause. He was not unsympathetic and when Brandon returned to court he conveyed to the king the poor health that Katherine was suffering.[52] This information clearly had no effect on the king and Brandon was left once more in the difficult situation of having to harass the former queen while secretly being sympathetic to her cause. Katherine continued to style herself as queen until her death almost three years later.

Now married to Henry VIII, with the future king (hopefully) of England in her belly, Anne Boleyn's magnificent coronation was set for Sunday 1 June. Wearing a gown of crimson velvet edged in ermine and a purple velvet mantle with her hair loose and hanging down to her waist, Anne Boleyn made the short journey barefoot from Westminster Hall to Westminster Abbey under a canopy of cloth of gold. Brandon's duty was to walk before the future queen carrying her royal crown and during the coronation he stood close to the queen holding a white staff of office.[53] Afterwards a great banquet was held at Westminster Hall where Brandon acted as Lord High Steward and Constable. It was his responsibility to organise all the details of the coronation, including Anne's procession through London the previous day. Wearing a doublet covered in pearls and riding a charger covered in crimson velvet, Brandon rode through the banquet where 800 people enjoyed courses amounting to approximately thirty-two dishes.[54] Whatever Brandon's thoughts on the new marriage, he performed his duties and Anne Boleyn's procession through London, her coronation and her banquet afterwards were of great opulence and no expense was spared.

It could not be missed that the king's sister Mary Tudor was not present at the coronation. Some have suggested that Mary's absence was an overt objection to the new queen. However, it was more likely that Mary was not in a fit enough state to attend the magnificent event. The Dowager Queen of France had been ill for some time and in May 1533 Brandon had returned to Westhorpe. It would be the last time he would ever see her alive. Brandon was soon recalled to London to continue with the preparations for Anne's coronation. Mary died between seven and eight o'clock in the morning on 25 June 1533.[55] Even by the standard of the time she had not reached old age.[56]

Mary's cause of death is unknown. A number of theories have been put forward, one being that she may have suffered from angina. Another proposal is that the pain in Mary's side that constantly bothered her throughout her life was due to an extreme kidney infection. In her younger years Mary may have suffered from a number of urinary tract infections, which had ultimately led to kidney failure. All of these suggestions are merely theories and without further recorded information it is simply impossible to say what caused her death.

It has also been proposed that Mary's death was due to her overwhelming grief over Henry's annulment of his marriage to Katherine and his wedding to Anne Boleyn.[57] A Spanish chronicler wrote that 'when the King left the blessed Queen Katherine the Queen Dowager of France, wife of the Duke of Suffolk, was so much attached to her that the sight of her brother leaving his wife brought on an illness from which she died.'[58]

There is no substance to his suggestion. Despite not agreeing to Henry's second marriage Mary still loved her brother deeply. Shortly before her death Mary wrote to Henry:

Has been very sick and 'ele ates' (ill at ease). Has been fain to send for Master Peter the physician, but is rather worse than better. Trusts shortly to come to London with her husband. Is sure, if she tarries here, that she will never 'asperre the sekenys.' Will be glad to see the King, as she has been a great while out of his sight, and hopes not to be so long again.[59]

Local church bells rang out at approximately eight o'clock in the morning to tell the world that Mary Tudor had died.[60] Mary's body was embalmed and she lay in state at Westhorpe Hall for three weeks. Her coffin was draped in deep blue velvet and surrounding the coffin, candles burned day and night. At Westminster Abbey, on 10 July, Henry VIII had a Requiem Mass held for his favourite sister.

Mary had continued to style herself Dowager Queen of France to the day she died. A delegation was sent from France to pay the nation's respects at the funeral. Mary's funeral was held on 21 July 1533 and was an affair befitting a woman of her status. Mary was to be buried at Bury St Edmund. Her daughter Frances was the chief mourner, accompanied by her husband Henry Grey and her younger brother Henry, Earl of Lincoln.[61]

Mary's coffin was taken from Westhorpe Hall to the abbey church at Bury St Edmund. The coffin was placed on a hearse covered in black velvet embroidered with Mary's coat of arms and motto 'the will of God is sufficient for me.' The coffin was draped in black cloth of gold and a white cross. On top of the coffin lay an effigy of Mary wearing robes of state, a golden crown and sceptre signifying her former status as Queen of France. The hearse was covered by a canopy, carried by four of Charles Brandon's knights, and pulled by six horses draped in black cloth. Around the hearse the coat of arms of the Tudor and Brandon families were carried by standard bearers.[62]

At the front of the funeral procession walked 100 torchbearers made up of members of the community, who had all been supplied with black clothing. Then followed several clergy, who carried a cross and behind them were members of Mary's household. Next came the hearse followed by knights and members of the gentry. One hundred men of Brandon's yeomen marched behind the nobility and then riding on a horse covered in black cloth came Mary's daughter Frances. She was accompanied by her husband Henry Grey, and behind rode Eleanor Brandon, Katherine Willoughby and other members of Mary's household. Members of local parishes joined the procession along the way.[63]

Mary's coffin arrived at the abbey at two o'clock in the afternoon and the coffin was brought up and placed upon the high altar. A Mass was held[64] and afterward a herald cried 'Pray for the soul of the right high excellent princess and right Christian queen, Mary, late French queen, and all Christian souls.'[65] Following the Mass a supper was held, attended by the noblemen and women of the funeral train.

During the night twelve men, eight women, thirty yeomen and a selection of clergy were chosen to watch over Mary's body. The following morning at breakfast a second Mass was held. During the Mass Frances and Eleanor Brandon, Mary's daughters, her two stepdaughters Anne and Mary, her ward Katherine Willoughby and Katherine's mother, Maria de Salinas, placed palls of golden cloth on the altar. The funeral address was given by William Rugg and when finished, the officers of Mary's household broke their white staffs and threw them into Mary's grave as a sign that their services to the late Dowager Queen were over. Mary was interred and her body lay at peace at the Abbey of Bury St Edmund until 1784, when her coffin was moved to the chancel of St Mary's Church. Mary's resting place is now marked by a slab on the floor.[66]

After the funeral, alms of meat, drink, and coin were given to the poor. Mary was beloved by the people of Suffolk and she was mourned deeply. It was customary that neither Mary's husband, Charles Brandon, nor her brother the king attended the funeral; therefore as Mary had been a Dowager Queen of France and princess of England, a funeral at court was required. Therefore previously on 10 and 11 July another funeral had been held at Westminster, attended by Henry VIII and Mary's husband, with all official duties being performed without the body.[67]

There are no personal records recording how Charles Brandon felt about the death of his wife of eighteen years. He had risked all, facing treason charges and the possibility of death because he married a member of the royal family without the king's permission. Mary and Brandon appeared to be close throughout their marriage, sharing similar views, especially regarding the casting aside of Queen Katherine of Aragon. They had four children together and it is reasonable to think that Brandon would be grieved the loss of his wife. How much may be estimated, perhaps, by his next decision. Or maybe that is too harsh.

Mary's death made very few waves across Europe. On 28 June 1533 Eustace Chapuys, Spanish Ambassador, wrote to Charles V, 'I have just been told that the duchess of Suffolk, the late queen dowager of France, is dead, in consequence of which the king of France will gain the 30,000 crs. a year, which he paid for her dower.'[68] On 30 June the Bailly of Troyes wrote to Francis I stating that he had written 'three days ago of the death of the queen Mary, duchess of Suffolk, who was much beloved in the country and by the common people of this town.'[69] On July 5 Marin Giustiniani wrote from Venice stating that 'news has been received from England of the death of the King's sister, the Duchess of Suffolk, widow of the late King Lewis of France.'[70]

Little more was recorded in Europe about Mary's death. Her passing made no difference to the affairs in England or Europe, except that Francis I would no longer have to ensure Mary received her dower payments.

For a woman who had lived much of her life in the spotlight, the most beautiful woman in all of Christendom passed into the shadows of death with barely a flicker.

12

Legacy

❧

'Queen Mary, duchess of Suffolk, who was much beloved in the country and by the common people of this town.'

With the death of Mary, Charles Brandon was left in an even more precarious financial situation. Mary's dower payment, worth £4,000 (£1,288,000) a year was no longer coming into the Brandon coffers and Brandon had two children to raise, in addition to various loans from the English Crown to repay. He was also required to maintain the visible trappings of being a duke. The king cancelled £1,000 (£322,000) of Brandon's debt as well as providing him the fruits of the vacant See of Ely for the year 1533/34, which amounted to around £2,000[1] (£644,000). But Brandon was still strapped for cash and the duke needed to look elsewhere for financial assistance. Fortunately, he did not need to look far.

Three months after Mary's death, on 7 September 1533, Charles Brandon married his ward Katherine Willoughby. Brandon's rushed marriage caused some controversy. He had originally acquired Katherine's wardship in order that he could marry her to his son and heir, Henry. However Henry was only eleven and since Brandon required money he decided to marry Katherine himself so that he could gain her inheritance and property.[2]

At the time of the marriage Brandon was aged forty-nine and Katherine fourteen. It was not unusual for an older man to marry a much younger woman. Despite it not being unusual, it is said that there were still some mutterings, and people were well aware of the real reasons why Brandon married Katherine Willoughby. Of the marriage, Imperial Ambassador Chapuys wrote to Charles V:

> On Sunday next the duke of Suffolk will be married to the daughter of a Spanish lady named lady Willoughby. She was promised to his son, but he is only ten years old; and although it is not worth writing to your Majesty the novelty of the case made me mention it.
>
> The Duke will have done a service to the ladies who can point to his example when they are reproached, as is usual, with marrying again immediately after the death of their husbands.[3]

Brandon's son, Henry, Earl of Lincoln, died on the morning of 1 March 1534,[4] nine months after the death of his mother. Rumour was that Henry died of a broken heart after having his wife stolen from him, but this seems more than faintly ridiculous. It has been suggested that young Henry may have been sick for a period of time leading up to his death. Whatever the cause of the young earl's death at the age of eleven, Brandon was left with four daughters but no male heir to succeed him. Anne Boleyn is reported to have said, 'My Lord Brandon kills one son to beget another.'[5] She still held a great deal of resentment towards the duke for trying to break her engagement to the king. Probably most wise of the duke, Brandon's thoughts on Anne Boleyn's comments are not recorded.

On 19 July 1535 Mary's debts were cancelled[6] but Brandon still had to repay the huge sum of £6,700 (£2,158,000). In an attempt to pay off this debt Brandon handed over a great deal of plate and jewels amounting to £4,360 (£1,400,000) as well as exchanging some of his lands and property with the king. Brandon lost his Oxfordshire and Berkshire manors as well as his house at Westhorpe. In return Brandon gained land in Lincolnshire which was worth a mere £175 (£56,400) a year, a manor in Essex, a house in London as well as £3,183 (£1,025,000) in cash and the final cancellation of his debts.[7] Brandon also wrote to Nicholas de St Martin in an attempt to obtain his French pension, which at the time of Mary's death was four months overdue:

I have written to Sir John Wallop to speak to the Great Master that I may have the arrears due to me at May last; trusting that the French king and his council will not stop my dues, if the King forbear his. If Sir John Wallop cannot obtain this from the Grand Master he is to speak with the King, and advertise you of the result. The king (of England) intends to send one of his Council shortly to Francis. When he arrives in Paris, you are to declare to him the effect of my business, and be ordered accordingly, as I wish to have all my causes determined. At the coming of the King's ambassador send me word, that I may give you directions.[8]

The duke's efforts came to naught. Despite having revenue of around £2,500–£3,000 (£805,000–£966,000) a year Brandon still owed money to the Crown.[9] He continued to live beyond his means because he was required to keep up appearances as one of the highest ranking peers of the land, and the duke's financial issues would continue to plague him throughout his life.

Charles Brandon, Duke of Suffolk, died on 22 August 1545 at four o'clock in the afternoon.[10] Despite wishing to be buried in the college church of Tattershall in Lincoln without any pomp or display, Brandon was buried at the king's expense in St George's Chapel, Windsor, near the south door of the choir.

Mary's second daughter Eleanor Brandon survived her mother by fourteen years. In 1533, before Mary's death, a wedding contract between Eleanor and Henry Clifford, 2nd Earl of Cumberland, had been organised. The wedding did not take place until the summer of 1537.[11] Eleanor and Henry Clifford were married at her father's home in London and it is reported that the king attended the wedding.[12] Certainly with the king in attendance it must have been a magnificent affair. In honour of the wedding and his son marrying such a high-born woman, Henry Clifford's father, the Earl of Cumberland, built an impressive gallery at his castle in Skipton.[13]

Despite her being fifth in line to the English throne, there are no records of any momentous events in Eleanor's life. She continued to live with her husband Henry Clifford, 2nd Earl of Cumberland. Clifford was a busy courtier acting as Sheriff of Westmoreland, Constable and Steward of the Castle and Honour of Knaresborough in 1542, and being made Councillor of the North in the same year.

He was made Captain of the West Marshes in 1544.[14] Eleanor's whereabouts during this time remain unknown, but it is likely that she spent some of her time at her husband's castle in Skipton. Eleanor had three children, a daughter named Margaret born in 1540 and two sons, Henry and Charles, who both died in infancy.[15] Eleanor died on 27 September 1547 at Brougham Castle, Westmoreland and was buried at Skipton, Yorkshire.[16]

Of all Mary's children it is probably her daughter Frances who is most remembered. Born on 16 July 1517, Frances was just sixteen years of age when she married Henry Grey, Marquis of Dorset.[17] Frances had three surviving daughters, Jane in October 1537, Katherine in August 1540, and Mary in 1545. Frances would be a regular member at court, attending the funeral of Henry VIII's third wife Jane Seymour and also being present at the festivities to celebrate the arrival of the king's fourth wife, Anne of Cleves. It has been suggested that Frances was with her father at Guildford when he died on 22 August, but there is no evidence to support this.

Upon his death Brandon left Frances £200 (£61,500) of plate in his will and should both her half-brothers die before her, she would inherit the lands and property that Brandon had left to them. As both boys died in 1551, Frances inherited a great deal of her late father's possessions and property. After the death of her half-brothers, her father's title of Duke of Suffolk passed to Frances' husband Henry Grey on 11 October 1551.[18]

Frances' eldest daughter, Jane, would become Lady Jane Grey, The Nine Days' Queen. Many books have been dedicated to Jane and her tragic journey to becoming queen and then her ultimate demise, therefore only a simple summary is given here to outline the context of Frances' role in her daughter's rise and fall. In 1553 Jane married Guildford Dudley, son of John Dudley, Duke of Northumberland and Protector of the Realm while King Edward VI was underage. It was soon clear that Edward was sick and would not live long and the king died on 6 July 1553.

Before his death the boy king wrote his 'Device for the Succession' in which he overlooked his half-sisters Mary and Elizabeth in favour of Lady Jane Grey, his cousin and the granddaughter of Mary Tudor, younger sister of Henry VIII. Edward was a staunch Protestant and wished for England to continue to follow the Protestant faith.

Mary, Edward's half-sister, was a devout Catholic and therefore he did not wish her to succeed to the throne and return England to Rome. But if the young king overlooked Mary, then he would also have to overlook his other half-sister Elizabeth. He did this on the grounds that she had been declared a bastard by Henry VIII.[19]

Lady Jane Grey, like her mother, was a devout Protestant and in her Edward saw a way to pass the line of succession on to a Tudor heir while keeping England a Protestant nation. What he did not anticipate was the support that his half-sister Mary Tudor would receive from the English people. At Jane's coronation, Frances carried her daughter's train. Frances was now mother to the Queen of England. While Jane was proclaimed queen in London, Mary was proclaimed queen in Norfolk and parts of Suffolk.[20] Mary soon gained the support of huge numbers of the common people and gentry, as well as members of the nobility. One by one the members of the council turned their back on Jane. On 19 July 1553 soldiers arrived at the Tower to inform Jane that she was no longer queen.[21]

As well as Jane, Frances and her husband, Henry Grey, were arrested for their roles in putting Jane on the throne. After a personal plea from Frances to the new queen, Mary I, Frances and her husband were released from the Tower. Henry Grey, Duke of Suffolk, returned to his house in Richmond while Frances attended court. It is interesting to note that Frances became a member of court despite her role in attempting to see her own daughter, rather than Mary, become queen.

In early 1554 Thomas Wyatt, son of the famous poet and courtier of the same name, led a rebellion against Mary I. The rebels wished to stop Mary's marriage to the Spanish king, Philip II, and the legalisation of Catholic Masses. Frances' husband Henry Grey attempted to raise men in the Midlands while Wyatt raised rebels in Kent.[22] Ultimately the revolt was a failure. Jane Grey was caught up in the revolt and many saw her as a figurehead and she would continue to be a dangerous threat to Mary I while she lived. Jane was executed within the Tower of London on 12 February 1554.[23] On 23 February Frances' husband Henry Grey was executed for his role in the rebellion.

Frances married Adrian Strokes, also a firm Protestant and her Master of the Horse.[24] Frances married far beneath her station, but there may have been good reason for this. It may simply be that Frances married for love; but a marriage so soon after her husband's death and to a man of such low standing certainly put Frances out of contention for the throne and distanced herself from any thought or idea of challenging Mary I for her throne.

For the short remainder of her life it is reported that despite the loss of her first husband and her daughter, Frances remained on good terms with Queen Mary. After her remarriage Frances spent little time at court and in the last years of her life she was reported as suffering from poor health. Frances died in London on 21 November 1559 with her two surviving daughters by her side. She was buried in St Edmund's Chapel in Westminster Abbey.[25]

Throughout the centuries Mary has often been referred to as Mary Brandon, or Mary Tudor Brandon. It is important to note that after the death of her first husband, King Louis XII, and her subsequent marriage to Charles Brandon, Duke of Suffolk, Mary never styled herself as Mary Brandon or even as Duchess of Suffolk. In her letters she always referred to herself as 'Mary' or 'The French Queen' or even 'Queen of France', but never as Duchess or Mary Brandon. Despite later marrying lower than her original station in life, Mary was determined that people should remember that she had once been Queen of France.

Until her death, Mary was always a queen.

13

Beautiful Without Artifice

❧

'The Princess is so well qualified that I have only to say again that alike in goodness, beauty, and age there is not the like in Christendom.'

Over the centuries there have been a number of portraits identified as Mary Tudor, Dowager Queen of France; however, only three of these have been authenticated.

The first authenticated portrait of Mary can be seen at Sudeley, Gloucestershire, UK. The portrait was painted by Joannas Corvus Flandrus, Joannas inscribed his name on the frame around the portrait.[1] Also inscribed on the frame was the Latin text '*maria soror illustrissio regi henrico VIII ac gallorum regina coniunxque illustri principi carolo duct suffociae. Ano aetatis suae xxxiiii*',[2] which loosely translates to 'Mary the sister of the illustrious King Henry VIII, and wife of the illustrious Prince Charles, Duke of Suffolk, age 34'. So we can safely estimate that the portrait was painted in 1529/1530.[3]

The portrait depicts a woman in the middling years of her life, wearing an English gable hood and a French gown dripping in jewels. The woman has similar almond-shaped eyes, the long nose and full lips to the portrait of Mary in her teens. It should also be noted that while little is known about the life of Joannas Corvus, he has been connected to Charles Brandon's household.[4] Mary holds an apple, which suggests a reference to the Greek myth of

The Judgement of Paris. In this fable Paris is given a golden apple to give to one of three goddesses, Hera, Aphrodite and Athena, whichever he deemed to be the fairest. Each of the goddesses sought to bribe Paris. Hera offered to make Paris the King of Europe and Asia, Athena offered wisdom and skills in war, and Aphrodite offered Helen of Troy, the most beautiful woman in all the world. Paris granted the golden apple to Aphrodite and claimed Helen as his own. Having Mary hold an apple within the portrait Corvus is comparing Mary's beauty to that of Helen of Troy.[5] Behind Mary there is an image of a man riding on horseback, which may represent her husband, the skilled jouster Charles Brandon who held the post of Henry VIII's Master of Horse.[6]

Perhaps the most well-known portrait of Mary Tudor by an unknown artist depicts Mary with her second husband, Charles Brandon, Duke of Suffolk. Sadly, it would seem that the original version of this portrait has been lost over time. However, there are four separate copies of this version.[7] The sitters in the portrait are holding hands. Their bodies seemed to be tilted towards each other, as though expressing their love and union. Mary appears to be tucked under Brandon's broad shoulder as if he is protecting her – Mary's knight in shining armour who came to rescue her from her unstable position in France after the death of her first husband. Brandon wears thick fur and richly decorated clothing, his eyes appear to be blue and he has a strong nose and thick lips. His brown hair is thick and he has a generous, square-cut beard. Brandon seems to stare out of the portrait, as though looking at something just out of range. He wears his Knight of the Garter chain. The Garter chain is bright and prominent, representing the highest order of chivalry in England. Brandon's hat has a medallion of a woman in flowing robes. She holds a rope or cord which points downwards and there is a motto inscribed '*Je tiens en sa cord*'. This may make reference to the motto that Brandon adopted during his time visiting Margaret of Austria, Regent of the Netherlands, where he famously flirted with the archduchess and stole a ring from her finger. The cord in the medallion may signify the princess giving her favour to St George, the patron saint of England, or it may signify the princess leading the dragon away from St George. It may signify that Mary Tudor is leading Brandon into marriage.[8]

The position of the subjects is interesting. In her Master's 2006 dissertation on Levina Teerlinc, Melanie Taylor highlights how in the Hilary Term of 1555 Queen Mary I is seated where the male would usually sit, namely on the left. This is to underscore the fact Mary is a queen regnant. In the marriage portrait, Mary Tudor, Dowager Queen of France and Duchess of Suffolk is also in the same position. The portraitist shows that Mary is a Dowager Queen of France, and a princess of royal blood, while Brandon, though a Duke, is lower than her in status. The significance of this would certainly not have been lost on Mary, or on Brandon. The painter, however, does not overlook Brandon and his imposing figure, with broad, square shoulders, noticeably taller than Mary, all point to his status as a man – although not higher than Mary in social status he was by gender.[9]

The most important piece of symbolism is what Mary is holding, an artichoke, something strongly associated with France. The shape of the artichoke and the way it is held in Mary's hand could also make reference to the orb held by royalty and thus reminds us that she was once Queen of France. Atop the artichoke is a caduceus, which is a symbol of negotiation and trade. Including a caduceus within the portrait most likely represents the successful negotiations that Mary and Brandon went through in order to have their marriage accepted and ratified by Henry VIII. The artichoke also had close associations with sexuality, seduction and fertility.[10] The fact that Mary holds the artichoke strongly suggests she is pregnant when this portrait was painted. This gives a possible date of late 1515. Mary gave birth to a baby boy in March 1516 at Bath Place, London (belonging to Cardinal Wolsey). The fact that Mary had married an English nobleman was also extremely important as any son she would bear would not only have a claim to the throne should her brother not produce a legitimate heir, but the line would be English and not tainted with foreign blood. For example, Mary and Henry's older sister Margaret Tudor had married King James IV of Scotland and their son and heir was James V. In his will Henry strictly barred Margaret's children from inheriting the English throne owing to their Scottish blood.[11]

On the subject of Cardinal Wolsey it is interesting to note that Mary gave birth at Wolsey's residence as well as naming him godfather of her first child. Mary and Brandon owed a great debt to Wolsey It may be that Cardinal Wolsey was behind the commissioning of the wedding portrait. Wolsey may have proposed to Henry the painting of a wedding portrait as a public statement of Henry's approval of the marriage, as well as the fact that Mary was quite possibly carrying the heir to the English throne. He would have then selected an appropriate painter and coaxed Mary and Brandon into having the portrait painted as a symbol of the King's approval.

The portrait so often assumed to be Mary Tudor may in fact not be the Tudor princess at all. In his work 'An Unknown Portrait of Isabel the Catholic' Pedro Flor provides strong evidence to suggest that the portrait once believed to be Mary Tudor is in fact a portrait of a young Isabella of Castile, Katherine of Aragon's mother.[12] It is not the woman in the portrait, but rather her jewellery that Flor examines. There are two strong pieces of evidence to support the idea that the woman in the portrait is Isabella of Castile and not Mary; these are a medallion representing Isabella and her tomb. In both the medallion and the carving on Isabella's tomb, the woman wears an almost identical necklace to the woman in the portrait. In fact the necklaces are so similar that there could be no mistaking they are the same. In no other known portrait of Mary Tudor does she wear such a necklace. Isabella of Castile is wearing the necklace in two known representations of her. It may be argued that Mary Tudor owned a similar necklace, although this is highly unlikely. In addition to the necklace the hairstyle and the coronet of the sitter in both the portrait and the Isabella of Castile medallion are almost identical. With the close similarity in the necklace, coronet and hairstyle it can strongly be argued that the portrait once believed to be Mary Tudor is, in fact, Isabella of Castile.

Another portrait believed to be Mary Tudor has often been attributed to Jean Perreal. Perreal was a painter, architect and sculptor who was a well-known portraitist at the courts of Louis XII and Francis I.[13] Towards the end of 1514 Perreal was sent by Louis XII to the English court to paint his new bride.[14] This portrait shows a beautiful young woman, clearly in the teenage years of her life with a small, full-lipped mouth and a long, delicate nose. The woman has almond-shaped eyes, thin eyebrows and golden-red hair. The woman is shown to be sliding a ring onto the ring finger of her left hand. If this is indeed Perreal's lost portrait of Mary Tudor then he is representing Mary's upcoming marriage to Louis XII. However the similarities between the sitters of this portrait and the portrait once believed to be Mary Tudor but now accredited to Isabella of Castile, are hard not to miss. Both women have thin eyebrows, long delicate noses and full-lipped mouths. Not only the hair colour but also the style of the hair is near identical. While portrait four is commonly seen as Mary Tudor by Jean Perreal, it may be that further examination needs to be undertaken to prove this.

Jean Perreal has also often been credited for a sketch of Mary Tudor. The sketch was most likely done while Mary Tudor was at the Hôtel Cluny where she was sent to mourn the death of Louis.[15] The sketch shows a woman wearing a plain bonnet with a solemn expression. At a later date the French words '*Marie Roin Dangleterre*'[16] (Marie Queen of England) were inscribed in brown ink on the sketch.

Another representation of Mary can be seen in a marvellous representation of the marriage of Louis XII and Mary Tudor. There is little information about the origins of this tapestry. Located at Hever Castle the tapestry covers the left-hand wall of the room containing Anne Boleyn's beautiful Books of Hours. This is ironic considering that Mary and Anne detested one another! The tapestry was purchased by William Waldorf Astor through his agent Partridge in the early twentieth century for 70,000 francs. Details of when it was made and where are unknown. Examination of the tapestry suggests that it was made before 1525.[17] It may have been made in Tournai, the centre of excellence for illumination and tapestry making. Tournai was captured by Henry VIII and his troops in 1513 and was handed back to France when Henry and Francis signed the treaty of Universal Peace in October 1518.[18] It may have been during the period when Tournai was in English hands that Henry ordered the making of this great tapestry to celebrate his sister's wedding. Another possibility is that Thomas Wolsey ordered the tapestry as a propaganda piece, which unfortunately missed the mark on the death of Louis XII in 1515.

It is generally assumed that Henry VIII's great flagship the *Mary Rose* was named after his beloved sister. The *Mary Rose* was built between 1509 and 1511. When Henry VIII succeeded to the throne after his father's death he decided to strengthen the English navy since the country was under the constant threat from a French invasion. Among other ships, Henry ordered the building of the *Mary Rose*. She sank on 19 July 1545 in the Solent during a battle with the French fleet. She was thirty-four years old, one of Henry's greatest warships carrying heavy guns and with a crew of more than 400 men. Nearly all of the 400 crew and soldiers perished when the *Mary Rose* went under. It has been proposed that she sank was because she was making too tight a turn and that the gun ports close to the water level were still open letting water in. It has also been suggested that there was disorganisation aboard ship with men either not obeying or not hearing orders. The order may have been given to close the gun ports before the ship turned, but unfortunately they were not heard or understood. The hull of the *Mary Rose* was raised in 1982 and is currently located at the Portsmouth Historic Dockyard.[19]

Mary Tudor was never known as or referred to as 'Mary Rose'. In the Tudor age ships were rarely named after people. The Mary Rose Trust, the organisation responsible for preserving and managing the wreck of the great ship, suggest that the *Mary Rose*'s sister ship, the *Peter Pomegranate*, was named after St Peter and the pomegranate to honour Queen Katherine of Aragon, the pomegranate being her emblem. If her sister ship was named after a saint it is likely that the *Mary Rose* received her name in honour of the Virgin Mary. The Trust also suggests that the Rose may come from the Virgin Mary springing forth like a rose from a bush of thorns.[20] The rose is a symbol of the Virgin. Although Mary was Henry VIII's favourite sister, there is no evidence that he ever named his great flagship after her.

On 6 September 1784,[21] more than 200 years after her death, Mary Tudor's body was moved from the Abbey at Bury St Edmunds to St Mary's Church, Bury St Edmunds.[22] The coffin was made of lead, '6 feet 2 inches long, nearly of the shape of the body, with a coarse representation of the face'.[23] The fact it was reported the coffin was 'nearly of the shape of the body' indicated that

Mary would have stood close to 6 feet tall. The average height of a woman of the time was 5 foot 2 inches.[24] Mary must have struck an impressive figure when alive. Henry VIII was also of above average height, standing at 6 foot 2 inches. Mary and her brother inherited their stature from their grandfather, Edward IV, who was 6 foot 4 inches tall.

Before the reburial Mary's coffin was opened and her body was found to be swathed in fine linen, her eyes had been removed and replaced with resin and the stomach cavity had sunk, exposing the embalming substance inside. It was reported that Mary's teeth, 'above and below' were 'entire and even'. However it was the length of her hair, reportedly almost 2 feet long, which struck observers. It was perfectly preserved and reported to be 'a beauteous golden colour'.[25]

Several locks of Mary's hair were cut as souvenirs. One of these was preserved in a locket that can be found at Strawberry Hill in the Beauclerk Closet. Another lock was sealed within a delicate ring, now part of the private collection of Geoffrey Munn. Almost 500 years after her death Mary's hair is still a vibrant golden-red colour, just as if it had been cut from her head only yesterday.

Timeline

'La volonte de Dieu me suffit.'

1443: 31 May – Birth of Margaret Beaufort (Mary's grandmother)

1456: 3 November – Death of Edmund Tudor (Mary's grandfather)

1457: 28 January – Birth of Henry Tudor

1462: 27 June – Louis XII of France is born

1471: 22/23 May – Death of King Henry VI

1483: 9 April – Death of King Edward IV

   26 June – Richard III is crowned King

   25 December – Henry Tudor vows to marry Elizabeth of York

1484: Charles Brandon is born

1485: 1 August – Henry Tudor and his troops leave France for England

   7 August – Henry Tudor and his troops land at Mill Bay six miles west of Milford Haven, Pembrokeshire

   22 August – The armies of Henry Tudor and King Richard III clash in the 'Battle of Bosworth Field'. Henry Tudor is victorious. Richard III is killed in battle

   3 September: Henry Tudor and his men enter London

   30 October: Henry Tudor is crowned at Westminster Abbey becoming King Henry VII and the first Tudor monarch

1486: 18 January – King Henry VII marries Elizabeth of York

   20 September – Arthur Tudor is born at Winchester

   24 September – Arthur Tudor is christened at Winchester Cathedral

1489: February – Lambert Simnel appears claiming to be Edward
Plantagenet, Earl of Warwick
24 May – Lambert Simnel is crowned King Edward VI at Dublin
1489: 28 November – Margaret Tudor is born
30 November – Margaret is christened at Westminster Abbey
1491: 28 November – Henry Tudor is born at Greenwich
1492: 8 June – Death of Elizabeth Woodville (Mary's grandmother)
2 July – Elizabeth Tudor is born (dies 14 September 1495)
1494: 1 November 1494 - Henry Tudor is created Duke of York
1495: 18 March – Mary Tudor is born at Sheen Palace
1496: September: Perkin Warbeck and James VI invade England.
Warbeck is pretending to be Richard, Duke of York
1497: 29 December – A fire burns through Sheen Palace destroying
much of the building. Henry VII rebuilds naming the new palace
'Richmond Palace'
1498: 26 March – Arthur Tudor is contracted to marry Katherine of
Aragon, youngest daughter of Isabella of Castile and Ferdinand
of Aragon
June – Perkin Warbeck is forced to make two public confessions
that he is not Richard, Duke of York
Duke Ludovico Sforza, Il Moro from Milan writes to King Henry
VII seeking Mary's hand in marriage for his son Massimiliano,
Count of Pavia. The marriage proposal is rejected by King Henry VII
23 November – Arthur Tudor is created the Prince of Wales
1499: February – Edmund Tudor is born (dies 19 June 1500 aged
just fifteen months).
Desiderius Erasmus visits Eltham Palace and meets Henry,
Margaret, Mary and Edmund Tudor.
August – Edward, Earl of Warwick is beheaded
23 November – Perkin Warbeck is hung at Tyburn
1500: June – King Henry VII and Phillip I of Castile negotiate a
treaty of friendship. As part of the treaty Mary is betrothed to
Prince Charles, Philip's son
1501: 2 October – Katherine of Aragon arrives in England
12 October – Mary, her sister Margaret and other members of
her family watch Katherine enter London from a high room
14 November – Katherine of Aragon and Arthur Tudor are
married in St Paul's Cathedral

1502: 2 April – Arthur Tudor dies

1503: 24 January – Margaret Tudor is betrothed to King James IV
of Scotland

2 February – Catherine Tudor is born

10 February – Catherine Tudor dies

11 February – Elizabeth Tudor dies

8 August – Margaret Tudor marries King James IV

1505/06: Charles Brandon is appointed to the King's Spears, a
group of men who participate in jousting and court events.

Brandon marries Anne Browne, daughter of Sir Anthony Browne

1506: 16 January – Philip I of Castile and his wife Juana sail for
Spain when a fierce storm blows them off course and they take
refuge in England

1 February – Mary dances and plays the lute for Philip I and her
father

9 February – The Treaty of Windsor is signed requiring England
and Castile to support one another in war

25 September – Philip I of Castile dies

1506/07: Brandon marries Margaret Neville, Dame Mortimer

1507: May and June – Multiple jousting events are held at
Henry Tudor's manor in Kennington. Mary plays the role of
Lady May.

Charles Brandon is appointed Esquire of the Body

21 December – The Treaty of Perpetual Peace is signed by
Maximilian, Holy Roman Emperor, Prince Charles of Spain and
Henry VII of England. The treaty outlines the betrothal of Mary
and Prince Charles

1508: Brandon remarries Anne Browne

17 December – Mary Tudor is married by proxy to Prince
Charles at Richmond Palace

18 December – Prince Charles writes to Mary

1509: 19 March – Henry VII writes his will, leaving £50,000 for
Mary's dowry

21 April – King Henry VII dies

23 April – Henry VII's death is announced and Henry Tudor
proclaimed King Henry VIII

11 June – Henry Tudor and Katherine of Aragon are married in
a quiet ceremony in the oratory of the Friar Observants' church

24 June – Henry and Katherine are crowned King and Queen at Westminster Abbey

29 June – Margaret Beaufort dies

9 July – Margaret Beaufort is buried in Westminster Abbey

13 October – Henry VIII orders gowns to be delivered Mary

5 November – Henry VIII orders gowns to be delivered to Mary

14 November – Henry VIII orders gowns to be delivered to Mary

1510: Shrove Tuesday – Mary participates in a masquerade with her brother and other members of the court

26 May – Henry VIII orders gowns to be delivered to Mary

29 November – Henry VIII orders gowns to be delivered to Mary

1512: 5 February – Erasmus writes of Mary's beauty

5 March – Henry VIII orders gowns to be delivered to Mary

23 March – Henry VIII orders gowns to be delivered to Mary

1 April – Henry VIII orders gowns to be delivered to Mary

29 April – Henry VIII orders gowns to be delivered to Mary

6 October – Brandon is created Henry VIII's Master of The Horse

John Palsgrave is assigned to Mary to support her in learning French

1513: 30 March – Charles Brandon is knighted

13 April – Mary writes to Margaret of Austria

23 April – Charles Brandon is elected into the Order of the Garter

15 May – Charles Brandon is contracted to marry Elizabeth Grey, Viscountess Lisle and created Viscount Lisle

15 October – A new treaty was signed between Henry VIII and Margaret of Austria, on behalf of Maximilian I, the Holy Roman Emperor. Part of the treaty instructs that Mary and Prince Charles are to marry before the 15 May the following year

28 November – Henry VIII orders gowns to be delivered to Mary

3 December – Henry VIII orders gowns to be delivered to Mary

18 December – Prince Charles write to Mary

1514: 1 February – Charles Brandon is created Duke of Suffolk

5 March – Philippe Sieur de Bergilies, ambassador to Margaret of Austria, writes of Mary's beauty

30 June – Derard de Pleine writes of Mary's beauty and manner The Holy League against France is formed.

Ferdinand of Aragon signs a one-year truce with the French King Louis XII.

Pope Julius II dies and is succeeded by Pope Leo X

30 July 1514 – Mary Tudor formally renounces her marriage to Prince Charles of Spain

1 August – Mary writes to King Louis XII

7 August – The treaty of 'Peace and Friendship' is signed between England and France

11 August 1514 – Dandolo, Venetian Ambassador in France writes of Mary's beauty

13 August – Mary is married via proxy to King Louis XII. The Duke of Longueville acts as proxy for the French king

14 September – Louis XII is married via proxy at the church of Celestines, the Earl of Worcester standing in for Mary

22 September – King Louis XII leaves Paris to Abbeville where he will meet Mary

23 September – Mary travels from London to Dover accompanied by her brother Henry VIII, Queen Katherine and other members of the English nobility

28 September – A grand tournament is held in France to honour Mary's upcoming arrival

2 October – Mary leaves Dover at four o'clock in the morning for Boulogne

4 October – Mary arrives at Boulogne, most of her ships blown off course during a huge storm

5 October – Mary and her entourage reached Montreuil

7 October – Mary and her entourage set out for Abbeville. Francis of Angouleme, son-in-law to Louis XII, greets Mary near the Anders Forest. Louis XII is out hawking with his men and 'happens' upon Mary, the pair meeting face to face for the first time. After this Mary and her entourage enter Abbeville.

8 October – Mary's revenue as Queen of France is approved and signed by King Louis XII

9 October – Mary and Louis marry at nine o'clock in the morning in the hall at Hôtel de la Gruthuse

10 October – King Louis XII dismisses most of the English women in Mary's household including Lady Guildford

12 October – Mary writes in distress to her brother and Thomas Wolsey regarding the dismissal of Lady Guildford

16 October – Mary, Louis XII and the court leave the Hôtel de la Gruthuse

18 October – Mary writes to Henry VIII regarding the possible ransom of a Frenchman

20 October – Mary writes again to Henry VIII regarding the possible ransom of a Frenchman

25 October – Charles Brandon, Duke of Suffolk meets with Louis XII, Mary sits by her husband's beside during the meeting

31 October – Mary arrives at St Denis outside of Paris

2 November – A French observer writes of Mary's beauty

5 November – Mary is crowned Queen of France at the Cathedral of St Denis

6 November – Mary makes her grand entrance into Paris

7 November – Mary attends Mass before travelling to the Hôtel des Tournells

11 November – Mary meets with the merchants of the city of Paris

13 November – The official tournaments begin to celebrate Mary's coronation.

13 November – Mary writes to Thomas Wolsey regarding her former tutor John Palsgrave

15 November – Mary writes to Henry VIII

17 November – Mary writes to Henry VIII regarding Mr Vincent Knight

24 November – Mary attends her first banquet as Queen of France at the Hôtel de Ville.

27 November – Mary, Louis XII and the court leave Paris for Saint-Germain-en-Laye.

Late December – Mary, Louis XII and the court returned to the Hôtel des Tournelles in Paris

28 December – Louis XII writes his last letter to Henry VIII

1515: 1 January – King Louis XII of France dies between ten and eleven o'clock at night

2 January – Mary retires to the Hôtel de Cluny in the Rue des Mathurins St Jaques. Here she wears white in mourning and is given the name '*La Reine Blanche*'

10 January – Mary writes to Thomas Wolsey

14 January – Henry VIII writes to Francis I sending his condolences and informing the new king that he would be sending Sir Richard Wingfield, Nicholas West and Charles Brandon, Duke of Suffolk to begin negotiations for Mary's return to England.

January – Mary writes to Henry VIII

28 January – Francis is crowned King Francis I at the ancient city of Rheims

31 January – Sir Richard Wingfield, Nicholas West and Charles Brandon, Duke of Suffolk meet with Mary in Paris

31 January – 3 February - Mary and Charles Brandon marry in a secret ceremony at the Hôtel de Cluny chapel before ten witnesses.

February – A number of letters are written by Mary and Brandon to Henry VIII and Thomas Wolsey

5 March –Brandon writes to Henry VIII

6 March – Mary writes to Henry VIII

March – Mary writes a public letter to Henry VIII handing over her dowry

31 March – Mary and Charles Brandon marry in a public ceremony in Paris.

5 April – A second peace treaty is signed between England and France

16 April – Mary and Brandon leave Paris and travel to Calais

22 April – Charles Brandon writes to Henry VIII from Montreuil

April – Mary writes her last letter to Henry VIII from France

2 May – Mary and Brandon land at Dover

13 May – Mary and Brandon are married for a third time at Greenwich

15 November – Thomas Wolsey is granted his Cardinal's hat by Rome

1516: 11 March – Mary gives birth to son at Bath Place, London, between ten and eleven o'clock at night

3 May – Margaret Tudor arrives in London

19 and 20 May – Mary watches a jousting event held in her sister Margaret's honour

June – Mary and Brandon visit Butley Priory, a favourite residence of Mary's

9 September – Mary writes to Henry VIII

End of the year – Mary suffers a bout of the ague

1517: March – Mary and Brandon host Queen Katherine of Aragon while the queen was on pilgrimage to the shrine of Our Lady, at the Austin Priory at Walsingham

17 March – Brandon writes to Henry VIII

16 May – Margaret Tudor leaves England, Mary never sees her sister again

July – Henry VIII entertains a delegation of Spanish Ambassadors, Mary is present wearing a gown of cloth of gold. She is nine months pregnant

16 July – En route to Our Lady at Walsingham Mary's labour comes on suddenly. She stops at Hatfield and between two and three o'clock in the morning gives birth to a daughter named Frances

1518: March – Mary is ill, suffering from a pain in her side. Both Brandon and Mary write to Henry VIII

23 September – French Ambassadors arrive in England

2 October – The treaty of Universal Peace is signed between France and England at St Paul's. Mary participates in a silent play to entertain the Ambassadors

1519: 28 July – Charles V is elected as the Holy Roman Emperor

27 September – Mary writes to Thomas Wolsey from Butley Priory

1520: 22 January – Mary writes to Thomas Wolsey

16 March – Brandon writes to Thomas Wolsey regarding arrangements for the Field of Cloth of Gold

26 May – Charles V lands at Dover; Mary sees her former fiancé for the first time

31 May – Henry VIII and his entourage, including Mary leave Dover for France

7 June to 24 June – The magnificent Field of Cloth of Gold is held between the English stronghold of Guînes and the French town of Ardres

11 June – Mary proceeds to the tiltyard, carried in a litter of cloth of gold, embroidered with lilies and monograms of L and M, signifying Mary's marriage to the late King Louis XIII

17 June – Mary accompanies her brother to dine at the French camp with Queen Claude

1518–1521: Mary gives birth to her third child, a daughter named Eleanor

1521: 25 August – Treaty of Bruges is signed between Charles V and Thomas Wolsey, pledging England's support against France

1522: March – Mary plays the role of Beauty in the pageant Château Vert, held for the Shrovetide celebrations

Mary's firstborn son, Henry dies aged just six years

Mary gives birth to her fourth child, a son named Henry

24 August – Brandon arrives at Calais in preparation for war against France

1525: February – Francis I is captured by Spanish forces

March – Anne Brandon marries Edward Grey, Lord Powis

18 June – Mary's three-year-old son is created Earl of Lincoln

August – Mary writes to Cardinal Thomas Wolsey regarding her French pension

30 August – The Treaty of More is signed between Cardinal Thomas Wolsey and Francis I's mother Louise of Savoy

1526: 14 January – Francis I and Charles V sign the Treaty of Madrid

17 March – Francis I is freed

9 May – Mary writes to Francis I congratulating him on his release

1527: 1 June – The City of Rome is ransacked by the Imperial Army.

Guillaume Gouffier de Bonnivet, the Lord Admiral of France writes that Mary is the 'rose of Christendom"

1527/28 – Mary Brandon marries Thomas Stanley, Lord Monteagle

1528: 15 January – Mary writes to Anne de Montmorency, Grand Master of France

March – Brandon purchases the wardship of Katherine Willoughby

18 June 1528 – Mary writes to Anne de Montmorency, Grand Master of France

20 June – Mary writes to her childhood friend Jane Popincourt

8 December – Cardinal Campeggio arrives in London

26 December – Mary writes to Anne de Montmorency, Grand Master of France

1529: A bull is finally granted from Rome legitimizing Brandon and Mary's marriage

31 May – The hearing regarding Henry VIII's annulment begins at Blackfriars

23 July 1529 – Cardinal Campeggio adjourns the court and refers Henry VIII's Great Matter back to Rome.

9 October – Cardinal Thomas Wolsey is charged with praemunire

1530: 20 September and 16 November – Mary visits Butley Priory for the last time

29 November – Cardinal Thomas Wolsey dies

1531: 7 February – Henry VIII demands to be called the 'Supreme Head of the English Church'

6 June – Spanish Ambassador Eustace Chapuys writes to Charles V stating he believes that Mary and Brandon would offer resistance to Henry VIII's marriage to Anne Boleyn

1532: 23 April – Mary speaks publically against Anne Boleyn resulting in a quarrel between Brandon's and the Duke of Norfolk's men

May – Frances Brandon marries Henry Grey

1533: 25 January – Henry VIII marries his second wife Anne Boleyn at Whitehall Palace

30 March – Mary writes to Viscount Lisle, Lord Lieutenant of Calais

9 April – Katherine of Aragon is informed that she is no longer Queen of England, and must style herself as the Dowager Princess of Wales

1 June – Anne Boleyn is crowned Queen

25 June – Mary dies between seven and eight o'clock in the morning

10 July – Henry VIII orders a Requiem Mass to be held for Mary at Westminster Abbey

21 July – Mary's funeral commences

22 July – Mary is laid to rest at the Abbey Church at Bury St Edmunds

7 September – Brandon marries his ward Katherine Willoughby

1534: 1 March – Henry Brandon, Earl of Lincoln dies

1535: 19 July – Mary's debts are cancelled

1536: 29 January – Katherine of Aragon dies

19 May – Anne Boleyn is beheaded at the Tower of London

1537: Summer – Eleanor Brandon marries Henry Clifford, 2nd Earl of Cumberland

October – Frances Brandon gives birth to a daughter named Jane

1545: 22 August – Charles Brandon, Duke of Suffolk dies

1547: 28 January – Henry VIII dies

27 September – Eleanor Brandon dies at Brougham Castle, Westmoreland

1554: 12 February – Lady Jane Grey is executed within the Tower of London

23 February – Henry Grey, Frances Brandon's husband is executed

1 March 1554/55 – Frances Brandon marries Adrian Strokes

1559: 21 November – Frances Brandon dies

1784: 6 September – Mary's coffin is moved to the chancel of St Mary's Church. Several locks of her hair are removed as souvenirs

Notes

Introduction
1. Calendar of State Papers Venice, Vol. 2, 500.
2. Medieval Lives: Birth, Marriage and Death.

The Rise of the Tudor Dynasty
1. Mary Tudor's date of birth is recorded as 18 March 1495. During the Tudor age the turn of the year did not happen until our 25 March. The Gregorian calendar is used today, brought into use by Pope Gregory XIII on 4 October 1584. Therefore we would say that the turn of the year starts on 1 January and thus Mary's year of birth would be 1496.
2. Loades 2012, p. 26.
3. Breverton 2014, p. 17.
4. Breverton 2014, p. 20.
5. Breverton 2014, p. 187.
6. Penn 2011, p. 2.
7. Bayani 2014, p. 156.
8. Skidmore 2013, 93.
9. Skidmore 2013, p. 94.
10. Bayani 2014, p. 175.
11. Breverton 2014, p. 203.
12. G. J. Meyer 2010, p. 6.
13. De Lisle 2013, p. 58.
14. De Lisle 2013, p. 60.
15. Skidmore 2013, p. 155.
16. Skidmore 20136, p. 339.
17. G. J Meyer 2010, p. 6.
18. De Lisle 2013, p. 63.
19. Penn 2011, p. 1.
20. Breverton 2014, p. 231.
21. Bayani 2014, p. 210.

22. Bayani 2014, p. 212.
23. Bayani 2014, p. 214.
24. Skidmore 2013, p. 274.
25. Bayani 2014, p. 215.
26. Breverton 2014, p. 242.
27. Jones 2015, p. 175.
28. Bayani 2014, p. 215.
29. Bayani 2014, p. 216.
30. Breverton 2014, p. 246.
31. Jones 2015, p. 197.
32. Meyer 2010, p. 12.
33. Skidmore 2013, p. 322.
34. Pronay 1986, p. 183.
35. Skidmore 2013, p. 335.
36. Licence 2013, p. 115.
37. Skidmore 2013, p. 353.
38. Bacon 1885, p. 14.
39. Skidmore 2013, p. 338.
40. Skidmore 2013, p. 339.
41. Skidmore 2013, p. 342.
42. Skidmore 2013, p. 358.
43. Licence 2013, p. 115.
44. Wilkinson 2013, p. 100.
45. Weir 2014, p. 200.
46. Bacon 1885, p. 10.
47. Cunningham 2016, p. 22.
48. Medieval Lives: Birth, Marriage and Death.

A Rose Blooms

1. Croom Brown 1911, p. 3.
2. Licence 2013, p. 151.
3. Cloake p. 2–3.
4. Orme 2013, p. 12.
5. Orme 2013, p. 16.
6. Licence 2012, p. 29.
7. Medieval Lives: Birth, Marriage and Death.
8. Licence 2012, p. 52.
9. Orme 2013, p. 16.
10. Medieval Lives: Birth, Marriage and Death.
11. Catholic Online.
12. Norton 2016, p. 16.
13. Orme 2013, p. 17–18.
14. Guillemeau, 1635, p. 84.
15. Medieval Lives: Birth, Marriage and Death.
16. Croom Brown 1911, p. 3.
17. Beaufort Book of Hours Royal 2 A XVIII f. 29.
18. Sim 2011, p. 85.

19. Encyclopædia Britannica.
20. CSPV 1499, 790.
21. Licence 2012.
22. Medieval Lives: Birth, Marriage and Death.
23. Vives 1523.
24. Erasmus, ed. Rummel 1996.
25. Norton 2016.
26. More ed. Baker-Smith 2012.
27. Vives 1523.
28. Erasmus ed. Rummel 1996.
29. Cunningham 2016, p. 21.
30. Cunningham 2016, p. 48.
31. Licence 2013, p. 154.
32. Licence 2013, p. 158.
33. Licence 2013, p. 160.
34. Norton 2016, p. 27.
35. Eltham Palace and Gardens.
36. Norton 2016, p. 22–23.
37. Norton 2016, p. 33.
38. Croom Brown 1911, p. 8.
39. Croom Brown 1911, p. 9.
40. Everett Green 1857, p. 4.
41. Croom Brown 1911, p. 9.
42. Everett Green 1857, p. 4.
43. Norton 2016, p. 35–36.
44. Everett Green 1857, p. 4.
45. Norton 2016, p. 34.
46. Richardson 1970, p. 13.
47. Croom Brown 1911, p. 9.
48. Hart 2009, p. 36.
49. Letters and Papers, Vol. 2, The King's Book of Payments Jan. 1513.
50. Bietenholz & Deutscher 2003, p. 47.
51. Everett Green 1857, p. 4.
52. Croom Brown 1911, p. 16.
53. Richardson 1970, p. 23.
54. Knox ed. Mason, R.A 1994, p. 9.
55. Knox ed. Mason, R.A 1994, p. 12.
56. Knox ed. Mason, R.A 1994, p. 12.
57. Jackson 1999, p. 231.
58. Cholakain and Cholakian 2006, p. 4.
59. Abernethy 2013b.
60. Licence 2013, p. 32.
61. Everett Green 1857, p. 3.
62. Spence, Aiston and Meikle 2009.
63. Mumby 1913, p. 4–5.
64. Richardson 1970, p. 17.
65. Calendar of State Papers, Milan 1498, 565.

Of Deaths, Marriages and Rebellions

1. De Lisle 2013, p. 81.
2. De Lisle 2013, p. 88.
3. De Lisle 2013, p. 89.
4. Bacon 1888.
5. De Lisle 2016, p. 89.
6. Bacon 1888, p. 28.
7. De Lisle 2013, p. 89.
8. Bacon 1888, p. 36.
9. Vergil 1555.
10. Vergil 1555.
11. De Lisle 2013, p. 93.
12. Trueman 2015.
13. Vergil 1555.
14. Vergil 1555.
15. Hutchinson 2011, p. 19.
16. De Lisle 2013, p. 97.
17. De Lisle 2013, p. 100.
18. De Lisle 2013, p. 102.
19. Cunningham 2016, p. 38.
20. Calendar of State Papers, Spain 1489, 34.
21. De Lisle 2013, p. 101.
22. De Lisle 2013, p. 101.
23. Licence 2013, p. 160.
24. Calendar of State Papers, Spain 1501, 305.
25. Croom Brown 1911, p. 12–13.
26. Perry 2002, p. 32.
27. Abernethy 2013b.
28. Perry 2002, p. 35.
29. Measuring Worth.
30. Vergil 1555.
31. Perry 2002, p. 35.
32. Russell 2011.
33. Bernard 2014.
34. Perry 2002, p. 39.
35. Hall 1809, p. 497.
36. Penn 2011, p. 86.
37. Perry 2002, p. 42.
38. Licence 2013, p. 211.
39. Licence 2012, p. 57.
40. Weir 2013, p. 416.
41. Perry 2002, p.44–52.

Princess of Castile

1. Medieval Lives: Birth, Marriage and Death.
2. Richardson 1970, p. 34.
3. Loades 2012, p. 45.

4. Loades 2012, p. 46.
5. Loades 2012, p. 47.
6. Everett Green 1857, p. 4.
7. Calendar of State Papers Spain, Vol. 1, 452.
8. Richardson 1970, p. 38.
9. Calendar of State Papers Venice, Vol. 1, 872.
10. Calendar of State Papers Venice, Vol. 1, 890.
11. Richardson 1970, p. 40.
12. Penn 2011, p. 285.
13. Cripps-Day 1918, p. 122.
14. Penn 2011, p. 289.
15. Sadlack 2011, p. 109.
16. Calendar of State Papers Spain, Vol. 1, 557.
17. Calendar of State Papers Spain, Vol. 1, 558.
18. Everett Green 1857, p. 8.
19. Everett Green 1875, p. 7–8.
20. The National Archives Currency Converter.
21. Letters & Papers, Vol. 4 5859.
22. Oxford Dictionary of National Biography – Charles Brandon.
23. Carmelianus (ed.) Gardiner 1893, p. 10.
24. Everett Green 1875, p. 10–11.
25. Everett Green 1875, p. 11–12.
26. Richardson 1970, p. 42–43.
27. Everett Green 1857, p. 13.
28. Perry 2002, p. 70.
29. Everett Green 1857, p. 13.
30. Richardson 1970, p. 43.
31. Everett Green 1857, p. 13.
32. Everett Green 1857, p. 14–15.
33. Carmelianus, (ed.) Gardiner 1893, p.xi.
34. Loades 2012, 54.
35. Mumby 1913, p. 116–120.
36. Mumby 1913, p. 116–120.

Thy Brother the King

1. Penn 2011, p. 273.
2. The Will of Henry VII, 1775, p. 38–42.
3. The National Archives Currency Converter.
4. Vergil 1555.
5. Richardson 1970, p. 58.
6. Calendar of State Papers, Spain, Vol. 2, 10.
7. Calendar of State Papers, Spain, Vol. 2, 11.
8. Hutchinson 2012, p. 118.
9. Hutchinson 2012, p. 119.
10. Vergil 1555.
11. Perry 2002, p. 86.
12. Hutchinson 2012, p. 121.

13. Hutchinson 2012, p. 124.
14. Hutchinson 2012, p. 125–126.
15. Richardson 1970, p. 60.
16. Hutchinson 2012, p. 127.
17. The National Archives Currency Converter.
18. Richardson 1970, p. 60.
19. The National Archives Currency Converter.
20. Letters & Papers Vol. 1, 84.
21. Penn 2011, p. 167–170.
22. Penn 2011, p. 376.
23. Hutchinson 2012, p. 129.
24. Hutchinson 2012, p. 139.
25. Richardson 1970, p. 61.
26. Everett Green 1857, p. 16.
27. Hall 1809, p. 513.
28. Hall 1809, p. 513–514.
29. Letters & Papers, Vol. 1, 202.
30. Letters & Papers, Vol. 1, 224.
31. Letters & Papers, Vol. 1, 237.
32. Letters & Papers, Vol. 1, 471.
33. Letters & Papers, Vol. 1, 629.
34. Letters & Papers, Vol. 1, 1086.
35. Letters & Papers, Vol. 1, 1115.
36. Letters & Papers, Vol. 1, 1125.
37. Letters & Papers, Vol. 1, 1165.
38. Letters & Papers, Vol. 1, 2487.
39. Letters & Papers, Vol. 1, 1777.
40. Richardson 1970, p. 67.
41. Letters & Papers, Vol. 1, 2366.
42. Letters & Papers, Vol. 1, 2370.
43. Letters & Papers, Vol. 1, 2445.
44. Letters & Papers, Vol. 1, 2515.
45. Richardson 1970, p. 68.
46. Richardson 1970, p. 73.
47. Camden Society 1838, p. 66.
48. Richardson 1970, p. 74.
49. Letters & Papers, Vol. 1, 2779.
50. Wilson 2009, p. 62.
51. Richardson 1970, p. 60.
52. Loades 2012, p. 64.
53. Hutchinson 2011, p. 186.
54. Perry 2002, p. 123.
55. Encyclopaedia of World Biography: Louis XII.
56. Jokinen 2007.
57. Letters & Papers, Vol. 1, 2791.
58. Letters & Papers, Vol. 1, 2957.
59. Letters & Papers, Vol. 1, 2958.

60. Calendar of State Papers Spain, Vol. 1, 558.
61. AE/III/24, *Grands documents de l'histoire de France*
62. Letters & Papers, Vol. 1, 3101.
63. Calendar of State Papers, Spain, Vol. 2, 183.
64. Perry 2002, p 126.
65. Richardson 1970, p. 81.
66. Calendar of State Papers, Venice, Vol. 2, 505.
67. Letters & Papers, Vol. 1, 3151.
68. Richardson 1970, p. 81.
69. Letters & Papers, Vol. 1, 3146.
70. Letters & Papers, Vol. 1, 3171.
71. Richardson 1970, p. 81–82.
72. Croom Brown 1911, p. 105.
73. Richardson 1970, p. 82.
74. Richardson 1970, p. 80.
75. Norton 2016, p. 87.
76. Norton 2016, p. 131.
77. Norton 2016, p. 86.
78. Letters & Papers, Vol. 1, 3151.
79. Mumby 1913, p. 272–273.

Nymph from Heaven

1. Letters & Papers, Vol. 1, 1050.
2. Loades 2012.
3. Fisher 2002, p. 21
4. Letters & Papers, Vol. 1, 2704.
5. Richardson 1970, p. 106.
6. Mumby 1913 p. 254–255.
7. Calendar of State Papers, Venice, Vol. 2, 470.
8. Mumby 1913, p 282–283.
9. Calendar of State Papers, Venice, Vol. 2, 508.
10. Calendar of State Papers, Venice, Vol. 2, 511.
11. Calendar of State Papers, Venice, Vol. 2, 509.
12. Calendar of State Papers, Venice, Vol. 2, 500.
13. Carroll 2010.
14. Calendar of State Papers, Venice, Vol. 2, 600.
15. Richardson 1970, p. 205.
16. Calendar of State Papers, Venice, Vol. 2, 500.
17. Mumby 1913 p. 263–264.
18. Letters & Papers, Vol. 1, 3147.
19. Letters & Papers, Vol. 1, 3147.
20. Letters & Papers, Vol. 1, 3202.
21. Mumby 1913, p. 274–276.
22. Mumby 1913 p. 276.
23. Loades 2012, p. 76.
24. The National Archives Currency Converter.
25. Letters & Papers, Vol. 1, 3326.

26. Richardson 1970, p. 85.
27. Letters & Papers, Vol. 1, 3332.
28. Letters & Papers, Vol. 1, 3333.
29. Letters & Papers, Vol. 1, 3343.
30. Perry 2002, p. 131.
31. Croom Brown 1911, p. 110.
32. Perry 2002, p. 132.
33. Letters & Papers, Vol. 1, 3294.
34. Loades 2012, p. 76.
35. Letters & Papers, Vol. 1, 3344.
36. Letters & Papers, Vol. 1, 3346.
37. Letters & Papers, Vol. 1, 3308.
38. Calendar of State Papers, Venice, Vol. 2, 482.
39. Mumby 1913, p. 282–283.
40. Mumby 1913, p. 282–283.
41. Richardson 1970, p. 88.
42. Mumby 1913, p. 310–311.
43. Loades 2012, p. 111.
44. Hall 1809, p. 570.
45. Loades 2012, p. 78.
46. Richardson 1970, p. 89.
47. Hall 1809, p. 570.
48. Richardson 1970, p. 90.
49. Perry 2002, p. 135.
50. Calendar of State Papers, Venice, Vol. 2, 511.
51. Loades 2012, p. 78.
52. Richardson 1970, p. 91.
53. Richardson 1970, p. 91.
54. Calendar of State Papers, Vol. 2, 511.
55. Bridge 1921, p. 255.
56. Calendar State Papers, Venice, Vol. 2, 511.
57. Richardson 1970, p. 94.
58. Calendar State Papers, Venice, Vol. 2, 511.
59. Calendar State Papers, Venice, Vol. 2, 511.
60. Perry 2002, p. 139.
61. Calendar State Papers, Venice, Vol. 2, 511.
62. Richardson 1970, p. 96.
63. Calendar State Papers, Venice, Vol. 2, 510.
64. Richardson 1970, p. 96.
65. Calendar State Papers, Venice, Vol. 2, 511.
66. Richardson 1970, p. 96.
67. Richardson 1970, p. 97.
68. Perry 2002, p. 140.
69. Richardson 1970, p. 97.
70. Calendar State Papers, Venice, Vol. 2, 508.
71. Bridge 1921, p. 260.
72. Calendar State Papers, Venice, Vol. 2, 511.

73. Mumby 1913, p. 287.
74. Calendar State Papers, Venice, Vol. 2, 511.
75. Gristwood 2016, p. 64.
76. Mumby 1913, p. 289–290.
77. Ellis 1825, p. 117–119.
78. Hall 1809, p. 570.
79. Letters & Papers, Vol. 1, 3376.
80. Mumby 1913, p. 291.
81. Letters & Papers, Vol. 1, 3357.
82. Perry 2002, p. 144.
83. Mumby 1913, p. 292–293.
84. Norton 2016, p. 131.

The French Queen

 1. Mumby 1913, p. 294.
 2. Hutchinson 2011, p. 191.
 3. Letters & Papers, Vol. 1, 3387.
 4. Loades 2012, p. 85.
 5. Letters & Papers, Vol. 1, 3580.
 6. Loades 2012, p. 95.
 7. Everett Green 1846, p. 174–175.
 8. Everett Green 1846, p. 176–177.
 9. Everett Green 1846, p. 180.
10. Everett Green 1846, p. 182–183.
11. Letters & Papers, Vol. 6, 293.
12. Richardson 1970, p. 112.
13. Everett Green 1857, p. 53.
14. Everett Green 1857, p. 53.
15. Richardson 1970, p. 114.
16. Letters & Papers, Vol. 1, 3424.
17. Everett Green 1857, 54–55.
18. Letters & Papers, Vol. 1, 3424.
19. Perry 2002, p. 147.
20. Croom Brown p. 135.
21. Perry 2002, p. 147.
22. Richardson 1970, p. 117.
23. Richardson 1970, p. 117.
24. Croom Brown 1911, p. 136–137.
25. Croom Brown 1911, p. 137.
26. Everett Green 1857, p. 59.
27. Richardson 1970, p. 118.
28. Everett Green 1846, p. 181.
29. Everett Green 1857, p. 61–62.
30. Perry 2002, p. 150.
31. Richardson 1970, p. 119.
32. Everett Green 1857, p. 62.
33. Letters & Papers, Vol. 1, 3461.

34. Richardson 1970, p. 119.
35. Hall 1809, p. 572.
36. Richardson 1970, p. 120.
37. Letters & Papers, Vol. 1, 3449.
38. Everett Green 1857, p. 66.
39. Richardson 1970, p. 121.
40. Everett Green, p. 70.
41. Richardson 1970, p. 123.
42. Everett Green, p. 69.
43. Mumby 1913, p. 305–306.
44. Everett Green p. 70.
45. Richardson 1970, p. 124.
46. Richardson 1970, p. 125.
47. Hutchinson 2011, p. 192.
48. Calendar of State Papers, Venice, Vol. 2, 560.
49. Bridge 1921, p. 270.
50. Bridge 1921, p. 269.
51. Richardson 1970, p. 126.
52. Morris & Grueninger 2013, p. 44.
53. Calendar of State Papers, Venice, Vol. 4. Additions and Corrections, p. 366.
54. Everett Green 1857, p. 73.
55. Richardson 1970, p. 128.
56. Calendar of State Papers, Venice, Vol. 2573.
57. Letters & Papers, Vol. 2, 139.
58. Richardson 1970, p. 132.

The White Queen

1. Letters & Papers, Vol. 2, 15.
2. Mumby p. 309–310.
3. Letters & Papers, Vol. 2, 24.
4. Richardson 1970, p. 166.
5. Oxford Dictionary of National Biography – Charles Brandon.
6. Richardson 2011, p. 297.
7. Richardson 2011 p. 368.
8. Richardson 2011 p. 369.
9. World Public Library – Charles Brandon.
10. Bayani 2014, p. 217.
11. Hutton 1813, p. 218.
12. Oxford Dictionary of National Biography – Charles Brandon.
13. Oxford Dictionary of National Biography – Thomas Brandon.
14. Loades 2012, p. 119.
15. Oxford Dictionary of National Biography – Charles Brandon.
16. Penn 2011, p. 171.
17. Hutchinson 2011, p. 95.
18. Wilson 2009, p. 85.
19. Richardson 2011 p. 369.
20. The National Archives Currency Converter.

21. Letters & Papers, Vol. 4, 5859.
22. Oxford Dictionary of National Biography – Charles Brandon.
23. Letters & Papers, Vol. 1, 1123 (65).
24. Baldwin 2015, p. 29.
25. Johnson 1969, p. 70.
26. Loades 2012, p. 122.
27. The National Archives Currency Converter.
28. The National Archives Currency Converter.
29. Gunn 2015, p. 30.
30. Loades 2012, p. 122.
31. Doran 2008, p. 94.
32. Gunn 2015, p. 28.
33. Oxford Dictionary of National Biography – Charles Brandon.
34. Letters and Papers Vol. 1 2941.
35. Velde, F 2014.
36. Oxford Dictionary of National Biography – Charles Brandon.
37. Perry 2002, p. 122.
38. Gunn 2015, p. 31.
39. The National Archives Currency Converter.
40. The National Archives Currency Converter.
41. Letters & Papers, Vol. 1, 1947.
42. Loades 2012, p. 102.
43. Loades 2012, p. 111.
44. Sadlack 2011, p. 237–238.
45. Vives 1523.
46. Mumby 1913, p. 310–311.
47. Letters & Papers, Vol. 2, 105.
48. Loades 2012, p. 103.
49. Sadlack 2011, p. 263.
50. Richardson 1970, p. 143.
51. Loades 2012, p. 103–104.
52. Perry 2002, p. 155.
53. Mumby 1913 p. 315–316.
54. Letters & Papers, Vol. 2, 80.
55. Richardson 1970, p. 172.
56. Everett Green 1857, p. 81–82.
57. Letters & Papers, Vol. 2, 80.
58. Letters & Papers, Vol. 2, 113.
59. Mumby 1913, p. 319–321.
60. Letters & Papers, Vol. 2, 139.
61. Letters & Papers, Vol. 2, 134.
62. Letters & Papers, Vol. 2, 135.
63. Mumby 1913, p. 321–323.
64. Letters & Papers, Vol. 2, 204.
65. Letters & Papers, Vol. 2, 203.
66. Mumby 1913, p. 324.
67. Letters & Papers, Vol. 2, 223.

68. Letters & Papers, Vol. 2, 343.
69. Letters & Papers, Vol. 2, 827.
70. Bryan.
71. Spears 2012.
72. Loades 2012, p. 114.
73. Mumby 1913, p. 325–327.
74. Mumby, 1913, p. 325–327.
75. Letters & Papers, Vol. 2, 230.
76. Letters & Papers, Vol. 2, 237.
77. De Savoie. Duchesse d'Angoulême, Louise p. 397.
78. De Savoie. Duchesse d'Angoulême, Louise p, 388.
79. Letters & Papers, Vol. 2, 281.
80. Letters & Papers, Vol. 2, 283.
81. Letters & Papers, Vol. 2, 284.
82. Letters & Papers, Vol. 2 304.
83. Letters & Papers, Vol. 2. 318.
84. Letters & Papers, Vol. 2, 319.
85. Letters & Papers, Vol. 1, 3129.
86. Letters & Papers, Vol. 1, 3139.
87. Letters & Papers, Vol. 2, 301.
88. Calendar of State Papers, Venice, Vol. 2, 606.
89. Mumby 1913, p. 333–334.
90. Richardson 1970, p. 185.
91. Everett Green 1846, p. 204–206.
92. Sadlack 2011, 309.
93. Everett Green 1857 p. 102.
94. Loades 2012, p. 117.
95. Calendar of State Papers, Venice, Vol. 2, 618.
96. Carroll 2010.
97. The National Archives Currency Converter.
98. The National Archives Currency Converter.
99. Loades 2012, p. 117.
100. The National Archives Currency Converter.
101. Evans 1784, p. 50–53.

As Wife and Mother

1. Chilvers 2010, p. 16.
2. Suffolk Place and The Mint.
3. Loades 2012, p. 131–132.
4. Richardson 1970, p. 189.
5. Letters & Papers, Vol. 3, 2856.
6. Loades 2012, p. 132.
7. Letters & Papers, Vol. 1, 134.
8. Loades 2012, p. 137.
9. Gunn 2015, p. 90.
10. Letters & Papers, Vol. 2, 436.
11. Gunn 2015, p. 68.

12. Richardson 1970, p. 215.
13. Loades 2012, p. 138–139.
14. Richardson 1970, p. 195.
15. Strickland 1850, p. 102.
16. Sadlack 2011, p. 353.
17. Letters & Papers, Vol. 2, 1652.
18. Loades 2012, p. 157.
19. Loades 2012, p.131.
20. Letters & Papers ,Vol. 4, 5859.
21. Richardson 1970, p. 201–202.
22. Loades 2012, p. 158.
23. Letters & Papers, Vol. 2, 1935.
24. Richardson 1970, p. 225.
25. Everett Green 1857, p. 113.
26. Richardson 1970, p. 225.
27. Letters & Papers, Vol. 2, 2170.
28. Everett Green 1857, p. 115–116.
29. Everett Green 1857, p. 115–116.
30. Everett Green 1857, p.114.
31. Baldwin 2015, p. 204.
32. Richardson 1970, p. 204.
33. Everett Green 1857, p. 116–117.
34. Richardson 1970, p. 204.
35. Everett Green 1857, p. 117–118.
36. Perry 2002, p. 194.
37. Letters & Papers, Vol. 2, 918.
38. Sadlack 2011, p. 355.
39. Loades 2012, p. 163.
40. Wodderspoon 1839, p. 61.
41. Wodderspoon 1839, p. 61–62.
42. Everett Green 1857, p. 121.
43. Everett Green 1857, p. 121–122.
44. Everett Green 1857, p. 122.

Concerning France

1. Perry 2002, p. 201.
2. Letters & Papers, Vol. 2, 4469.
3. Perry 2002, p. 201.
4. Letters & Papers, Vol. 2, 4481.
5. Letters & Papers, Vol. 2, 4481.
6. Ward 1907, p. 139.
7. Sadlack 2011, p. 356.
8. Everett Green 1846, p. 242–243.
9. Sadlack 2011, p. 368.
10. Sadlack 2011, p. 470.
11. Sadlack 2011, p. 344.
12. Richardson 1970, p. 228–229.

13. Calendar of State Papers Venice, Vol. 3, 50.
14. Calendar of State Papers Venice, Vol. 3, 50.
15. Richardson 1970, p. 229.
16. Hall 1809.
17. Calendar of State Papers Venice, Vol. 3, 50.
18. Richardson 1970, p. 230.
19. Calendar of State Papers Venice, Vol. 3, 50.
20. Doran 2008, p. 114.
21. Wilson 2009, p. 122.
22. Calendar of State Papers Venice, Vol. 3, 50.
23. Letters & Papers, Vol. 3, 869.
24. Calendar of State Papers Venice, Vol. 3, 83.
25. Starkey 2009, p. 94.
26. Loades 2011, p. 113.
27. Gunn 2015, p. 60.
28. Sadlack 2011, p. 350.
29. Calendar of State Papers Venice, Vol. 3, 84.
30. Calendar of State Papers Venice, Vol. 3, 69.
31. Calendar of State Papers Venice, Vol. 3, 69.
32. Perry 2002, p. 211.
33. Ives 2005, p. 37.
34. Ives 2005, p. 38.
35. Loades 2012, p. 164.
36. Oxford Dictionary of National Biography – Charles Brandon.
37. Loades 2012, p. 164.
38. The National Archives Currency Converter.
39. Letters & Papers, Vol. 2, 529.
40. Richardson 2011, p. 372.
41. Emerson 2015.
42. Oxford Dictionary of National Biography – Charles Brandon.
43. The National Archives Currency Converter.
44. Wilson 2009, p. 124.
45. The National Archives Currency Converter.
46. Loades 2012, p. 132.
47. Letters & Papers, Vol. 1, 3429.
48. Gunn 2015, p. 67.
49. Letters & Papers, Vol. 3, 3281.
50. Wilson 2009, p. 141.
51. Letters & Papers, Vol. 3, 3288.
52. Loades 2011, p. 172.
53. Oxford Dictionary of National Biography – Charles Brandon.
54. Loades 2012, p. 150.
55. Oxford Dictionary of National Biography – Charles Brandon.
56. Wilson 2009, p. 141.
57. Loades 2011, p. 172–173.
58. Wooding 2015, p. 121.
59. MacCulloch 1995, p. 45.

60. All Kinds of History 2014.
61. Kadouchkine 2014.
62. Wooding 2015, p. 122.
63. The National Archives Currency Converter.
64. The National Archives Currency Converter.
65. All Kinds of History 2014.
66. MacCulloch 1995, p. 45.
67. Wilson 2009, p. 144.
68. Betteridge & Freeman 2012.
69. Staging the Henrician Court 2015.
70. Kadouchkine 2014.
71. Everett Green 1846, p. 241–242.
72. The National Archives Currency Converter.
73. The National Archives Currency Converter.
74. Loades 2012, p. 131–132.
75. Letters & Papers, Vol. 4, 1431.
76. Loades 2012, p. 153.
77. Calendar of State Papers, Venice, Vol. 3, 1141.
78. Knetch 1996, p. 246–247.
79. Sadlack p. 475–476.

The Final Years

1. Perry 2002, p 237.
2. Ives 2005, p. 95.
3. Loades 2011, p. 192.
4. Ives 2005, p. 96.
5. Fraser 2002, p. 181.
6. Letters & Papers, Vol. 4, 4851, 4857.
7. Ives 2005, p. 96.
8. World Heritage Encyclopaedia – Arthur Bulkeley.
9. Letters & Papers, Vol. 8, 894.
10. Oxford Dictionary of National Biography – Charles Brandon.
11. Richardson 1970, p. 204.
12. Oxford Dictionary of National Biography – Charles Brandon.
13. Baldwin 2015, p. 23.
14. Ives 2005, p. 18.
15. Letters & Papers, Vol. 2, 529.
16. Wilkinson 2010, p. 115.
17. Sadlack 2011, p. 365.
18. Sadlack 2011, p. 481.
19. Letters & Papers, Vol. 4, 5064.
20. Everett Green 1857, p. 134–135.
21. Everett Green, Vol. 2, 1846, p. 87.
22. Weir 1991, p. 204.
23. Calendar of State Papers, Vol. 3, 621.
24. Calendar of State Papers Spain, Vol, 3, Part 2, 1527–1529, 621.

25. Loades 2012, p. 178.
26. Letters & Papers, Vol. 4, 5535, 5547.
27. Letters & Papers, Vol. 4, 5597, 5598.
28. Letters & Papers, Vol. 4, 5635.
29. Letters & Papers, Vol. 4, 5733.
30. Fraser 2002, p. 204.
31. Du Bellay, i. 115.
32. Richardson 1970, p. 214.
33. Phillips 1578.
34. Weir 2015, p. 36.
35. Letters & Papers, Vol. 5, 287.
36. Hume 1905 p. 137.
37. Letters & Papers, Vol. 5, 340.
38. Letters & Papers, Vol. 5, 287.
39. Calendar of State Papers, Venice, Vol. 4, 761.
40. Letters & Papers, Vol. 7, 1498, 37.
41. Perry 2002, p. 267.
42. Reformation Parliament.
43. The National Archives Currency Converter.
44. Calendar of State Papers, Spain, Vol. 2, 2 880.
45. Richardson 1970, p. 253.
46. Letters & Papers, Vol. 6, 324.
47. Letters & Papers, Vol. 6, 759.
48. Letters & Papers, Vol. 6, 780.
49. Letters & Papers, Vol. 6, 1541.
50. Weir 1991, p. 262–263.
51. Letters & Papers, Vol. 6, 1541.
52. Weir 1991, p. 263.
53. Letters & Papers, Vol. 6, 548.
54. Letters & Papers, Vol. 6, 601.
55. Sadlack 2011, p. 403.
56. Norton 2016, p. 272.
57. Loades 2012, p. 187.
58. Richardson 1970, p. 256.
59. Letters & Papers, Vol. 6, 693.
60. Letters & Papers, Vol. 6, 693.
61. Loades 2012, p. 188.
62. Loades 2012, p. 189.
63. Richardson 1970, p. 261.
64. Loades 2012, p. 190.
65. Richardson 1970, p. 261.
66. Sadlack 2011, p. 407–408.
67. Loades 2012, p. 191–192.
68. Calendar of State Papers Spain, Vol. 4, 1091.
69. Letters & Papers, Vol. 6, 723.
70. Letters & Papers, Vol. 4, 934.

Legacy
1. Loades 2012, p. 192.
2. Baldwin 2015, p. 40.
3. Letters & Papers, Vol. 6, 1069.
4. Letters & Papers ,Vol. 7, 281.
5. Weir 2008, p. 349.
6. Letters & Papers, Vol. 9, 1063.
7. Loades 2012, p. 193.
8. Letters & Papers, Vol. 9, 437.
9. Loades 2012, p. 194.
10. Letters & Papers, Vol. 20, 197.
11. Richardson 2011, p 372.
12. Urban 1803, p. 528.
13. Burke 1833, p. 36.
14. Richardson 2011, p. 372.
15. Emerson 2015.
16. Richardson 2011, p. 372.
17. Perry 2002, p. 267.
18. Richardson 2011, p. 168.
19. De Lisle 2013, p. 259.
20. De Lisle 2013, p. 273.
21. De Lisle 2013, p 276.
22. De Lisle 2013, p. 283–284.
23. De Lisle 2013, p. 286.
24. Richardson 2011, p. 168.
25. Emmerson 2015.

Portraits
1. Hervey 1909, p. 152.
2. Fisher 2002, p. 26.
3. Waterhouse 1994, p. 15.
4. Ainsworth 1998, p. 37.
5. Homer. *The Iliad* with an English Translation by A. T. Murray.
6. Fisher 2002, p. 26.
7. Fisher 2002, p. 20.
8. Fisher 2002, p. 24.
9. Fraser 2006.
10. Fisher 202, p. 23.
11. Lipscomb 2015, p. 117.
12. Flor 2012.
13. Encyclopaedia Britannica – Jean Perreal.
14. Richardson 1970, p. 82.
15. Fisher 2002, p. 23.
16. Ashmolean Museum.
17. Hever Castle 2016.

18. Campbell 2006.
19. The Mary Rose Trust 2017.
20. The Mary Rose Trust 2014.
21. The Lewis Walpole Library 2009.
22. Richardson 1970, p. 266.
23. The Proceedings of the Suffolk Institute of Archaeology, Vol. 1, pp. 55–56
24. Brooke 2007.
25. The Proceedings of the Suffolk Institute of Archaeology, Vol. 1, pp. 55–56

Bibliography

All Kinds of History, *1525: Amicable Grant 2014*, viewed 8 January 2017, <https://tudorrebellions.wordpress.com/2014/11/23/1525-amicable-grant/>.

Abernethy, Susan, *Arthur Tudor, Prince of Wales*, viewed 1 December 2016, <http://thefreelancehistorywriter.com/2013/04/01/arthur-tudor-prince-of-wales/>, 2013a.

Abernethy, Susan, *Margaret of Austria, Duchess of Savoy and Regent of the Netherlands*, viewed 26 November 2016, < https://thefreelancehistorywriter.com/2013/06/28/margaret-of-austria-duchess-of-savoy-and-regent-of-the-netherlands/>, 2013b.

Ackroyd, Peter, *The History of England Volume II Tudors* (London: Macmillan, 2012).

Ainsworth, Maryn Wynn, *Gerard David: Purity of Vision in an Age of Transition* (New York: The Metropolitan Museum of Art, 1998).

Ashdown-Hill, John, *The Last Days of Richard III and the fate of his DNA* (United Kingdom: The History Press, 2013).

Ashmolean Museum of Art and Archaeology, Anonymous, French (sixteenth century) *Portrait of Mary Tudor* (Oxford University).

Bacon, Francis & Lumby, Joseph Rawson, *Bacon's History of the Reign of King Henry VII* (University of Michigan: University Press, 1885).

Baldwin, David, *Henry VIII's Last Love The Extraordinary Life of Katherine Willoughby, Lady-in-Waiting to the Tudors* (Gloucestershire: Amberley Publishing, 2015).

Bayani, Debra, *Jasper Tudor Godfather of the Tudor Dynasty* (USA, Self-Published, 2014).

Beaufort Book of Hours Royal 2 A XVIII f. 29, *Calendar page for March with an added date of the birth of princess Mary, daughter of Henry VII*, viewed 4 November, <www.bl.uk/catalogues/illuminatedmanuscripts/ILLUMIN.ASP?Size=mid&IllID=33306>.

Beaufort Book of Hours Royal Ms. 2 A xviii, f.30v, *Margaret Beafort Book of Hours Page showing Henry's birth 1491*, viewed 4 November, <www.bl.uk/learning/timeline/item100630.html>

Bernard, Jared, *The Dreaded Sweat: the Other Medieval Epidemic,* viewed 13 April 2017, <www.historytoday.com/jared-bernard/dreaded-sweat-other-medieval-epidemic>, 2014.

Betteridge, Thomas & Freeman, Thomas, *Henry VIII and History* (England: Ashgate Publishing Limited, 2012).

Bibliothèque Nationale de France AE/III/24

Bietenholz, Peter.G and Deutscher, Thomas Brian, *Contemporaries of Erasmus: A Biographical Register of the Renaissance and Reformation Volumes 1–3,* (Toronto: University of Toronto Press, 2003).

Breverton, Terry, *Jasper Tudor Dynasty Maker,* (Gloucestershire: Amberley Publishing, 2014).

Bridge, John Sergeant Cyprian, *A History of France from the Death of Louis 11,* (United Kingdom: Oxford Clarendon Press, 1921).

Brooke, Chris, *Myth debunked: Our medieval ancestors were just as tall as us says a new study,* viewed 5 July 2017, <www.dailymail.co.uk/news/article-457506/Myth-debunked-Our-medieval-ancestors-just-tall-says-new-study.html>.

Bryan, Lissa, *The Mirror of Naples,* viewed 13 January 2017, <http://under-these-restless-skies.blogspot.com.au/2013/12/the-mirror-of-naples.html>.

Bunbury, Selina, *Star of the court; or, The maid of honour & queen of England, Anne Boleyn, Grant* (Available from the collections of Harvard University, 1844).

Burke, John, *The Portrait Gallery of Distinguished Females Including Beauties of the Courts of George IV. and William IV.* (London: Bull and Churton, 1833).

Calendar of State Papers and Manuscripts in the Archives and Collections of Milan 1385–1618 (London: Originally published by His Majesty's Stationery Office, 1912).

Calendar of State Papers Spain (London: Her Majesty's Stationery Office, 1871).

Calendar of State Papers Relating To English Affairs in the Archives of Venice (London: Her Majesty's Stationery Office, 1871).

Camden Society, *The Chronicle of Calais in the Reigns of Henry VII and Henry VIII to the year 1540* (Great Britain: J. B. Nicholas & Son, 1838).

Campbell, *Tapestry in the Renaissance: Art and Magnificence* (New Haven: Yale University Press, 2006).

Carmelianus, P. (ed.) Gardiner , James, *'The spousells' of the Princess Mary, daughter of Henry VII, to Charles Prince of Castile, A.D. 1508* (London: The Camden Society, 1893).

Carroll, Leslie, *Notorious Royal Marriages: A Juicy Journey Through Nine Centuries of Dynasty, and Desire* (New York: New American Library, 2010).

Catholic Online, *St Margaret of Antioch,* viewed 12 February 2017, <www.catholic.org/saints/saint.php?saint_id=199>, 2017.

Chapman, H. W., *Anne Boleyn* (London: Jonathan Cape, 1974).

Charles Brandon, 1st Duke of Suffolk, World Public Library, viewed 3 January 2016, <www.worldlibrary.org/articles/Charles_Brandon,_1st_Duke_of_Suffolk>.

Chilvers, Allan, *The Berties of Grimsthorpe Castle* (Bloomington Indiana: Author House, 2010).

Cholakain, Patricia Francis and Cholakian, Rouben C., *Marguerite de Navarre* (New York: Columbia University Press, 2006).

Cloake, Dr John, *Richmond Palace* (Local Studies Collection: Richmond Libraries), viewed 10 October 2016, <www.richmond.gov.uk/local_history_richmond_palace.pdf>.

Correspondance du Cardinal Jean du Bellay, *Tome Premier 1529-1535* (Paris: Librairie C. Klincksieck, 1969).

Cripps-Day, Francis Henry, *The history of the tournament in England and in France* (London: B. Quaritch, 1918).

Croom Brown, Mary, *Mary Tudor Queen of France* (London: Methuen, 1911).

Cunningham, Sean, *Prince Arthur The Tudor King Who Never Was*, (Gloucestershire: Amberley Publishing, 2016).

De Lisle, Leanda, *Tudor The Family Story* (London: Chatto & Windus, 2013).

De Savoie. Duchesse d'Angoulême, *Louise Journal de Louise de Savoye, duchesse d'Angoulesme, d'Anjou et de Valois*, viewed 13 October 2016, <https://books.google.com.au/books?id=P7cPAAAAQAAJ&printsec=frontcover&dq=inauthor:%22Louise+(De+Savoie.+Duchesse+d%27Angoul%C3%A9me)%22&hl=en&sa=X&ved=0ahUKEwi1kf-RsdfPAhUBbSYKHa-VCfAQ6AEIHTAA#v=onepage&q&f=false>.

Doran, Susan, *The Tudor Chronicles* (London: Quercus Publishing, 2008).

Ellis, Henry, *Original Letters, Illustrative of English History; Including Numerous Royal Letters: From Autographs in the British Museum, and One or Two Other Collections: Volume 1* (London: Harding, Triphook, and Lepard, 1825).

Emerson, Kathy Lynn, *A Who's Who of Tudor Women*, viewed 20 June 2015, <www.kateemersonhistoricals.com/TudorWomenIndex.htm>, 2015.

Encyclopædia Britannica, *Gregorian calendar*, viewed 12 February 2017, <www.britannica.com/topic/Gregorian-calendar>, 2010.

Encyclopedia of World Biography, *Louis XII* (The Gale Group Inc.), viewed 22 December 2016, <www.encyclopedia.com/people/history/french-history-biographies/louis-xii>, 2004.

English Heritage, *Eltham Palaces and Gardens*, viewed 4 November 2016, <www.english-heritage.org.uk/visit/places/eltham-palace-and-gardens/history/>.

Erasmus, Desiderius ed. Rummel, Erika, *Erasmus on Women* (Toronto: University of Toronto Press, 1996).

Evans, Thomas, *Old ballads, historical and narrative. Collected, with notes* (Taylor Institution, 1784).

Everett Green, Mary Anne, *Letters of royal and illustrious ladies of Great Britain, from the commencement of the twelfth century to the close of the reign of Queen Mary Vol. 1* (London: H. Colburn, 1846).

Everett Green, Mary Anne, *Letters of royal and illustrious ladies of Great Britain, from the commencement of the twelfth century to the close of the reign of Queen Mary Vol. 2* (London: H. Colburn, 1846).

Everett Green, Mary Anne, *Lives of the Princesses of England, from the Norman Conquest* (Loondon: Longman, Brown, Green, Longman, & Roberts, 1857).

Fisher, Celia, *The Queen and the artichoke: A study of the portraits of Mary Tudor and Charles Brandon* (The British Art Journal, Vol. 3, No. 2, pp. 20-27, 2002).

Flor, P., *UN RETRATO DESCONOCIDO DE ISABEL LA CATÓLICA* (Universidade Nova de Lisboa: Universidade Aberta de Lisboa, Instituto de Historia da Arte, 2012).

Fraser, Antonia, *The Six Wives of Henry VIII* (London: Phoenix Press, 2002).

Grands documents de l'histoire de France, Musée, armoire de fer et Musée, AE/III/24, 1514, viewed 4 July 2017, <www.culture.gouv.fr/public/mistral/caran_fr>.

Gristwood, Sarah, *Game of Queens The Women Who Made Sixteenth-Century Europe* (New York: Basic Books, 2016).

Fraser, Melanie (now Melanie V Taylor), *Master of Arts dissertation on The Life and Works of Levina Teerlinc: 1546–1576* (University of Kent at Canterbury: Templeman Library, 2006).

Guillemeau, Jacques, *Child-birth; Or, The Happy Delivery of Women: Wherein is Set Downe the Government of Women ... Together with the Diseases, which Happen to Women in Those Times, and the Meanes to Help Them. With a Treatise for The Nursing of Children* (1635).

Gunn, Steven, *Charles Brandon* (Gloucestershire: Amberley Publishing, 2015).

Haigh, Christopher, *English Reformations: Religion, Politics, and Society Under the Tudors* (Oxford: Clarendon Press, 1993).

Hall, Edward, *Hall's chronicle: containing the history of England, during the reign of Henry the Fourth, and the succeeding monarchs, to the end of the reign of Henry the Eighth, in which are particularly described the manners and customs of those periods. Carefully collated with the editions of 1548 and 1550* (London: J. Johnson, 1809).

Harris, Barbara, *Power, Profit, and Passion: Mary Tudor, Charles Brandon, and the Arranged Marriage in Early Tudor England* (Feminist Studies, Vol. 15, No. 1, pp. 59–88, 1989).

Hart, Kelly, *The Mistresses of Henry VIII* (Gloucestershire: The History Press, 2009).

Hervey, Mary, *Notes on Some Portraits of Tudor Times* (The Burlington Magazine, Vol. 15, pp. 151–160, 1909).

Hever Castle, *Marriage Tapestry Goes in for Conservation*, viewed 12 January 2017, <www.hevercastle.co.uk/news/marriage-tapestry-goes-conservation-2/>, 2016.

Homer. The Iliad with an English Translation by A.T. Murray, Ph.D. in two volumes (London: Cambridge, MA, Harvard University Press; London, William Heinemann, Ltd. 1924, 2016).

Hume, Martin, *The Wives of Henry the Eighth and the Parts They Played in History* (London: Eveleigh Nash, 1905).

Hutchinson, Robert, *Young Henry The Rise of Henry VIII*, (London: Orion Books, 2011).

Hutton, William, *The Battle of Bosworth Field, Between Richard the Third and Henry Earl of Richmond, August 22, 1485* (Fleet Street: Nichols, Son, and Bentley, 1813).

Ives, Eric, *The Life and Death of Anne Boleyn* (Oxford: Blackwell Publishing, 2005).

Jackson, G.M. 1999, Women Rulers Throughout the Ages: An Illustrated Guide, ABC-CLIO, California.

Jean Clouet (Encyclopaedia Britannica), viewed 11 January 2017, <www.britannica.com/biography/Jean-Clouet>.

Jean Perréal, (Encyclopaedia Britannica), viewed 11 January 2017, <www.britannica.com/biography/Jean-Perreal>.

Johnson, David, *Southwak and the City*, (United Kingdom: Oxford UP, 1969).

Jokinen, A, *Louis XII King of France (1462-1515)*, (The Luminarium Encyclopaedia Project), viewed 22 December 2016, <www.luminarium.org/encyclopedia/louis12.htm>, 2007.

Jones, Michael, *Bosworth The Battle that Transformed England* (New York: Pegasus Books, 2015).

Kadouchkine, Oliver, *The Amicable Grant, 1525*, viewed 8 January 2017, <http://jwsmrscott.weebly.com/tudorpedia/the-amicable-grant-1525>, 2014.

Knetch, R. J., *Renaissance Warrior and Patron: The Reign of Francis I*, (Cambridge: Cambridge University Press, 1996).

Knox, John ed. Mason, Roger Alexander, *Knox: On Rebellion*, (New York: Cambridge University Press, 1994).

Laing, David (ed.), *Selected Writings of John Knox: Public Epistles, Treatises, and Expositions to the Year 1559*, (Edinburgh, 1864).

Letters and Papers, Foreign and Domestic, of the Reign of Henry VIII, 1509–47, ed. J. S. Brewer, James Gairdner and R. H. Brodie, (His Majesty's Stationery Office, 1862–1932).

Licence, Amy, *In Bed with the Tudors The Sex Lives of a Dynasty from Elizabeth of York to Elizabeth I* (Gloucestershire: Amberley Publishing, 2012).

Licence, Amy, *Elizabeth of York: The Forgotten Tudor Queen* (Glouestershire: Amberley Publishing, 2013).

Licence, Amy, *Red Roses: Blanche of Gaunt to Margaret Beaufort* (United Kingdom: The History Press, 2016).

Lipscomb, Suzannah, *The King is Dead, The Last Will and Testament of Henry VIII* (London: Head of Zeus, 2015).

Loades, David, *Henry VIII* (Gloucestershire: Amberley Publishing, 2011).

Loades, David, *Mary Rose* (Gloucestershire: Amberley Publishing, 2012).

MacCulloch, Diarmaid, *The Reign of Henry VIII Politics, Policy and Piety* (New York: St Martin's Press, 1995).

Measuringworth, viewed 12 February 2017, <www.measuringworth.com/>.

Medieval Lives: Birth, Marriage and Death (Scotland, BBC, 2013).

Meyer, G. J., *The Tudors The Complete Story of England's Most Notorious Dynasty* (New York: Delacorte Press, 2010).

More, Thomas ed. Baker-Smith, Dominic, *Utopia* (United Kingdom: Penguin Books, 2012).

Morris, Sarah & Grueninger Natalie, *In the footsteps of Anne Boleyn* (Gloucestershire: Amberley, 2013).

Mumby, F, *The Youth of Henry VIII: A Narrative in Contemporary Letters* (Boston New York: Houghton Mifflin Company, 1913).

Norton, Elizabeth, *The Lives of Tudor Women* (London: Head of Zeus, 2016).

Ormen, Nicholas, *Medieval Children*, (New Haven: Yale University Press, 2013).

Oxford Dictionary of National Biography, *Brandon, Charles, First Duke of Suffolk (c.1484–1545)* (Oxford University Press), viewed 3 January 2017, <www.oxforddnb.com/>.

Oxford Dictionary of National Biography, *Brandon, Sir Thomas (d. 1510)* (Oxford University Press), viewed 3 January 2017, <www.oxforddnb.com/>.

Oxford Dictionary of National Biography, *Grey [other married name Stokes], Frances [née Lady Frances Brandon]* (Oxford University Press), viewed 3 January 2017, .

Penn, Thomas, *Winter King, The Dawn of Tudor England* (London: Penguin Group, 2011).

Perry, Maria, *Sisters to the King* (London: André Deutsch, 2002).

Phillips, John, *A Commenoration of the Right Noble and virtuous Lady Margaret Douglas's good Grace, Countess of Lennox* (London, 1578).

Pronay, Nicholas & Cox, John, *The Crowland Chronicle Continuations: 1459-1486* (USA: Sutton for Richard III and Yorkist History Trust, 1986).

Reformation Parliament, United Kingdom Parliament, viewed 15 April 2017, <www.parliament.uk/about/living-heritage/evolutionofparliament/originsofparliament/birthofparliament/overview/reformation/>.

Richardson, Douglas, *Plantagenet Ancestry: A Study In Colonial And Medieval Families, 2nd Edition* (USA: CreateSpace, 2011).

Richardson, Walter C., *Mary Tudor The White Queen* (Great Britain: University of Washington Press, 1970).

Roud, Steve, *The English Year A month-by-month guide to the Nations Customs and Festivals, from May Day to Mischief Night* (London: Penguin Books, 2006).

Russell, Gareth, *April 2nd, 1502: The Death of Arthur Tudor, Prince of Wales* (Confessions of a CI-Devant), viewed 1 December 2016, <http://garethrussellcidevant.blogspot.com.au/2011/04/april-2nd-1502-death-of-arthur-tudor.html>, 2011.

Sadlack, Erin, *The French Queen's Letters* (New York: Palgrave Macmillan, 2001).

Sim, Alison, *Pleasures and Pastimes in Tudor England* (Gloucestershire: The History Press, 2011).

Skidmore, Chris, *The Rise of the Tudors The Family That Changed English History* (New York: St Martin's Press, 2013).

Spears, JoAnn, *The Cheapside Hoard*, viewed 13 January 2017, <http://onthetudortrail.com/Blog/2012/02/23/the-cheapside-hoard/>, 2012.

Spence, Jean, Aiston, Sarah and Meikle, Maureen M., *Women, Education, and Agency, 1600–2000* (New York: Routledge, 2009).

Starkey, David, *Man & Monarch Henry VIII* (London: The British Library, 2009).

'Suffolk Place and the Mint', in Survey of London: Volume 25, St George's Fields (The Parishes of St George the Martyr Southwark and St Mary Newington), ed. Ida Darlington (London, 1955), pp. 22–25, viewed 2 January 2017, <www.british-history.ac.uk/survey-london/vol25/pp22-25>.

Strickland, Agnes, *Lives of the Queens of England: From the Norman Conquest; with Anecdotes of Their Courts* (Philadelphia: Lee and Blanchard, 1850).

The Amicable Grant 1525, Staging the Henrician Court bringing early modern drama to life, 8 January 2017, <http://stagingthehenriciancourt.brookes.ac.uk/historicalcontext/the_amicable_grant_1525.html>.

The Lewis Walpole Library, *Hair of Mary Tudor in a Gold Locket* (Yale University) 21 December 2016, < http://images.library.yale.edu/strawberryhill/oneitem.asp?i=1&id=662>, 2009.

The National Archives, *Currency Converter*, <www.nationalarchives.gov.uk/ currency/default0.asp#mid>.

The Will of Henry VII, 1775, London.

The Mary Rose Trust, *Who Was 'Mary Rose'?*, viewed 12 January 2017, <www. maryrose.org/who-was-mary-rose/>, 2014.

The Mary Rose Trust, The Mary Rose Museum, viewed 12 January 2017, <www. maryrose.org/>, 2017.

The Proceedings of the Suffolk Institute of Archaeology, Quarterly Meetings, 1846, Vol. 1, pp. 55–56.

Urban, Sylvanus, *The Gentleman's Magazine and Historical Chronical* (London: Nichols & Son, 1803).

Velde, François, *'List of the Knights of the Garter'*, viewed 7 January 2015, Available from Internet <www.heraldica.org/topics/orders/garterlist.htm>, 2014.

Vergil, P., *Anglica Historia*, viewed 1 December 2016, <www.philological.bham. ac.uk/polverg/>, 1555.

Vives, Juan Luis, *A very fruteful and pleasant boke called the Instruction of a christen woman tourned out of latyne into Englishe by Rychard Hyrde* (London, 1523).

Ward, Adolphus William, *The Cambridge Modern History Volume II The Reformation* (Cambridge: The University Press, 1907).

Waterhouse, Ellis K., *Painting in Britain, 1530 to 1790* (Hong Kong: Yale University Press, 1994).

Weir, Alison, *The Six Wives of Henry VIII* (New York: Grove Press, 1991).

Weir, Alison, *Henry VIII King & Court* (London: Vintage Books, 2008).

Weir, Alison, *Elizabeth of York, The First Tudor Queen* (London: Vintage Books, 2014).

Weir, Alison, *The Lost Tudor Princess* (London: Vintage, 2015).

Wilkinson, Josephine, *Mary Boleyn, The True Story of Henry VIII's Favourite Mistress* (Gloucestershire: Amberley Publishing, 2010).

Wilson, Derek, *A Brief History of Henry VIII* (London: Constable and Robinson Ltd, 2009).

Wodderspoon, John, *Historic Sites and Other Remarkable and Interesting Places in the County of Suffolk* (Cornhill: R. Root, 1839).

Wooding, Lucy, *Henry VIII* (Oxon: Routledge, 2005).

World Heritage Encyclopaedia, *Arthur Bulkeley*, viewed 11 January 2017, <http:// self.gutenberg.org/articles/arthur_bulkeley>.

Index